1992

american FILM genres

american F I L M genres

second edition

Stuart M. Kaminsky

Nelson-Hall nh **Chicago**

Library of Congress Cataloging in Publication Data

Kaminsky, Stuart M.
  American film genres.

  Includes bibliographies, filmographies, and index.
  1. Moving-pictures—United States—History.
2. Moving-picture plays—History and criticism.
I. Title.
PN1993.5.U6K34 1984   791.43'0973   84-1037
ISBN 0-8304-1048-1 (cloth)
ISBN 0-88229-826-7 (paper)

Manufactured in the United States of America

10 9 8 7 6 5 4 3 2 1

The paper in this book is pH neutral (acid-free).

CONTENTS

145, 229

PREFACE

The first edition of this book appeared in 1974 and, at that time, was the first book in English to be devoted specifically to the issue of genre and film. While the basic ideas of the original remain sound, a decade of new films has come and gone, and an updating is very much in order. In addition, the author's interests and ideas expanded and changed, and it seems reasonable to incorporate those interests in a new edition.

Those familiar with the earlier edition may note that the chapters on the big-caper film and the musical have been removed. The big-caper film has not continued as a significant generic form, and the original chapter on the musical has been superseded by excellent book-length studies published since the first edition.

I have made a number of additions to this volume. I have added an analysis of film and realism to the introduction. I have included a chapter in which I examine the narrative structure of a very recent film, *Once upon a Time in America*. Another chapter on comparative forms has been added—this one dealing with the phenomenon of Kung Fu films. An additional chapter on literary adaptation has been included in which I discuss the adaptation to film of B. Traven's novel *The Treasure of the Sierra Madre*. There is a new chapter devoted to Sergio Leone as genre director. Finally, the chapter on comedy and social change now includes material on Woody Allen and Mel Brooks.

Throughout the book, examples, photographs, charts, and bibliographies have been brought up-to-date to reflect the historical and theoretical changes of the past decade.

Stuart M. Kaminsky

ACKNOWLEDGMENTS

My primary thanks go to Tom Snyder, who assisted me and contributed to the changes in this edition. I also wish to thank Steve Fagin for his many hours of research on the original text and John Cawelti for his valuable criticism of my original manuscript. My thanks also go to the late Paddy Whannel for his support and encouragement in this effort; to Douglas Lemza and Films, Incorporated, for their cooperation in providing research material; and to the *Journal of Popular Film,* in which three chapters of this book have been published in a somewhat different form.

1
INTRODUCTION

What Is Film Genre?

Criticism and Genre

In film criticism, the concept of genre has emerged as an important tool. Those who use the term usually mean that, in film, broad forms of popular expression are identifiable, each with a specific tradition. They also indicate that the works are related and that this relationship is worth examining. It has been assumed that, by examining these broad *forms*—Westerns, horror films, gangster films, art films, costume dramas, war films—we can gain some knowledge about the *individual films* that exist within them. Generally, this is where any discussion of genre ends. Few books that discuss genre go much beyond this point.

One of the problems of dealing with genre is that, to make essential generalizations that have any meaning, one must have seen enough films to make speculation valid. Another problem is that genre theory must be systematic, a critical tool. It is not primarily a means of validating one's likes and dislikes. Value judgment is a matter of aesthetics beyond (or apart from) basic genre study. Taste and judgment change. As Northrop Frye has pointed out, genre study can be of little value if we start trading in the stock of various artists, selling George Lucas this year and buying George Cukor next.

Genre study in film is based on the realization that certain popular narrative forms have both cultural and universal roots—that, for example, the Western of today is related both to folk tales of the past two

1

hundred years in the United States and to the archetypes of myth. A major value in examining particular genres of film is in discovering what the elements are to which we are responding in the form—what makes it popular, makes it survive, relates it to forms that have existed before it, and informs us about what there is in film to which we respond.

The argument that people go to films simply for entertainment is fine, as far as it goes, but it does not answer the question of why certain forms persist, why others rise and fade, why a person may respond to detective stories and not to romances, why one society's dominant form is violent while another's is passive. In essence, what is the nature of the entertainment to which one is responding? Film and television genres occupy much of our entertainment time; yet few of us ever come to terms with what this means. On one level, one can argue that genre film, television, and literature to a great extent have replaced more formal versions of mythic response to existence, such as religion and folk tale. This is not a new idea. It exists in literature, anthropology, and psychology, in the writings of Kenneth Burke, Northrop Frye, Sir James Frazer, Sigmund Freud, and Carl Jung, to name a few.

Most of us recognize and feel uneasy with our inability to cope with popular film. We like the form, perhaps even realize that it has a basic importance in our lives and in society, but we do not know how to approach it. For the teacher who wants to deal with film on a level of its significance for society and student, popular film becomes an essential tool; but too often the teacher, unable to approach genre and popular film, will fall back on the idea of the film as art. By so doing, he or she is very likely failing to deal with the very films that most affect him or her and the students. Many teachers and critics feel it is their responsibility to ''elevate'' taste rather than to understand the films to which the students and public actually respond. All too often, teachers or critics display a strange internal or external discord stemming from the knowledge that they really like Westerns or detective stories or situation comedies better than the staid, literary adaptations that they often foist upon themselves and their students. Telling the students that Federico Fellini, Ingmar Bergman, or Michelangelo Antonioni are worth their attention—and that *Terror Train* or *Airplane* are not—is a negation of reality and an imposition of taste; it is not analysis.

All too often, the critic or teacher turns to the ''art'' film because it is so much easier to deal with such films. The art-film approach assumes the existence of a creative author, and in-depth analysis of authors and their work has been the primary tool of literary education and criticism for several hundred years. The approach also provides a form for literary analysis that too often ends in justification of the creative artist whose literary stock is up and who can be examined as a conscious creator of high purpose—one who deals knowingly with issues of life, death, God, and politics.

In contrast, the genre approach need make no qualitative judgment. It is an examination of popular forms, an attempt to *understand,* not to *"sell"* films or directors. On one level, the more popular a film (the more people who see it), the more attention it deserves as a genre manifestation. If a film is popular, it is a result of the fact that the film or series of films corresponds to an interest—perhaps even a need—of the viewing public.

The genre critic does not castigate society for responding to the popular work; he or she examines the work to determine why it evokes response. The contributors to that work—director, writer, producer—are discussed in terms of their ability to produce a meaningful, popular work.

There is a question of depth in this approach, and it is one that ultimately, I believe, leads to a greater complexity of analysis than almost any art-film approach. Genre analysis can involve an attempt to understand the milieu and background of the work through its relationship with religion, mythology, the social sciences, psychology, and anthropology. The roots of genre are not solely in the literary tradition but in the fabric of existence itself. Genre films deal just as surely and deeply with social issues, considerations of life and death and the unknown, as do art films. The very persistence of genre films argues that they must be dealing with basic aspects of existence and social/psychological interaction, or they could not continue to be made.

Genre films (or formulas, if the genres are limited) quite often originate in the adaptation of a novel, short story, or play. If the public responds to the original film form, other films in the same form are made. If the genre is deeply rooted—as it is in the horror film or the Western, for example—the numerous works comprise a tradition that can be examined. Artists in tune with their society and culture arise just as surely within the confines of genre as outside it, and these artists can be fully appreciated only in terms of the tradition and time in which they worked.

Valid genre criticism does not impose a belief on a form or dictate what it should be. Valid genre criticism recognizes that a form exists and then examines it to see what it means. To those who would argue that meaningful creation must be individual, I respond in two ways. First, I say, ''Why?'' I am opposed to arbitrary definitions of what creativity should be. If a society or a culture can produce, can create, its creations are worth examination and appreciation. After all, we do not talk about specific Egyptian artists but about ancient Egyptian art. Second, some creators can work best within genre; they need genre, need a form, to create best. A prime example of this type of artist is William Shakespeare.

Genre analysis can be approached in a variety of ways. One method is to devote an entire study, or book, to a particular genre. This is a worthwhile method, because it implies an examination of the form or works, not just a listing of films and descriptions. Another method of genre analysis is to list a large number of genres and examine their elements, or categorize them. This approach, too, can be very valuable. Genre criticism can contribute a measure of scientific stability to criticism. Science is essential to film criticism because it implies the use of orderly, verifiable thought. Although science should be of no particular consequence for the creator, the person who examines creative works should use a systematic approach. This idea, once again, is Northrop Frye's; but it is as valid for film criticism as it is for literary criticism.

The method I have adopted in this book is to examine various ways in which one can approach the idea of genre analysis. In one case, I may take an individual film and indicate some of its contributions. In another case, I may deal with comparisons of source and film versions.

This book is not an exhaustive look at all American film genres. It is not meant to be. In the concluding chapter, I have dealt briefly with a few genres not described in more detail earlier. These additional genres might well merit entire books. Although I have dealt almost not at all with the fantasy film, for example, almost any of the approaches indicated in the chapters in this book could be applied to an analysis and understanding of that genre. In addition, this is not an exhaustive application of approaches. I am sure many other approaches to genre analysis exist. This book is an attempt to deal with the concept of film genre as a tool and to apply approaches to genre to actual works.

I have dealt exclusively with American films and non-American generic films that have been quite popular in the United States (martial-arts films, Italian Westerns) for a number of reasons. First, genre is a particularly strong element in American creative work, dating back to the 1920s in film and earlier than that in literature and theater. Genre does exist in other countries, but both its tradition and its impact on society—due to its pervasiveness in popular media—are most demonstrable and powerful in America. Second, this work is written primarily for those who view American films. For that reason, it deals mainly with films with which I am particularly familiar and to which I respond.

There are other points that should be emphasized. My choice of popular genre films and approaches does not indicate a qualitative judgment. In short, I am not saying that American genre films are superior in quality to, let us say, a European art film. Their difference is in kind, not quality. I would say, however, that the European art film is not *per se* superior to the American genre film. Both require understanding. The American genre film, though, from the point of view of its impact, often merits more attention than it has been given as a creative form.

The auteur critics of *Cahiers du Cinema* and Andrew Sarris, among others, recognized and helped to bring serious critical recognition to the American popular film. This delayed recognition, however, often has come only as a result of raising individual directors to the auteur level, and this approach offers little in the way of historical continuum and relegates important films by unknown directors to oblivion. Still, one must recognize auteur criticism as valid and important because it can rely on analysis of content with a minimum of prejudice.

Authorship and Genre

The concept of authorship in film study is not, I believe, a consideration that should or need be set in opposition to the concept of genre. Both are of value. A genre consideration might yield more understanding of certain films, especially those whose directors, writers, producers, and or cinematographers have not displayed enough consistency or produced enough work to consider them in terms of authorship. Auteur approaches might be most fruitful in considering works of highly productive, dynamic directors whose work offers distinctions (Alfred Hitchcock, Ingmar Bergman, Federico Fellini, Samuel Fuller, Charlie Chaplin, Steven Spielberg, John Carpenter, Stanley Kubrick, Francois Truffaut, John Ford, and many others). This does not exclude the value of looking at a John Ford film, for example, in terms of the Western genre (see chapter 12). In fact, I believe a consideration of any film should recognize (a) that it is the creation of a person or group of persons reflecting the contribution of that person or persons (author-ship); and (b) that the film does not exist in a cultural vacuum—that it must, of necessity, have roots in other works that surround it or have appeared before it (genre).

In general, one must first consider a work in terms of understanding its genre—and the work's relationship to that genre—before attempting to discern what the creator of the work has added to the genre, or given it beyond its accumulated historical-cultural definition. One reason this dual consideration is seldom undertaken is, I believe, the complexity of the task.

Because auteur study appears to be a relatively easy way to examine a work or body of works, more ''good'' studies have concentrated upon the director as author than upon the works as genre creations. After all, it is far easier to gather the several films of Arthur Penn—or even the many films of King Vidor—and to explore the consistencies and pat-terns of expression in them than to attempt to assimilate hundreds of horror films, Westerns, science-fiction films, war films, love stories, or historical epics. The task of a genre study is monumental—but not insur-mountable. As in a consideration of quantitative research in the social sciences, one can begin with a few case studies, constantly expanding, so that one's conclusions after 100 examples become less tentative than they were after the first several dozen. It is doubtful that one can ever be truly comprehensive in a film genre study. The conclusions will remain tentative; but so, too, are conclusions in the social sciences. Such con-clusions exist to be tested, tried, strengthened, modified, or discarded if they prove invalid.

All too often, film critics make use of a broad context of generic defi-nition and, for reasons of haste, substitute tentative definitions for criti-cal criteria. This problem of tentative value judgment also exists among the social scientists in their analysis of a medium (see Leo Lowenthal's Voice of America studies), a period (see Siegfried Kracauer's *From Ca-ligari to Hitler)*, or any other cultural entity. The film critic, however, too often proceeds from the assumption that genre exists only to provide a means of evaluation, a way to say that something is good or bad. In theory, at least, the social scientist has no such preconceived goal.

An additional problem in attempting to apply social science analysis to film analysis, however, is that the body of works selected for tenta-tive definition in film must incorporate at least the possibility of a crea-tive presence. The reason for examining a television series, the politics of a country, or radio transmissions over a period of time is that such studies can provide an understanding of social phenomena. A film genre study can, indeed, add to this understanding; but it runs the risk of reducing the individual contributions within the genre to mere social phenomena. In general, the film critic is not interested in such phenomena but in the creativity of the medium. That the film is a means of mass communication is at the center of most communications research and film analysis. That the film can be a creative medium, can produce art—high or popular—is at the center of the critic's consideration. Since some concept of art is operative for the film critic, he or she is anxious to get on with a consideration of the works as art.

This brings us again to the question of whether the study of a genre is purely descriptive or is critically useful. Genre studies in film are, as I have said, minimal in number. In addition, a number of these studies (William Everson's study of the Western and John Baxter's consideration of the gangster film, for example) have been weak—although gallant—analyses of film genre. In literature, however, genre studies have helped define broad creative concerns and the traditions in which creative artists work. Genre in literary criticism, therefore, appears to be quite different from genre in film studies.

Genre in film, if it is to have meaning, must have a limited scope, a limited definition. The films must have clearly defined constants so that the traditions and forms within them can be clearly seen and not diluted into abstraction. A study of the "crime film," for example, will yield a number of valid generalizations; but the breadth of work within this category is so great that it is impossible to form any valid tentative conclusions about such a genre. Therefore, the "crime film" is too broad to be considered as a workable genre. Any actual comparison of Lawrence Kasdan's *Body Heat* and Gordon Douglas' *The Detective* is limited, if not impossible. A narrowing of definition, on the other hand, not only limits the scope of works to be examined (and, in so doing, limits the number of films necessary for valid tentative conclusions) but also makes the examination more manageable. Thus, studies of the private-eye film, the cop film, the big-caper film, the gangster film, and the bandit film all can reveal specific themes, settings, icons, and motifs existing in an archetypal situation. John Cawelti suggests that, instead of calling these categorical breakdowns *genres,* it might be more fruitful to call them *formulas* and allow a more literary definition of *genres* to stand. Unfortunately, the term *genre* in film studies has become so accepted that a clarification at this point seems futile. What is more likely is that usage will result in a change of meaning for the word *genre,* particularly when the word is applied to film analysis.

As to whether the study of genre is purely descriptive, I agree with Northrop Frye that, at its best, a genre study should be just that—but as thorough as possible. The establishment of the validity of a particular symbol (e.g., the white horse) or motif (e.g., betrayal by a female) as a means of expression—and with a history of connotations—are examples of how a pure genre study can contribute to a critical understanding of film.

I am not sure genre study contributes to any attempt to solve the problem of evaluations, but an increase in understanding is a factor contributing to evaluation. Understanding a film does not always lead to appreciation of it. Even if it were possible to comprehend a work fully, one's opinion of the value of that work may be radically different from that of someone else who also "understands" it.

Because of the difficulty in arriving at a common evaluation of a film, I have experienced a decreasing interest in defining any specific criteria of evaluation to use based on auteur observations or genre studies. I am now more interested in coming to an understanding of the works through whatever means are available. Increased understanding means increased appreciation: the value judgment that arises from appreciation comes from finding in a film new methods of expression that I find effective or in discovering that a work has nothing, or very little, new to offer in terms of presentation or understanding.

I also am increasingly unwilling to accept stated criteria for evaluation that exist outside the works themselves. Therefore, a statement such as Ernest Lindgren's, that, to be valid art, a work must represent an individual creator, is insupportable by any real evidence. And André Bazin's aesthetic of in-depth and limited montage filming should be considered as a possibility, rather than a prerequisite, of a film, depending upon what the film's director is trying to express. In-depth and limited montage filming might not ruin a work of Blake Edwards, for example, but these techniques would make of it quite a different film. For similar reasons, I also question the theories of art of Rudolf Arnheim, Siegfried Kracauer, V. I. Pudovkin, and Béla Balázs.

In addition, although I believe that authorship studies are of great value in understanding a film, it may be of even more importance at the present state of film study to encourage additional descriptive generic studies.

Several terms used in this book should be understood in the way I will be using them. Thus:

- *Theme*—a basic conceptual or intellectual premise underlying a specific work or body of works.
- *Motif*—a dominant, generally recurring idea or dramatization designed, in most cases, to enhance the theme or themes of the director. Such motifs may be peculiar to the director, writer, or cinematographer of a particular work but, more often, are common to related works in the same medium.
- *Genre*—a body, group, or category of similar works, this similarity being defined as the sharing of a sufficient number of motifs that we can identify works that properly fall within a particular kind or style of film.
- *Archetype*—the manifestations in image, dialogue, or character recognizable as basic symbolic elements of a culture's experience as a whole.

Realism, Naturalism, and Genre

A major criticism of the popular generic film is that such films are not "real." The question of genre and reality, therefore, merits attention. When people speak or write of reality in film (or any other medium), they tend to mean one of three things:

1. The film is documentary reality, actually *cinema vérité*, which reflects a belief that somehow that which is shown has actually taken place or is taking place before the camera and is an event that could exist or would have existed even had the camera not been there. Examples: sports (the Super Bowl), a performance of some kind (*Gimme Shelter*), a historical event (*Primary*). It seems simple, but it really isn't. We will return to this later.

2. The film is recognized as "fictional," but there is some personal or cultural response that impels the critic or viewer to say that it is real— that it conforms somehow to one's expectation of experience. Examples sometimes cited include: *All the President's Men; Saturday Night Fever; Grand Illusion;* and *Ordinary People.*

3. The film is part of a tradition of naturalism that is accepted as more "real" than films that are not part of the tradition. Example: *Raging Bull.*

These ideas of reality are highly problematic, and it is difficult to get a given group of people to agree in the "reality" of any of the ideas when a particular film is involved.

Documentary Reality

We shall deal first with the idea of documentary reality. The filming of *actualities* (the term used by two French brothers, Pierre and August Lumiere, in the late 1800s) took place at the beginning of film history. The Edison company took pictures of the Fifth Avenue elevated trains in New York, Admiral Dewey on his yacht, and an Easter parade. The Lumieres shot pictures of workers coming out of their father's factory, a train pulling into a station, and one of the Lumiere children eating breakfast. Eventually, the Lumieres and Edison sent crews all over the world to shoot and show actualities.

Initially, there was no theory. Films of people playing cards or rowing boats were shown on the same bill with strong men flexing their muscles, belly dancers, or vaudeville acts. Had someone asked where the line between actuality and intervention began, the filmmakers would no doubt have had some difficulty answering. For example, W. K. L. Dickson put a woman on a stage in Edison's Black Maria and told her to bathe a baby for the camera. Is that an actuality? What if the Lumiere brothers directed the workers how to walk out of the factory or where they should go? Is that an actuality? What if we do not know if such directions are given? Are we totally dependent upon outside information about the film to know if it is "real" in this sense? If so, the idea ceases to have meaning, because we know so little about how such works were set up.

It wasn't until the late 1920s and early 1930s that people began to try to identify and establish a difference between those films that were, somehow, real (documentary) and those that were not. Several Englishmen and one or two Americans came up with definitions of *documentary*. The term itself as applied to film was coined by an Englishman named John Grierson.

Grierson said that *documentary* is "the creative treatment of actual-

Corbett and Courtney in an early Edison film.

Robert De Niro in *Raging Bull*.

ity.'' He later admitted that this was a weak definition, though he didn't come up with anything more helpful. It is weak because it can be applied to any movie ever made, even *Stir Crazy* and *Flash Gordon.* What is "creative"? What are the principles for determining it? And what aspect of "actuality"? People? People behaving in a particular way that we accept as "real"?

Basil Wright tried, "Documentary is a method of approach to public information, and its function is to be at the forefront of policy." All films contain information made public, but what has reality necessarily to do with policy? What policy issue is raised in a film about Linda Ronstadt preparing for a recording session? Since such a film is not about policy, is it therefore not a documentary? If it is not, what is it?

Few of the definitions of the 1930s really help when pushed to application. Historically, one simple way out of the definition dilemma, in literature and journalism, has been to divide all acts of creation into fiction and nonfiction. There is actually a book by Richard Barsam called *Non-Fiction Film,* which, rather curiously, is only about those nonfiction films other people call documentaries; it is not about scientific films, newsreels, or instructional films. It is perhaps rather strange that the films we somehow wish to equate with reality are described by a negative; they are "not fiction," as if fiction itself were so easily defined and everything left over were real.

There is one perfectly reasonable way out. The whole idea of the need to separate reality and nonreality—as if there were some line for doing so and everything could be dropped in one bin or the other—seems particularly Anglo-Saxon—a concept accepted in England, the United States, Canada—a belief that the world is neatly divisible into real and nonreal. The way out is essentially the way of many French filmmakers, such as Louis Malle, Chris Marker, and Jean Luc Godard. They simply see each film as an artifact of personal expression. They don't worry about distinctions. But since we are in an American milieu and most of us have been taught that the distinction is valid, we'll keep at it for a while.

Our democratic journalistic tradition (at least until recently) has been one in which we have been taught to believe that truth/reality can be obtained or found if the searcher/filmmaker is impersonal and objective. In journalism and documentary-film courses, this is often reduced to a formula: (1) Observe the event. (2) Determine what the most important aspects of that event are. (3) Report those aspects clearly in descending order of importance.

The problems with this approach can be reduced to a few questions. First, don't people observe events differently, depending upon who they are, where they are, whom they talk to, and what questions they ask? Doesn't "importance" vary from one individual to another, one culture to another? Is "importance" self-evident and the same for everyone?

Nonetheless, one can say that things called documentaries exist. One can say, "I recognize them, know them." The TV series "60 Minutes" is documentary. *National Geographic* specials are documentary. They are real. The news is "real." But how do we know?

Let's take a hypothetical situation. Supposing I give you evidence that the last "60 Minutes" show was actually staged, beginning to end, with actors and a script. Would it cease to be a documentary? If it would, then how do we know in any case without outside information that this hasn't happened, that the situation hasn't been scripted and created from someone's imagination? You might answer that you can tell in a film when someone is acting. But you can't always. Capable actors or even amateurs can look authentic. The Abscam tapes are a prime example, as were the Mirage kickback films of several years ago. There are a number of films, including *No Lie* by Mitchel Block, *Daughter Rite* by Michelle Citron, and *David Holzman's Diary,* which appear to be "real" and are only revealed as otherwise when the credits at the end tell us that we have been seeing actors in a work of "fiction."

I'll propose a definition: *Documentary film is film which, through convention, creates the illusion that the events depicted are taking place or have taken place uncontrolled by those engaged in making the film.* The individual viewer will be more likely to accept the film as documentation to the degree that he or she accepts the illusion.

The next question then is, What are the conventions in film that create the illusion of reality? Almost all such conventions evolve from technology; or, simply put, there are certain things that will happen to image and sound when an event is filmed that suggest the authenticity of the image. Thus, documentary film is often authenticated by the long take, grainy images resulting from high A.S.A. film which must be used in poor lighting conditions, variable sound levels and quality, and a lack of conventional narrative editing which results in ellipses of information.

But these and other information in each film are conventional only. They do not prove or validate actuality. In fact, they are so clearly recognized that they can be duplicated with great skill. See, for example, Martin Scorsese's *Raging Bull* or the films of Peter Watkins.

The Assumption of Verified Experience

The second use of the word *realism* in film study refers to the belief that the events could happen within the realm of our projected experience. To call a film "realistic" is usually to praise it, to make the assumption that the goal of the work, somehow, is to relate directly to one's expectation of experience. To say a film is "unrealistic" generally is a condemnation. "Realism" becomes a kind of touchstone of quality. A crucial question becomes, Where did we get the idea that film or any medium ought to strive for something the audience will accept as within its experience or potential experience? A second crucial question: Why do we think it important that a film be "realistic"? What are we supposed to get from that "realism"? Vicarious experience? New knowledge of how to cope with the world? Do we need a realistic context for this?

Can't just as much be "said" about politics in *Stir Crazy* or about attitudes toward religion in *The Empire Strikes Back* as in a tale about people in an urban setting who are in anguish over these issues?

It has also been argued that being realistic is not so much a matter of how the action conforms to our expectations or experience, but whether what takes place is "unbelievable" or not. Again, what do we mean by "believable"? That it conforms with our expectation of what a character will do or say in a given situation? Is Obi-Wan Kenobe believable or unbelievable because he elects to let himself die? Is Christ believable or unbelievable in the same situation?

If a character says something you don't accept as coming from his or her lips, is it unbelievable because you've never experienced someone talking like that? Because you haven't experienced it, does that perhaps mean your experiences may be limited?

I would, in fact, argue that the so-called plausibility we often demand in fiction films is a contradiction of the reality we experience. We know madmen exist, that people often act without apparent motive, that nature confounds reason; yet in most fiction films, a visual presentation of a UFO or the theft of a ferris wheel or a two-ton elephant might be labeled unreal even though such events happen.

A French critic of the late 1940s and early 1950s, André Bazin, spent some time thinking about such problems. Bazin eventually came to the following key conclusion stated in *What Is Cinema I:*

> A very faithful drawing may actually tell us more about the model but despite the promptings of our critical intelligence it will never have the irrational power of the photograph to bear away our faith.

The key here is "bear away our faith." Reality or realism in a photograph or moving picture for Bazin, who was prone to religious allusions, lies in the ability of the image to "bear away our faith," to convince us of an illusion about the image. It is not a matter of information in the picture. As he pointed out, a drawing can give more information. It is an illusion.

Bazin did not completely abandon the idea that the content of the image—what's in the picture—will affect an individual's willingness to have faith borne away, but an essence of the art of photography is its ability to make a viewer believe that he or she is watching something in undirected time and space.

The key is this idea of undisturbed time and space. Bazin argued that, in silent film, there were two opposing tendencies:

1. The dominant tendency was toward montage and plasticity to interpret events viewed. (Bazin said the most gifted practitioners were people like D. W. Griffith in the United States, Abel Gance in France, and Sergei Eisenstein in the Soviet Union.) This became dominant filmmaking technique. In such films, the meaning of film, according to Bazin, is not in the content of the image, but in how images are related to each other. The viewer, he argued, is led through the film without even the illusion that he is making choices. There is no illusion of ambiguity. Sets, makeup, limitation of frame, all detract, according to Bazin, from the inherent power of the photographic image.

2. The second tendency in silent film, which Bazin thought largely unrecognized, was the one he liked and which he thought had even greater potential for "artistic expression." These films did not tend to break up the tale into shots which recognized and respected the integrity of time and space. Put simply, they explored an existing space indoors or outdoors by camera movement or use of depth and let time continue, let it be real time by allowing longer takes, shorter shots. Bazin's examples included the work of Robert Flaherty, F. W. Murnau, Erich von Stroheim, and Jean Renoir.

In short, Bazin said movies are more likely to carry the illusion of reality—an illusion that convinces the viewer to suspend disbelief—if the artificial elements are minimized. So, the less editing, sets, manipulating the viewer can see, the better.

It is important to emphasize that Bazin believed all this operated subconsciously—that is, the viewer doesn't say, "Ah, that is a plastic scene; it is broken up into many shots, and I recognize that a set is being used and that the frame is relatively fixed." Bazin believed that the process operated at a different level—that we are aware of not believing but cannot necessarily put into words why this is so.

Bazin gave the example of the man being chased by the lion. If the man and the lion never appear in the same shot, he argued, the illusion of time and space is ruptured, and the viewer will not believe as strongly that they shared the same time and space. Thus Bazin would argue that the sequence in Flaherty's *Louisiana Story* of the alligator chasing the boy does not sustain the illusion because it is accomplished through editing, while the sequence in *Nanook of the North* involving the struggle to pull the walrus from the sea carries the illusion of realism because of minimal editing, deep focus, and a "long take." The kind of tale told can contribute to the illusion, he argued, but the handling of time and space is most essential, as it was to silent comedians, especially Buster Keaton.

Since the filmmaker is not confined to what actually takes place (as supposedly is true in documentaries), it is possible to convert or use deep focus and long takes as a tool. Renoir in *Rules of the Game,* for example, can place people at various levels of the frame or follow a character down a hallway preserving time and space as much as possible and creating the illusion that we are watching a location that actually existed. It *suggests* the ambiguity of experience; it is not *actually* ambiguous. To Bazin, these illusions of reality are illusions, not necessarily consciously recognized by viewers, but helping to bear away their faith in the film seen.

A value in this approach, as mentioned earlier, is that it does not depend upon all the problems of experience I raised. Realism is not an objective truth in narrative fiction or documentary film; it is a series of conventions that can be used, examined, analyzed, and discussed.

Naturalism and Film

The final test of "realism" in film is the concept of "naturalism," which derives from literature and theater and is relatively recent. Before the eighteenth century, journalism did not really exist. Stories were recognized as accounts of mythology or acts of religious metaphor or entertainment. However, there was little attempt to equate them with the immediate experience present.

A sense of the importance of the present in European literature came clearly with the rise of populism, popular journalism, and sociopolitical participation of the middle classes. The initial impulse seems to have been an overt social one, an impulse to underline the immediate social and political problem and put it in the context of entertainment. One could have social import in the form of narrative.

At first, the line between fact and fancy was indiscernible. In England, the rise of the newspaper (*Bee, Tatler*) brought no clear distinction. Defoe's novels (*Diary of the Plague Years, Moll Flanders, Robinson Crusoe*) were presented as if they were actualities—acts of journalism, not acts of fiction. An early step in this process of the supposed depiction of the immediate reality was the inclination toward negativism associated strongly with the impulse toward social and economic change rather than societal documentation.

The first major recognition of naturalism as a generic form came in France. In essence, philosophers like Auguste Comte and H. A. Taine articulated the idea that all human action was the result of material causes. People were responsible for what they did. More generally, it was held that all existent phenomena are in nature and thus within the sphere of scientific knowledge. There is no supernatural. The first naturalistic novel was *Germaine Lacerteux* (1865) depicting the sordid life of a servant girl. It was Emile Zola who used the term *naturalistic* to describe this movement. Because of Zola's interest in the overt depiction of social problems and his pessimism about solving these problems, he concentrated on the lower classes—slums, poverty, dirt. This became the model: negativism as reality.

The naturalistic movement was widespread. In England, Charles Dickens was a forerunner of the school of naturalism. In Russia, Maxim Gorky and Leo Tolstoy were advocates of naturalism. In the United States, it became a major literary movement. Upton Sinclair, Theodore Dreiser, and John Dos Passos were interested in middle-class naturalism. In Germany, playwright Gerhardt Hauptman worked in naturalistic theater. In Russia, the Moscow Art Theater, under the direction of Konstantin Stanislavski, produced naturalistic plays.

Reaction to naturalism continues today, and one can find it in reviews of films like *On the Waterfront* or *Raging Bull*. Such reactions are not far removed from Alfred Lord Tennyson's in *Locksley Hall Sixty Years After:*

> Feed the budding rose of boyhood with the drainage of your sewer;
> Send the drain into the fountain, lest the stream should issue pure.
> Set the maiden fancies wallowing in the troughs of Zolaism,—
> Forward, forward, ay, and backward, downward too into
> the abysm.

In early American film, the influence of Charles Dickens' naturalism was an important factor. For example, D. W. Griffith's early films dealt heavily with the plight of the poor and the conditions surrounding poverty.

One principal example of film naturalism has been Erich von Stroheim's *Greed,* based on a consciously naturalistic novel, *McTeague,* by Frank Norris. It is interesting, perhaps, that Bazin should fix on von Stroheim and later on neorealism, a clear form of naturalism and an attempt to correlate the process of filmmaking with the analysis of meaning.

The association of the idea of documentary/realism has, I think, significantly affected the depiction of naturalism in American film. In the United States, a movement toward American naturalism emerged strongly in the 1940s, right after World War II and paralleling neorealism. Interestingly, perhaps, American naturalism concentrated heavily on crime and the lower middle class rather than the lower classes. Inspiration for this movement came largely from the socially conscious American theater of the 1930s.

Film, Illusion, and Reality

All three of the assumptions explored in this section are based, not on any external verification in truth, but on a set of conventions and illusion—aesthetic depictions and self-deceptions. My goal has been to suggest that the very concept of realism, which we so often assume to be self-evident, is so highly problematic and questionable as to be of dubious aesthetic value. It is more important to understand the process by which we—critics, teachers, and students—make assumptions about reality and the history of the concept in film than it is actually to assert its existence.

Readings on Film Genre

Books

Bodkin, Maud. *Archetypal Patterns in Poetry.* Oxford, England: Oxford University Press, 1934.

Bryson, Lyman, editor. *The Communication of Ideas.* New York: Harper, 1948.

Campbell, Joseph. *The Hero with a Thousand Faces.* Princeton, New Jersey: Princeton University Press, 1973.

Cawelti, John G. *The Six-Gun Mystique.* Bowling Green, Ohio: Bowling Green State University Popular Press, 1970.

Cawelti, John G. *Adventure, Mystery, and Romance.* Chicago: University of Chicago Press, 1976.

Dexter, Lewis Anthony, and David Manning White, editors. *People, Society and Mass Communications.* Glencoe, Illinois: Free Press, 1964.

Edinger, Edward. *Ego and Archetype.* Baltimore: Penguin Books, 1980.

Festinger, Leon. *A Theory of Cognitive Dissonance.* New York: Harper, 1957.

Freud, Sigmund. *Totem and Taboo.* Penguin, 1938.

Frye, Northrop. *Anatomy of Criticism.* Princeton, New Jersey: Princeton University Press, 1957.

Jung, Carl G., editor. *Man and His Symbols.* Garden City, New York: Doubleday, 1964.

Klapper, Joseph T. *The Effects of Mass Communication.* New York: Free Press, 1960.

McConnell, Frank. *Storytelling and Mythmaking: Images from Film and Literature.* New York: Oxford University Press, 1979.

Payne Fund Study of Motion Pictures and Social Values 1933–1939. 13 vols. New York: Arno Press, 1970.

Propp, V. I. *The Morphology of the Folktale.* Bloomington: Indiana University Research Center in Anthropology, Folklore, and Linguistics, 1958.

Schatz, Thomas. *Hollywood Genres: Formulas, Filmmaking, and the Studio System.* Philadelphia: Temple University Press, 1981.

Schramm, Wilbur, editor. *The Process and Effects of Mass Communication.* Urbana: University of Illinois Press, 1954.

Slotkin, Richard. *Regeneration through Violence.* Middletown, Connecticut: Wesleyan University Press, 1973.

Todorov, Tzvetan. *The Poetics of Prose.* Ithaca, New York: Cornell University Press, 1977.

Whannel, Paddy, and Stuart Hall. *The Popular Arts.* New York: Pantheon Books, 1964.

White, David Manning, and Bernard Rosenberg, editors. *Mass Culture: The Popular Arts in America.* New York: Free Press, 1964.

2
THE INDIVIDUAL FILM
Little Caesar as Prototype

Scarface [and] *Little Caesar* are archetypal gangster movies.
—Robert Warshow, *The Immediate Experience*

[*Little Caesar*] caused a long-lasting controversy but sold a lot of tickets and produced a host of imitators.
—Leslie Halliwell, *The Filmgoer's Companion*

Little Caesar realistically and uncompromisingly depicted the rise of the egoist through aggressiveness, ruthlessness, and organized large-scale racketeering. It was shocking, it was hard, it was not pleasant, but it was real. Lack of sentimentality, brutal assault on the nerves with gunplay, violence, chases, tense struggles over big stakes, callousness toward human feelings, appealed to a public suddenly insecure in their own lives . . . .
—Lewis Jacobs, *The Rise of the American Film*

The gangster existed in silent film, but the films in which he appeared were essentially romances. *Little Caesar* is the first clear depiction of the elements which have been evident in the gangster-film genre for more than forty years. The genre elements (motifs, themes, and icons) in *Little Caesar* have developed gradually since 1930, but they still remain persistently recognizable today.

The gangster films of the 1930s, of which *Little Caesar* was the first,

21

were generally semiconscious attempts to deal with the depression and the public's shaken confidence in American economics, politics, and myths of the self-made man. This was the first stage of the genre. In the 1940s, the next stage emerged, carrying with it the basic elements, with some slight changes, of the first. The gangster became a conscience-stricken American, anxious to help his country, willing to put aside his ruthless quest "to be somebody" so that he could join in the battle against the common enemy *(All Through the Night, Hitler: Dead or Alive)*. The depression had ended, and fear of the Axis had replaced fear of hunger.

After the war, the gangster figure returned as an object of psychological displacement, painful self-awareness, and uncertainty. Often, the returning gangster could be seen in the character of Humphrey Bogart *(Dark Passage)* or Burt Lancaster *(I Walk Alone)*. By the mid-1950s the film gangster had become less lost and disillusioned and more directed toward aggressive destruction of the society that had made him and the psychosexual problems with which he had to exist *(Machine Gun Kelly; Bonnie and Clyde;* in *The Dark Past,* gangster William Holden is actually given psychotherapy treatments by psychiatrist Lee J. Cobb, in whose house he has taken refuge).

The assessment of the genre elements in Mervyn LeRoy's *Little Caesar,* the evolvement of these elements in subsequent gangster films, and the examination of the meaning of such elements are the goals of this section. As the first and possibly the most elemental of the true gangster films, *Little Caesar* was the template on which others that followed were placed. As Robert Warshow states, *Little Caesar* is archetypal. Other important elements of the gangster-film genre clearly evolved from Howard Hawks's *Scarface* (1932) and William Wellman's *Public Enemy* (1931). Although *Public Enemy* and *Scarface* may be far better films than *Little Caesar,* we are concerned here, not with the quality of the film, but with its contributions to a genre—contributions that, I believe, are considerable in the case of *Little Caesar.*

The Title: "Caesar" and "Little"

"Little Caesar" refers to Caesar Enrico Bandello (Edward G. Robinson). Initially, Rico's rise to power is an ironic parallel to the rise of a

truly historic figure, an emperor, in more "classical" works of literature. Both *Macbeth* and *Julius Caesar,* for example, can be viewed on
one level simply as elevated gangster films. Indeed, *Macbeth* was used
as the basis for a gangster film, *Joe Macbeth* (1955), directed by Ken
Hughes and starring Paul Douglas. Shakespeare's *Caesar* is presented
on a consciously grand scale of humanity's view of itself. LeRoy's *Caesar* shows the human self-image on an intentionally reduced scale—and
the resulting tragedy. LeRoy's film was initially aimed at lower-class
and solidly middle-class audiences and designed as a work of popular
entertainment featuring vulgar behavior and images that would bring a
response of social recognition to the viewer. Part of the irony of the situation in a gangster film is that the gangster feels he is operating on a
grand scale. The irony is pushed toward its limit when, in John Huston's
Key Largo (1948), Humphrey Bogart sarcastically says of Rocco
(Edward G. Robinson in a role that is clearly an extension of Rico in
Little Caesar) that he "was more than a king; he was an emperor."
Johnny Rocco's pleased response is, "That's right."

The irony of the tie-in to grand tragedy can be seen in the regal titles of
many gangster films which followed *Little Caesar: Queen of the Mob,
King of the Underworld, King of the Roaring Twenties, The Rise and
Fall of Legs Diamond.* To carry the ironic grandeur of the title to perhaps its most ambitious conclusion, we have the gangster as God's surrogate in Francis Ford Coppola's *The Godfather.*

The use of the gangster's name as the title of the film, which appears
to have originated with *Little Caesar,* is common in the genre and also is
reminiscent of the practice of naming tragic plays for the central figure
*(Al Capone; Baby Face Nelson; Mad Dog Coll; Machine Gun Kelly;
Dillinger; Roger Touhy, Gangster; Bonnie and Clyde).* The frequency
with which real gangsters are the subject—and title—of the films also
tends to elevate the fictional gangster to a media-folk status. The most
frequently used real gangster in the genre is Al Capone, who appears in
picture after picture (sometimes answering to a slightly disguised
pseudonym) complete with his icons: cigar, fedora, topcoat, and big
black car. *Little Caesar* is based upon Capone's life; so, too, are, to
name a few, *Scarface, Al Capone, Bullets or Ballots,* and *The St. Valentine's Day Massacre.* As the genre evolved, Capone became more of a
folk symbol—a truly tragic figure, surrounded by those who wished to
kill him and take his empire (a story which was also told in several of

Shakespeare's royal gangster plays, including *Julius Caesar* and *Macbeth*).

The *Little* of *Little Caesar* also is central to an understanding of the gangster genre. The title is ironic, because it points out the contrast between the tragic figure's aspirations and the actual possibilities of his life. As Flaherty, the cop, says of Rico, "The conceit of that guy!" If Rico is Caesar, he is indeed a little one; little in the possibility of attaining his dreams and little in size.

The two representative gangster figures of the 1930s, Robinson and James Cagney, were extremely short. Consciously or unconsciously, their smallness emphasized the affinity between the cocky gangster and the "little" man in the audience who identified with the gangster on the screen and was, at the same time, told to shun him.

Robinson and Cagney are, in the gangster films from 1930–31 (*Little Caesar* and *Public Enemy*) to 1948–49 (*Key Largo* and *White Heat*), quick to attack with their fists people bigger than they are, even if they have to kick them in the shin (Robinson in *Bullets or Ballots*) to get them low enough to land a punch. The size of such protagonists is, of course, an added ironic overtone, considering their aspirations. It is also an identification image of great power. The small gangster automatically gains our sympathy. We know part of his problem and tend to react by thinking, "If that little guy on the screen can push his way to the top, why can't I?"—at least for the duration of the cathartic experience of seeing the movie. In *Our Movie-Made Children,* published in 1933, a number of teenaged slum children were interviewed about their identification with Rico. According to the book, a great many boys, instead of denying Rico, identified with him, especially if they, too, were small. The book states that the identification was so strong in several cases that the boy adopted the name Rico and wound up being shot or jailed while attempting to duplicate the film gangster's acts.

George Raft, who soon joined Robinson and Cagney as a gangster hero, also was short. Paul Muni *(Scarface)* was of average height. As the genre evolved and heroes become more seriously considered as worthwhile figures with whom to identify, Humphrey Bogart emerged as the primary gangster figure. Whenever a director or producer has chosen consciously to reassert the irony, he has gone back to the small actor (Mickey Rooney in *Baby Face Nelson,* Alan Ladd in *This Gun for Hire,* Peter Falk in *Murder, Incorporated,* John Cassavetes in *Machine Gun McCan,* Al Pacino in *The Godfather,* Richard Dreyfuss in *Dillinger).*

Time and Fate

Little Caesar opens with the robbery of a gas station. The instant the film begins, Rico is committing a major crime. There is no turning back for him after the first few seconds. His fate is sealed by the moral conviction of the audience and the moral code of the 1930s, which required that the criminal be punished for his crimes. Many gangster films begin with such an irrevocable act, often that of a murder during the course of a robbery (*White Heat, The Grissom Gang*). The viewer is warned that, once the first step has been taken, one's fate is sealed; there is no turning back. This idea of not being able to turn back is carried through in another genre motif. (See the next major section of this chapter for an extended analysis of "time" in a specific gangster film.)

"Once in the gang . . .," Joe Masara (Douglas Fairbanks, Jr.) begins in *Little Caesar,* and then trails off. "You know the rest. I've never seen the guy who could get away from it." The gangster's fate is decided. He can no more evade the gang, break away from it, than Oedipus could have avoided the wrath of the gods. Later, Joe echoes his early statement, saying, "Can't a guy ever quit?" Finally, Olga (Glenda Farrell) tells Joe to go to the police, that the world is not large enough to escape from Rico and the gang. "Where do we run to?" she asks. "There is no place to hide." This attempt, always futile, to hide, to escape from the gang and one's destiny, is repeated constantly in gangster films (*Tight Spot, The Enforcer, The Brothers Rico, Kiss of Death, The Valachi Papers*).

In the scene immediately following the initial robbery in *Little Caesar*, Rico and Joe are in a diner. Rico turns back the diner clock to establish an alibi. Joe admires him for being smart: "Got to hand it to you, Rico. The old bean's working all the time." We do not see the alibi called into question in the film, but the original screenplay (published in John Gassner's *Twenty Best Film Plays)* carries the scene through to a confrontation with the police in which Rico's faith in his turned-back clock does save him. The visual attempt to arrest time is a generic warning in the gangster film. Time, for a gangster, goes quickly. His chances of reaching old age are almost nonexistent, and he knows it. His life is lived at a rapid, precarious pace, not the cautious one-step-at-a-time of the viewer's. For this reason, the criminal tries to "live" as much as possible and to hold back time while he is doing so. Coppola plays upon this feeling in *The Godfather,* when he shows us that Sonny (James Caan), the overtly emotional man of action who reminds us of the film

145, 229

gangsters of the 1930s, is, like Rico (and Tony in *Scarface,* and Tom in *Public Enemy)*, gunned down at an early age. Marlon Brando, who shows little public emotion and displays great caution throughout the film, manages to survive much violence, and finally dies an ironically *natural* death.

Closely allied to the holding back of time is the gangster's reliance upon specific timing, being at a particular location at a specific time. The gangster must control time, as Rico does with the diner clock, or it may elude him and send his world crashing down. Practically, timing is important because, if things are not done quickly and precisely, the police will arrive before the gangsters can get away. The element of control of time is evident in *Little Caesar,* when Rico insists that the Bronze Peacock robbery take place at midnight on New Year's Eve. It does; and, precisely at that moment, Rico murders the crime commissioner. In *Bullets or Ballots,* Robinson sets 10 P.M. as the time he will deliver marked money to the bosses; even though he is mortally wounded, he keeps the appointment. Again, Robinson in *Key Largo* checks his watch and insists on the phone that Ziggy (Marc Lawrence) keep their appointment on time or "the deal's off." In Don Siegel's *The Line-Up,* Dancer (Eli Wallach) has to deliver heroin to The Man at a precise moment; to miss it is to die for his failure.

To the Big City

Another motif of the genre established in *Little Caesar* is closely tied to the concept of the self-made man, an ideal that has existed in American popular fiction since the time of the Revolution (see John Cawelti's *Apostles of the Self-Made Man,* University of Chicago Press, 1964). We first meet Rico and Joe in a small town (which was not the case in W. R. Burnett's novel), where we learn that Rico wants to go to the big city, "East," and make something of himself like "Diamond" Pete Montana, about whom he has just read in a newspaper.

Rico leaves rural America, the last vestige of frontier echoes, to make his way in the new American frontier—the big industrial urban complex. It is the exact reversal of the other primary American film genre, the Western, in which the hero frequently has come from the East to escape the constrictions of the urban scene, the new America. *(The Virginian* is the classic example of this motif, which is still used in films such as *Something Big,* in which Dean Martin is an easterner trying to avoid the need to return to the city.)

The advantage of the gangster in going to the big city is that he knows, from the fiction he's read about the American dream, that the city is *the* place of opportunity. There, an enterprising young man with nothing but nerve, drive, and loyalty for sale can get ahead, whether he comes from rural America (Rooney in *Baby Face Nelson*, Shelley Winters and her sons in *Bloody Mama*, Bogart in *High Sierra*, Scott Wilson in *The Grissom Gang*), another country (Capone in all the Capone films, Henry Silva in *Johnny Cool*, Robinson in *Key Largo*, Marlon Brando in *The Godfather*), or the alienated slums of the city itself, from which the audience often is not more than a generation removed (Cagney in *Public Enemy* and *Angels with Dirty Faces*, Bogart in *Dead End*, John Davis Chandler in *Mad Dog Coll*, Wallace Beery in *The Secret Six*, Clark Gable in *Manhattan Melodrama*).

Gangsters and Dancers

A minor but interesting motif in gangster films first appears in the diner scene in *Little Caesar*. Joe is a dancer who wants to dance professionally; at one point in the film, we see him dance on the stage of the Bronze Peacock. Both Cagney and Raft were professional dancers before becoming movie gangsters and they continued to dance in films, sometimes tying the skill directly to the gangster film (Cagney in *Battling Hoofer* and Raft in *Bolero*). The motif of the gangster and dance is also present in *Quick Millions*, *The George Raft Story*, and *The Rise and Fall of Legs Diamond*.

The dancer as criminal allows the genre to include a nervous, graceful sense of movement, or hypervitality. The motif is used specifically for this purpose in *The Line-Up*, in which Dancer (Eli Wallach) intentionally moves like a dancer as he goes through his series of brutal murders. The dancer's vitality of motion is important to the American sense of affirmation, dynamism, and spontaneous expression. Few moments are as clearly expressive of this vitality in American films as the one in which Cagney (in *Public Enemy*) actually breaks into a dance step on the street after meeting Jean Harlow.

The dancer as criminal also ties in to the musical genre of the 1930s. In films from *The Gold Diggers of 1933* through *The Ziegfeld Girl* (1941), the dancer, usually female (perhaps the dance musical gave females of the 1930s audience a protagonist with whom to identify in much the same way gangster films of that period gave males ambiguous figures with whom to identify), rises ruthlessly to the top over her competitors "who don't have it any more." The dancer's rise, like the gangster's, is often halted just when success is within her reach. It is snatched suddenly from the hands of the dancer and gangster and, vicariously, from the audience because the rules of the game of "getting ahead" have somehow been violated. There is an interesting ambivalence in both gangster films and dance films concerning the protagonist's quest for success. The self-made man is expected to move ahead ruthlessly, to accept power, to be dynamic; but this lauded behavior is contrary to Christian ethics. Society worships ruthless ambition but insists that we love our neighbor. The gangster and dancer, by deserting the limbo existence between these clashing concepts, are writing their own doom. We root for the gangster—and are guiltily gratified when he is gunned down.

Sex and the Gangster

Combining dancer and criminal also invites a kind of simple-minded aspersion on his masculinity. Rico calls Joe a "sissy." "Dancin's all right for a sideline," says Rico, "but it ain't a man's game." Rico, however, clearly protests too much. His attachment to Joe and, to a great extent, Joe's to Rico, can be seen most clearly in terms of latent homosexuality. Rico works hard to keep Joe from going back to Olga. Without knowing how much he is revealing, Rico says, after he cannot shoot Joe, "This is what I get for liking a guy too much." The subdued sexual undercurrent also can be seen, as Robin Wood points out, in *Scarface,* in Tony's fairly overt incestuous feeling for his sister. Oedipal overtones are evident in such gangster films as *Machine Gun Kelly, Baby Face Nelson, Gun Crazy, Bloody Mama,* and *The Grissom Gang.* These sexual undercurrents accomplish two things. First, they may render the gangster somewhat impure in conventional social/moral terms, although his is an impurity that may well touch the repressed sexual concerns or guilts of the viewers, who both identify with and condemn the gangster. Second, the sexual nuance of homosexuality or depravity elevates the tragic elements of the genre, for such problems are not normally associated with the antisocial figure in drama but with the lofty tragic figure (for example, in the Oedipal relationship in *Hamlet*).

Women and Acquisitions

Women do have an important function for the gangster, but it is not a sexual one; at least, it wasn't until more recent films, such as *Once Upon a Time in America.* Women are, as Warshow points out, acquisitions for the gangster, who has no conscious interest in sex. He is an ascetic. Rico does not drink; we seldom see a Capone figure actively interested in women as sexual objects. Women and liquor are to be displayed—but not trusted. Both can betray the gangster. In *Little Caesar,* Rico, in his speech at his testimonial banquet, says: "The liquor is good. I don't drink it, myself. . . .Good to see you gents with your molls." In *Key Largo,* Rocco proudly calls Gay (Claire Trevor) out of a dark room to display her to Ziggy, his old gangster friend. Rocco then dismisses her and gets down to business. The "pure" gangster disdains women as sex objects. "Women—dancin'—where do they get you?" says Rico with a sneer. One reason we know early in *The Godfather* that James Caan will make a poor "Don" is his interest in sex; Caan's overt passions are contrasted with the control of Al Pacino, who emerges as the properly ascetic "Don" to whom Brando passes his mantle.

Women are rewards, proofs of success, like the stickpin and the ring Rico admires on Pete Montana in *Little Caesar* and the $1,500 painting he looks at in awe in the Big Boy's home. Women, jewels, paintings, big houses, flashy cars, tuxedos, cigars are all evidence that the gangster has "made it" in his business—and in American society. He engages, quite simply, in a parody of conspicuous consumption.

Getting Up in the World

Getting ahead is the gangster's simple goal. No matter how high he gets, the gangster always wants to get higher, until he has gone so high that he is sure to fall (rather like Charlie Chaplin as Hitler on the rising barber chair in *The Great Dictator).* In *Little Caesar,* Rico keeps talking about how Sam Vettori, Diamond Pete, and even the Big Boy "can't take it." In *Key Largo,* Bogart says he knows what Rocco wants, even though Rocco can't articulate it. "He wants more," says Bogart. Rocco beams and says, "That's right. I want more." "And will you ever have enough?" "No," responds Rocco seriously; "I never have."

The higher the gangster gets, the more dangerous is his position, not unlike the situation of an aggressive young man in a corporate structure—but the gangster can't turn back. "You're getting up in the world, aren't you, Rico?" says Flaherty, the cop in *Little Caesar* at the banquet. Rico smiles. Later, Rico preens himself in his first tuxedo before a mirror as he gets ready to meet the Big Boy. Otero (George E. Stone) says with admiration, "You're getting up in the world, Rico." Rico nods.

Sidney Blackmer and Edward G. Robinson in *Little Caesar.*

Posing for a wedding photograph in *The Godfather.*

Getting up in the world is tied to the idea of aspiration and social success. The gang, in gangster films, is very often an efficient business, a corporation.

The Gang as a Business

Although the gang is a business in the gangster genre, it is a very special kind of business which has been created in American fiction and in Hollywood. When Roger Corman states in a title at the beginning of *The St. Valentine's Day Massacre* that "this is what really happened," he is both making a joke and being quite serious at the same time, for Corman's films, like much of the genre since *Little Caesar,* are an attempt, not to re-create reality, but to create a legend that can be used for a thematic purpose. To draw an establishment of legend, the viewer might consider the response of the newspaper editor in John Ford's *The Man Who Shot Liberty Valance.* Given the truth about the death of Valance, he prefers to ignore it and to print the legend, which is more meaningful to the public and has already been accepted by the readers as reality. The gangster genre is, possibly, more a part of life in America than is the real gangster; often, a film has more to do with shaping our views of society than with any real criminal activity and has more to do with our behavior than with any contact with criminals through the news media.

Specifically, the business milieu of the gangster film reflects our view of American business enterprise in general, even if we happen to be part of a business structure that does not conform to this image. In no film is this viewpoint more evident than in *The Godfather,* in which Brando and, later, Pacino repeatedly refer to the activities as "business"—a family business supporting many employees for whom they are responsible.

In the gangster film, the gang is often a loose feudal system with individual warlords held in tow by one strong regent who reports to a mysterious boss or mysterious bosses. The bosses remain above the gang, anonymous, aloof, but in control. When the bosses are revealed, we find they are "upper class," influential, wealthy. They may be idle rich (Sidney Blackmer in *Little Caesar*), bankers and government officials *(Bullets or Ballots; Once upon a Time in America),* or apparently respectable middle-class businessmen (Jack Elam in *Baby Face Nelson;* Fred Clark in *White Heat*). It is these upper- and middle-class bosses, hiding behind a gang leader of courage, whom we are taught to hate in the gangster films. They, in the midst of the depression we know exists in the films of the 1930s (but seldom see), are accumulating wealth, taking what there is of available money, wearing tuxedos, and living off the labor of ambitious gangsters who have risen from the working classes. We see the gangster take the risks, hold the small gang bosses in line, protect his own position, exact tribute from the workers who don't have enough for themselves, and, finally, inevitably, fall—only to be replaced by another like himself—while the top bosses continue to be protected. This pattern is apparent in *Little Caesar,* in which the Big Boy is not caught or punished, and can be seen, strikingly, in the quasi-gangster film *On the Waterfront,* where Lee J. Cobb is the ambitious gangster who fronts for the bosses.

In contrast to the upper-class manipulators—the social chairmen of the board of crime—are the workers, the on-the-line gangsters. Between these extremes are the tragic figures of the genre: the Ricos, the members of the minority trying to get ahead. The attainable goal for such men is to replace the man who reports to the bosses, to replace a man who, like himself, has also risen from a lower class. More recently, in films like *The St. Valentine's Day Massacre, The Godfather, The Valachi Papers,* and *Honor Thy Father,* we see an ironic twist—the immigrant gangsters as bosses, controlling destinies and dividing spoils at businesslike meetings of the board.

In the early gangster films, the gang itself was often composed of first- or second-generation immigrants, like the people who made up much of the movie audience of the 1930s. In *Little Caesar,* the gang members are clearly Italian. They meet at Palermo's and have names like Bandello, Masara, Passa, and Otero. Arnie Lorch doesn't have a particularly Italian name; but he and his assistant have the only Italian accents in the film (outside of "yellow" Tony's mother), although Arnie, in Burnett's novel, was Jewish. Most often over the years, when protests did not rise too loudly, gang members have been Italian (*Little Caesar; Scarface; The Brothers Rico; The Brotherhood; The Godfather; The Valachi Papers*), but they can be Irish (*Public Enemy; The Roaring Twenties*), rural whites (*Pretty Boy Floyd; Bloody Mama; Bonnie and Clyde; The Grissom Gang; Dillinger*), or Jewish (*Murder, Incorporated; King of the Roaring Twenties;* Nails Nathan in *Public Enemy*). Black gangs, it might be added, although they existed from 1910 on, did not appear in an American film until the 1970s (*Dirty Harry; Cotton Comes to Harlem; Shaft*). Hollywood clearly felt that black aspirations were not such that they had to be included in the genre as a mainstream element, and the black moviegoer did not protest not being depicted as a criminal.

Law Abiders and Middle-Class Americans

The social forces against which the gang fought in the 1930s and which have been carried into the present were invariably represented by people with middle-class American names. In *Little Caesar* the crime commissioner Rico kills is Alvin McLure. In *Bullets or Ballots,* Bogart kills a wealthy crusading publisher named Bryant. Even within the gang structure, the upper-middle echelons usually are manned by middle-class Americans like *Little Caesar*'s Pete Montana.

The middle management and upper levels of the criminal structure are solidly American, as are the forces of "good" that battle the gangster. Whether a man is law-abiding or not, there is a level above which the lower class cannot rise, a point at which the American dream draws the line. Rico's downfall is partly a matter of his aspiring too high, to a level of society and business filled by more "American" Americans. An audience viewing a gangster film in the 1930s, especially if they were members of the working class, may well have felt that there was something to be despised in a system in which they could not possibly get ahead, as they had been led to believe they might. At the same time, however, the audience might have been reinforced in their belief that this is the way things are and will inevitably remain.

Surroundings and Ceremonies

The gangster's very aspirations and their manifestations are parodies of American business, although the American public of the 1930s had been conditioned through films to accept these aspirations without question. The middle-echelon gangster boss has a comfortable, even plush, office (Sam Vettori and Arnie Lorch in *Little Caesar*) from which he conducts his business—although one may ask why gangsters need offices other than to display their possession of them. The offices often are unsafe places that have to be heavily guarded to protect the always-threatened gangster from those who would take his place.

The gangster's office is often in a nightclub or bar (*Little Caesar; I Walk Alone; Angels with Dirty Faces; Bullets or Ballots; The Grissom Gang; King of the Roaring Twenties; Once upon a Time in America),* a location that ties in the gangster with entertainment, a colorful way of life, an exciting, but slightly unsavory, social endeavor that both at-

Table 2.1
Observations on American Gangster Film History since 1930

	1930–1933	1934–1938	1939–1945	1946–1959	1960–1970	1971–Present
Some Key Films	*Little Caesar; Scarface; Public Enemy; The Secret Six; Beast of the City; Quick Millions*	*Bullets or Ballots; Angels with Dirty Faces; Marked Woman; Manhattan Melodrama; Dead End*	*High Sierra; The Roaring Twenties; All through the Night*	*White Heat; Baby Face Nelson; I Walk Alone; Gun Crazy; They Live by Night*	*The St. Valentine's Day Massacre; Bonnie and Clyde; Bloody Mama; Underworld U.S.A.*	*The Godfather; The Valachi Papers; The Getaway; The Grissom Gang; Honor Thy Father; Once upon a Time in America*
Context	Start of depression; rise of unions; uncertainty of American dream in literature; fear of immigrant	Deep depression; rise of Roosevelt; search for strong individual leader in politics	Preludes to war and war itself; threat of isolation and ideological and military defeat	War ends; A-bomb; Korea; fear of Armageddon; disillusionment over American power	Vietnam; internal political unrest; lack of confidence in solidarity of state	Nixon; detente with Russia, China
Primary Form	Rise and fall of the lower-class gangster	Heroic self-sacrifice	Disillusionment with American ideals	Fall of criminal individual	Mythic elevation of gangsters	Search for affirming ideals
Era	1920s	Contemporary	Contemporary	Contemporary	1920s–1930s	Contemporary

Protagonist	Grotesque; small urban, lower-class ethnic background; tough; ironic	Same as earlier, but torn between social responsibility and friendship; contrast between being a criminal and a responsible friend	More conventional looking, but psychologically flawed	Taller, not handsome; loner in gang; jeopardized by others in gang; cynical, but with hopes for love; faith in American ideals	Young, antisocial, antiestablishment, unconscious revolutionary against shallow, frightened society	Responsible, family head; patriarchial businessman
Protagonist's Goals	Business success; to see self and to have others accept and see him as successful	Save others of his class	Sanity for self; understanding of world of confusion	Protect and affirm ideals of country	Gratification of animal needs; celebration of self; living for the moment	Affirmation of old values; desire for order in father figure above law
Problems	Little man in society; American dream vs. American reality; ambivalence between audience's identification with criminal and need to reject him	Social-political responsibility, poverty, and morality in face of temptations of society (social pseudo-documentary)	Fear of loneliness; Freudian alienation	Search for family, loved ones in gang; seeking values to which gangster already is alien	Questioning of accepted ideals of society and simplistic responses to violence; evaluation of and questioning of past, picturing of gangster as lone heroic figure	Fear of moral and social chaos
Icons and Settings	Guns, machine guns, flashy suits, black limousines, cigars, tuxedos, blondes; *Settings:* offices, nightclubs, lower-class homes	Icons same, but settings include slums, small apartments, jails, D.A.s' offices	Dark offices, taverns, middle-class homes, alleys, nightclubs	Older cars, country roads, isolated cafes, farmhouses	Return to icons of early 1930s	Upper-middle-class homes, older settings revisited, church

James Caan, Marlon Brando, Al Pacino and John Cazale in *The Godfather.*

Rico (Edward G. Robinson) in the shootout at the end of *Little Caesar.*

tracts and frightens the viewer. The entertainment tie-in becomes explicit in *The Godfather,* with the Corleone family moving into the movie business and Las Vegas nightclubs.

A funeral can be both a ceremony and a surrounding in a gangster film. Quite frequently, a funeral is an occasion for the central gangster to bid a fond, expensive farewell to the man he has replaced or to a rival gang leader he has eliminated. The gangster sends the biggest wreath; often there is a joke made by him or the members of his gang about how deeply touched the boss is. The funeral foreshadows the death of the boss himself (who mocks the sacred image of the funeral), and it contrasts with the central figure's eventual downfall and ignoble death (Rico behind the billboard in *Little Caesar;* Cagney mummified and dropped through his front doorway in *Public Enemy;* Muni in the bullet-riddled room in *Scarface;* Rooney coughing blood in the graveyard as he dies in *Baby Face Nelson).* James Caan's death and the funeral parlor sequence in *The Godfather* are grim reminders of the tradition and clearly identify Caan as having been part of it. In a sense, the ignoble death of the gangster has a greater effect upon the audience than the death that resulted in the grand funeral. In most gangster films, this apparent contradiction of values becomes a comment upon a society that falsely mourns those it has discarded or, to paraphrase Howard Hawks, those who have shown by their death that "they aren't good enough."

Another frequent ceremony in the gangster genre is the banquet, which often is held as a testimonial for the gangster when he has "made it." There is always an element of parody in such a banquet—a mocking of the businessman's testimonial for service (*Little Caesar; The St. Valentine's Day Massacre; Some Like It Hot;* the wedding feast at the beginning of *The Godfather,* the initiation ceremony in *The Valachi Papers;* the dinner party in *Honor Thy Father).* In *Little Caesar,* "Loyalty and Friendship" are printed on the banner behind Rico at his banquet, a dinner at which he is given a stolen watch. Rico has displayed neither loyalty nor friendship, and he can expect neither. Business is not a matter of loyalty and friendship. He who displays such traits is certainly doomed in the gangster film—and, by extension, perhaps in life. This element is intentionally reversed in *The Godfather,* as are so many of the *Little Caesar* archetypes; the loyal gang members, Robert Duvall and Richard Castellani, survive and are rewarded, while all who have betrayed the Corleones are executed.

A church is often shown in gangster films—but only briefly. The church is a place on whose steps the gangster dies. The church is a place of irrelevance and ineffectuality in the society of the genre and in life. Nowhere is this irrelevance more evident than in *The Godfather,* in the sequence of quick cuts between the church at which Pacino is serving as godfather for his sister's baby and the violent murders Pacino has arranged to take place while he establishes his alibi. It is only in death that the film gangster finds himself concerned about God; and even then, his arrival at the church is less a matter of choice than of chance (Tony's death in *Little Caesar;* Cagney's death in *The Roaring Twenties,* Weiss's death in *The St. Valentine's Day Massacre).*

The Gangster's Decline and Fall

The downfall of the gangster comes about rapidly, either just after he has reached his goal or, ironically, when he has almost reached it. The downfall often is a loss of social position, not just death. In *Little Caesar,* Rico is reduced to poverty (as are Cagney in *The Roaring Twenties,* Raft in *If I Had a Million,* and DeNiro in *Once upon a Time in America),* emphasizing what happens to those of lower classes who dare to challenge society on its own terms. Rico's fall to poverty, one should note, does not take place in Burnett's novel—only in the film. The gangster's downfall is complete so that the audience can pull away at the end, to realize that we are not like Rico, that we are not so foolish as to aspire beyond our known limits. It is questionable, however, whether the downfall of the gangster always works to this end, as it clearly has been intended to do. According to Warshow, the audience identifies with the central figure: we immerse ourselves in his antisocial behavior, but we are purged of our guilt for admiring him by drawing away from him as he falls. It is difficult, however, to pull away so quickly. The fall is sudden, and the memory of the gangster's rise and vitality are still vivid. Thus, when Cagney staggers through the rain in *Public Enemy* after attacking the rival gang alone and being shot, he says, "I ain't so tough." Certainly, we are supposed to agree with him; but agreement is difficult, for he has been admirably tough. We do not feel that he is worthless. So, too, Rico's dying words in *Little Caesar* are supposed to be pathetic, and his fate, deserved. "Mother of Mercy," says Rico, "is this the end of Rico?" We are supposed to marvel at Rico's turning to God after all he has done and to remark upon his vanity for thinking of himself in the third person as someone above the normal traffic of existence.

The problem is—and it is part of the ambivalence of the genre, which both admires and rejects the gangster—that before his death, even faced with a return to poverty, Rico has gone down in a blaze of glory; he has once again challenged society, even though he couldn't win. Death is the result for the gangster, but ambivalence is our reaction to his existence and demise. This ambivalence exists with irony in *The Godfather,* in which it is not the gangster's death that causes our unease, but his survival and success.

Weapons and Style

It is interesting to contrast the use of weapons in gangster films and in Westerns. "Shoot first, and argue afterwards," says Rico in *Little Caesar.* Muni says approximately the same thing in *Scarface.* For the gangster, the gun is a means to an end, not an object of style. There is no fast draw, no moment of decision. You get as close as possible, with as big a gun as possible, and shoot your enemy as full of lead as you can. It is best if the man you are shooting is unarmed. The gun, like a typewriter or telephone, is a tool of business, not an object through which the gangster can express himself. It is an extension of his matter-of-fact character, the only skill he knows and the one upon which he must build his career. Of his gun, Rico says, "That's all I got between me and them, between me and the whole world."

The Public

For all the lip service given to "the public and its protection" in gangster films, it is remarkable how little of the public is actually seen on the screen. The public, the ordinary man, remains in the background of a gangster film; he seldom steps out to be identified, seldom is harmed, and often admires the gangster (newsboys and manicurists always smile sincerely and say "come back again" to the gangster). The public is not really relevant to the genre. In the gangster film, the audience views the working out of a myth, a process that can be repeated with infinite variations depending upon the social and political milieu of the time or country. The myth does not deal with the effect of crime upon real people. It is concerned with the persona of the gangster and the qualities in him and our society with which we identify and against which we react.

The elements of the gangster genre, the motifs with which we have been dealing, can be controlled and explored to make an aesthetic statement or critique. Defining the genre as it emerged from *Little Caesar* helps us to appreciate films that draw upon the tradition. An understanding of the generic roots of a film like *The Godfather, The Valachi Papers,* or *The St. Valentine's Day Massacre* helps us to appreciate the ironies of a filmmaker.

Readings on the Gangster Film

Books

Bergman, Andrew. *We're in the Money.* New York: New York University Press, 1971.

Burnett, William Riley. *Little Caesar.* New York: Dial Press, 1929.

Cawelti, John. *Apostles of the Self-Made Man.* Chicago: University of Chicago Press, 1965.

Cawelti, John, editor. *Focus on Bonnie and Clyde.* Englewood Cliffs, New Jersey: Prentice-Hall, 1973.

Clarens, Carlos. *Crime Movies: From Griffith to* The Godfather *and Beyond.* New York: W. W. Norton, 1980.

Everson, William K. "The Gangster Film" In *Film Review, 1969-70,* edited by Maurice Speech. London: W. H. Allen, 1970.

Forman, Henry James. *Our Movie Made Children.* New York: Macmillan, 1933.

Gassner, John, and Dudley Nichols, editors. *Twenty Best Film Plays.* New York: Crown Publishers, 1943.

McArthur, Colin. *Underworld U.S.A.* New York: Viking Press, 1972.

Rosow, Eugene. *Born to Lose: The Gangster Film in America.* New York: Oxford University Press, 1978.

Shadoian, Jack. *Dreams and Dead Ends: The American Gangster/ Crime Film.* Cambridge, Massachusetts: MIT Press, 1977.

Thrasher, Frederic. "The Screen Speaks Out." In *Okay for Sound.* New York: Duell, Sloan and Pearce, 1946.

Warshow, Robert. "The Gangster as a Tragic Hero." In *The Immediate Experience.* New York: Atheneum Press, 1970.

Periodicals

Sacks, Arthur. "An Analysis of Gangster Movies of the Early Thirties." *The Velvet Light Trap,* no.1 (1970).

Whitehall, Richard. " 'Crime, Inc.,' A Three-Part Dossier on the American Gangster Film." *Films and Filming,* January-March 1964.

Table 2.2
Key Gangster Films

Year	Title	Director	Principal Actors
1930	*Little Caesar*	Mervin LeRoy	Edward G. Robinson
1931	*Quick Millions*	Rowland Brown	Spencer Tracy, George Raft
1931	*The Secret Six*	George Hill	Wallace Beery, Clark Gable
1931	*Public Enemy*	William Wellman	James Cagney
1932	*Scarface*	Howard Hawks	Paul Muni, George Raft
1933	*Blood Money*	Rowland Brown	George Bancroft
1934	*Manhattan Melodrama*	W. S. Van Dyke	Clark Gable, William Powell
1936	*Bullets or Ballots*	William Keighley	Edward G. Robinson
1937	*Dead End*	William Wyler	Humphrey Bogart
1937	*You Only Live Once**	Fritz Lang	Henry Fonda, Sylvia Sidney
1938	*Angels With Dirty Faces*	Michael Curtiz	James Cagney, Humphrey Bogart
1939	*The Roaring Twenties*	Raoul Walsh	James Cagney, Humphrey Bogart
1941	*High Sierra**	Raoul Walsh	Humphrey Bogart, Ida Lupino
1941	*All Through the Night*	Vincent Sherman	Humphrey Bogart, Conrad Veidt
1944	*Roger Touhy, Gangster*	Robert Florey	Preston Foster
1945	*Dillinger*	Max Nosseck	Lawrence Tierney
1947	*Kiss of Death*	Henry Hathaway	Richard Widmark, Victor Mature
1947	*They Live by Night**	Nicholas Ray	Farley Granger
1947	*I Walk Alone*	Byron Haskin	Burt Lancaster, Kirk Douglas
1948	*Key Largo*	John Huston	Edward G. Robinson, Humphrey Bogart

*These films are arranged chronologically to accompany Table 2.1. They are possibly best described as bandit gangster films. They include many of the same elements of the more archetypal rise-and-fall gangster films, but they have a number of distinguishing characteristics. They are essentially love stories. The protagonist escapes or is released from jail, often through the machinations of a powerful but corrupt figure who needs his talent. The hero either meets, or falls in love with a woman, or returns to his old girl; and they embark on a life of crime, usually following a killing during a robbery—a killing which is not their fault. The films in this subgenre are essentially rural, as opposed to the urban setting of the dominant genre. The couple find themselves living a dangerous, nomadic existence, their love reaffirmed with each onslaught. A substantial part of the film is devoted to showing the couple in their automobile, living within the machine. The police are generally cold, faceless creatures who allow them no respite. Ultimately, the couple are destroyed at the peak of their exhaustion and love, redeemed in what can be seen basically as a Romeo and Juliet fulfillment, in much the same way as the rise-and-fall gangster films can be seen in relationship to heroic tragedies. *The Getaway* is an interesting example of the subgenre and one that very clearly plays upon our expectations from this type of gangster film.

Table 2.2 *(Continued)*

Year	Title	Director	Principal Actors
1948	*The Dark Past*	Rudolph Mate	William Holden, Lee J. Cobb
1949	*White Heat**	Raoul Walsh	James Cagney
1950	*Gun Crazy**	Joseph Lewis	John Dall, Peggy Cummins
1951	*The Enforcer*	Bretaigne Windust	Humphrey Bogart
1955	*The Big Combo*	Joseph Lewis	Cornel Wilde, Richard Conte
1955	*Joe Macbeth*	Ken Hughes	Paul Douglas, Ruth Roman
1957	*Baby Face Nelson**	Don Siegel	Mickey Rooney
1958	*Machine Gun Kelly*	Roger Corman	Charles Bronson
1959	*Some Like It Hot*	Billy Wilder	Jack Lemmon, Tony Curtis, Marilyn Monroe
1960	*Pretty Boy Floyd*	Herbert Leder	John Erickson
1960	*The Rise and Fall of Legs Diamond*	Budd Boetticher	Ray Danton
1960	*Murder, Incorporated*	Burt Balaban	Stuart Rosenberg, Peter Falk
1960	*Underworld U.S.A.*	Sam Fuller	Cliff Robertson
1960	*The George Raft Story*	Joseph Newman	Ray Danton
1964	*Johnny Cool*	William Asher	Henry Silva, Brad Dexter
1967	*Bonnie and Clyde**	Arthur Penn	Warren Beatty, Faye Dunaway
1967	*The St. Valentine's Day Massacre*	Roger Corman	Jason Robards, Jr., George Segal
1970	*Bloody Mama*	Roger Corman	Shelley Winters, Don Stroud
1971	*The Grissom Gang*	Robert Aldrich	Scott Wilson, Tony Musante
1972	*The Godfather*	Francis Ford Coppola	Marlon Brando, Al Pacino
1973	*The Valachi Papers*	Terence Young	Charles Bronson, Lino Venturi
1973	*Honor Thy Father*	Paul Wendkos	Joseph Bologna, Raf Vallone
1973	*The Getaway**	Sam Peckinpah	Steve McQueen, Ali McGraw
1973	*Dillinger**	John Milius	Warren Oates, Ben Johnson
1974	*The Godfather, Part II*	Francis Ford Coppola	Al Pacino, Robert DeNiro
1974	*Thieves Like Us**	Robert Altman	Keith Carradine
1984	*Once upon a Time in America*	Sergio Leone	Robert DeNiro

3
THE INDIVIDUAL FILM
Once upon a Time in America as Narrative Model

Assumptions

The author has several generic assumptions that should be brought to the fore in beginning an analysis of *Once upon a Time in America*. As the introduction to this book suggests, my basic position is relativist. I do not believe that the history of aesthetic thought has brought us one step closer to being able to differentiate qualitatively between works. That judgments will continue to be made is obvious; that they reflect anything beyond the acquired taste of an individual or culture segment is doubtful; that they can be substantiated with any kind of detachment is alchemical.

My point in making the above assertions is not to claim originality—the argument has been made by others, including Northrop Frye, John Cawelti, and Norman O. Brown—but to make clear that I am not trying to present an argument that *Once upon a Time in America* is particularly elevated by my analysis. I am not claiming something unique for the film but citing it as an example of how a particular means of structural analysis can be used to aid an understanding of both an individual gangster film and the totality of film. Conversely, it should be clear that I am not concerned with any assertion that *Once upon a Time in America* is not worth singular attention because it is neither high art nor folk art.

Several years ago, Gerard Gennette engaged in a fine analysis of narrative time in Marcel Proust's *Remembrance of Things Past* (*Figures,*

Young gang members in *Once upon a Time in America.*

The Williamsburg Bridge above New York's streets in *Once upon a Time in America.*

Robert De Niro in *Once upon a Time in America*.

Elizabeth McGovern and Robert De Niro in *Once upon a Time in America*.

Paris: Edition du Seuil, 1966). Gennette, dealing with an already canonized work, argued that Proust's use of narrative time was a touchstone to his genius, that a structural analysis would yield evidence of that genius. I think, as fine as Gennette's essay is and as much as it has influenced me, he succeeded in doing nothing of the kind. That which he wrote is as applicable to Proust as to Stephen King.

I wish also to recognize that I do not think the kind of structural analysis in which I will engage is particularly objective. It is "a" way, not "the" way. It is, as I believe all structural analysis is, not a discovery of a buried skeleton of truth, but a template created by the critic, which he or she proposes will be a useful one in pursuing a particular line of inquiry. The legacy of Claude Levi-Strauss has been that of grail seeking. If the world is, indeed, divided into good and bad, up and down, here and there, past and future—in fact, if the world is actually a series of oppositions—then the structure is clearly there to be discovered. If, however, as Ken Wilber (*No Boundary,* Boulder, Colorado, and London: Shambala, 1979) and others have suggested, the oppositions are not there but are created by the human imagination to establish an order needed by the ego, then such structural truths are not ultimate at all, but revelations of the mind of the creator.

Put another way, if a critic discovers that the works of Vladimir Nabokov all reveal the same basic pattern of opposing relationships and follow the same "structure," the critic is dealing with his or her imposition upon that work. The critic came looking, chose the tools, and discovered himself. I have no real quarrel with this procedure, however. Later, I will indulge in it myself. What I object to is the assumption upon the part of the critic that a discovery has been made that blots out other analysis—that objectifiable truth has been discovered about the work and, possibly, about literature, film, or other acts of creation. I find it far more acceptable and valuable for critics to recognize that they are engaged in an essentially creative act. The critic's process is created or borrowed and then applied to a created work; the result, one hopes, is illuminating for both critic and reader. The criticism is a modification of the original work and should illuminate the relation of the critic—and the reader—to it. It is neither a justification, a condemnation, nor a vindication of the original creative act.

The reason so many "artists" are unhappy even with affirmative criticism is that they recognize, even if they are unable to articulate, that another personality, another ego, in the process of converting the creative act to an analysis, has taken the original creation a step away and made it part of someone else's imagination. The novel, coupled with the criticism, becomes a new creative act: the novel/criticism. It is the critic's unwillingness to recognize this, to believe in a quasi-science called criticism, that causes difficulty.

In consideration of the above argument, I will take a specific course in dealing with the issue of time in *Once upon a Time in America.* First I will indicate my relationship to the project, next, I will move to a structural analysis of time transitions in the context of reservations indicated above, and then I will conclude with a brief criticism of my own analysis.

Creation

In the summer of 1981 Sergio Leone got in touch with me. He had read some of my fiction published in Italy and thought I might be an appropriate person to write the dialogue for *Once upon a Time in America.* The film was scheduled to be (and was in 1982) shot in English using the dialogue I wrote. The project had been in development for more than six years before I was approached and ultimately hired.

Based originally on a rather little-known book, *The Hoods,* by Harry Grey (New York: Crown Publishers, 1952), early scripts were attempted by various writers, including Norman Mailer. When I came to the project in 1981 and subsequently worked on the script for more than six months, the principal screenwriters were Enrico Medioli, Leo Benvenuti, and Piero DeBernardi. Medioli, whose best-known credits are for scripts for Luchino Visconti *(The Damned; Death in Venice; Rocco and His Brothers),* was the only Italian writer who spoke English. Leone, at the time, spoke little English. The working procedure for *Once upon a Time in America* was for the Italian script to be translated into English and given to me. I would rewrite dialogue and make other suggestions for cutting, change, and defining character; and the script would be retranslated into Italian. This process was followed through five versions with supervision by Leone and input by the film's star, Robert DeNiro. Writing took place in Los Angeles, Rome, and New York. A final four-week session before shooting began was a line-by-line discussion of the English dialogue. Leone supervised this session.

Various changes in the script were made during shooting. The first script I received from Leone indicated in a covering note[1] that he was quite concerned with two aspects of the script: the fantasy/fairy-tale nature of the story and the importance of time as both a theme of the dialogue and an element in the presentation. It was, in his view, to be a film dealing with the ephemeral nature of time and human interaction.

The Tale

Recognizing that there are many ways to tell the story or give the plot, here is a summary of my version of what transpires in the final version of the script of *Once upon a Time in America.* Gangsters looking for Noodles Aaronson, a Jewish gangster in New York in 1934, kill Eve, the woman with whom he has been living, and beat his friend Moe. Noodles barely escapes from them by hiding in a Chinese opium den. He then flees New York.

At this point, we leap forward to 1968 and Noodles's return to New York City. Through various leaps from 1968 to 1933–34 and 1922–24 and back (see Figure 3.1), we discover that Noodles was once the co-leader of a small gang on the Lower East Side. As a child, he went to jail for killing another gang leader. Out of prison, Noodles and his partner, Max, have a disagreement about which direction to take the gang after the end of Prohibition. Noodles wants to stay small; Max wants to align the gang with the "syndicate." The gang does a few syndicate jobs, particularly backing a union organizer named Jimmy in his bid to move up in union leadership.

When Max appears to go mad and insists that the gang tackle a federal bank, Noodles turns himself and the gang in to the police to keep them from getting killed in what is sure to be a disastrous robbery. However, there is a shootout as the police close in; and all the gang members, except for Noodles, who has been left behind, are killed. It is at this point in 1934 that the syndicate comes after Noodles to punish him for his betrayal of the gang.

Noodles's 1968 return to New York is the result of having been lured

---

[1] "Time and the years are one other essential element in the film. In the source of them, the characters have changed, some of them rejecting their past identities and even their names—and yet in spite of themselves, they have remained bound to the past and to the people they knew and were. They have gone separate ways; some have realized their dreams, for better or worse; others have failed. But growing from the same embryo, as it were, after the careless self-confidence of youth, they are united again by the force that had made them enemies and driven them apart—Time."

This quote is taken from a note given to the author and other members of the writing and production staff by Leone in August 1981. Note the paragraph begins and ends with the word, the idea, the reference to "Time" with a capital "T."

from his hiding place by a cryptic message. Various events take place that force Noodles to deal with the memory of his old friends and the woman whom he loved and lost.

Near the end of the tale, Noodles discovers that Max was not killed in the shootout, that the entire event had been staged with syndicate help, and that Max, who has summoned Noodles back to New York, is a high-ranking government official under congressional investigation. Max's purpose in summoning Noodles is to give his old friend the opportunity to even scores and execute him, since the syndicate and Jimmy have now decided Max must go to prevent scandal. Noodles refuses and, apparently, the mob does kill Max.

The film ends back in the opium den in 1934 with a bedrugged Noodles who may or may not have imagined the entire core of the film as a fantasy to relieve himself of the responsibility for the death of his friends.

The above summary, as I have said, is, like all summaries, the result of an individual's imagination at work upon the material.

The Analysis

There are, in the final script of *Once upon a Time in America*, fifteen separate sequences (presentations within a continuing time block).[2] There are a total of 151 scenes within these fifteen sequences. A scene involves, essentially, a continuing action without apparent break in time or space. The script was written in scenes, not shots (as most scripts are, in spite of textbooks to the contrary). Normally, the director decides upon the shots, not the writer. In other words, how the scene will be broken down into angles, duration of shots, distance of shots (long shot, medium shot, close-up) is the director's province. Normally, each scene is shot in its entirety first (the master shot), and then the director breaks the scene into alternative angles and distances, from which the director and the editor can draw later. The writer(s) can, of course, suggest; but the final decision is made by the director.

As a writer, I found it interesting to envision a scene with the other writers and then, later, see the set not as we had imagined it, but as Leone and his long-time art director, Carlo Simi, had seen it. In at least

---

[2]All quotes and examples here and following in this chapter are taken from the script approved by Leone in New York City in May of 1982. Shooting began in Rome on June 14, 1982. There will surely be variations and changes from that which is reported here and that which is both shot and edited.

one instance, the writers had to rewrite a scene to accommodate the vision of the set.

Figure 3.1 indicates how the script moves among time periods. Each point on the graph indicates a change in time: Scene 1 begins in 1933; the tale remains in 1933 until scene 23, when we leap forward; then we remain in 1968 from scene 23 to scene 34.

At this point, one might be tempted to suggest from looking at the chart that we have a film whose time orientation is bizarre indeed. In fact, a random examination of popular American film will often show leaps forward and backward, although the leaps will often be in hours, days, or weeks rather than decades. For example, a chart of D. W. Griffith's *Broken Blossoms* (1919) would show similar discontinuities and, in fact, would present an additional problem at the conclusion, when simultaneous time is shown in three consecutive sequences. A film such as *Halloween* presents similar leaps in time. The difference, however, between *Broken Blossoms* and *Halloween* and *Once upon a Time in America* is that the breaks in time in the Leone film are foregrounded, as they are in many more-self-conscious films, such as Fellini's *8½*. Each major transition is underlined by a foregrounded visual metaphor that accentuates its chronological position. The normal procedure in film for such leaps in time is to make the transition as conventionally invisible as possible, to avoid calling attention to it. However, a breakdown of even the most transparent and seemingly simple feature film reveals the flexibility of conventional time in film terms.

The comparison of literary time with film time is somewhat helpful but can be misleading. A continuing analytical problem in dealing seriously with film is the comparison of film with literature. Obviously, there are many points of comparison. Normally, however, the reduction of the film to a narrative leaves one with, not a work of literature, but an art stripped of its context. No film is its story. The tale is both the story and its telling. The artifice of leaping in time and space is an accepted part of film narrative and has been since at least 1903. *The Great Train Robbery* is not the simple story of a group of men who rob a train and then are gunned down in the woods as they count their loot. *The Great Train Robbery* is a series of moving images in which we see an action and a tale. The imaginary experience is in the viewing—not in the words to which we reduce the experience. The literary experience is quite different from the filmic experience.

By the same token, there is much a novelist can do that a filmmaker

Figure 3.1
Time Periods and Scenes in
Once upon a Time in America

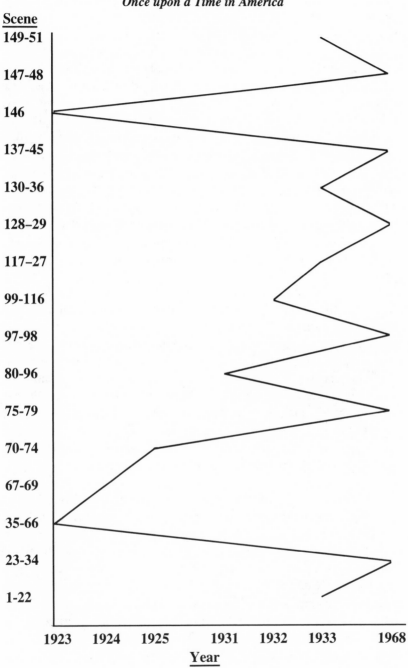

Scene

149-51

147-48

146

137-45

130-36

128–29

117–27

99-116

97-98

80-96

75-79

70-74

67-69

35-66

23-34

1-22

1923   1924   1925   1931   1932   1933   1968

Year

can only do with difficulty. The novelist has ready access to interiority—the thoughts of the characters. This interiority can be achieved in film, but only with difficulty.

Thus, when we return to the question of time, we see that time functions quite differently in film from how it functions in literature, and vice versa. For example, Gennette deals with Proust's use of the iterative in literature—the phrase that connotes a repeated action. Every day, Miles went to town; whenever Anne ate a sandwich, she picked up the spoon in her left hand; etc. There is no visual equivalent for this in film. Every envisioned act is an individual one, for we see specific clothing, specific actions—a moment arrested in time, not a verbal comment about repeated time. Thus, the approximation of the iterative becomes quite difficult in film. Conversely, the film has no need to describe in words. The description is in the visual experience. The experience of reading is linear. It takes time. When reading, you cannot experience thoughts, dialogue, and description at the same time. In film, however, you can.

There is no suggestion of superiority of one medium over the other in the above observation. It is, on one point only, an attempt to point out that each medium has its own parameters and those parameters indicate what has been done and perhaps what can be done within them. Nor am I suggesting, as did Gottfried Lessing, that each medium has its own destiny which cannot be violated, that vision should not be attempted in novels or that interiority should not be done in film. It is one thing to point out the boundaries of the form and quite another to make aesthetic prescriptions.

Let's examine the points at which the film script of *Once upon a Time in America* contains major transitions in time. They are:

1. 1933, scene 22. Noodles, after escaping from New York, hitches a ride with a truck driver. The driver asks, ''Where are you going?'' as Noodles gets into the truck. A long train approaches, blocking our vision of the truck. The cars on the long train are 1933 Fords. When the train passes, we see Noodles, now thirty-four years older, returning to New York City on the same road.

2. 1968, scene 34. Noodles is in the toilet of Fat Moe's bar. He stands on the toilet seat and looks through a vent. He is ''peering into his past.'' We see his point of view of a young girl, Deborah, dancing. We are carried back to 1923, and a 14-year-old Noodles is looking through the same vent.

3. 1923, scene 66. The police are taking a rival gang member away in a sunlit alley. Max shouts down to the rival; and there is a straight cut to 1924, one year later, and the interior of a paper plant.

4. 1924, scene 74. Noodles is in the back of a paddy wagon, being taken to jail for the murder of the rival gang leader. The prison gates clang shut, leaving the four remaining gang members on the street. They do not see the inscription at the arch of the entrance reading, "Your men will fall by the sword, your heroes in the fight" (Isaiah, 3:25). The camera moves down from the inscription, which we now see at the entrance to a tomb in 1968, before which stands Noodles, who has been brought here by an enigmatic message. It turns out to be the tomb of three of the gang members, the ones Noodles is supposed to have betrayed.

5. 1968, scene 79. Noodles, carrying a suitcase full of money mysteriously given to him, is walking down the street, when a Frisbee hits him and flies on. "A hand reaches out of nowhere and grabs it." This is matched by a hand reaching out to take the suitcase from Noodles. As the camera pulls back, we see that it is June, 1933, and the hand is that of Max, who is greeting Noodles upon his release from prison.

6. 1934, scene 96. After a job in Detroit, the killing of an out-of-favor syndicate gangster, Noodles angrily tells Max that he was not "let in" on the real purpose of the job; he had been led to believe it was a jewelry robbery. Noodles drives their car off a bridge. Max emerges from under water looking for Noodles but cannot see him. Nearby, a steam shovel is dragging the river bottom, lifting debris. As the debris drops into a truck, the camera reveals that it is no longer Detroit and no longer 1934, but 1968. It is Long Island, and Noodles is watching a truck picking up garbage at a mansion.

7. 1968, scene 71. Noodles is watching television at Fat Moe's bar and sees on the screen a familiar face, that of Jimmy Conway, the president of the Transport Union. Jimmy, who is being badgered by the media because of alleged corruption in his union, is saying, "If mistakes have been made in this situation, don't look at us." We cut to gasoline being sprayed in the face of the young Jimmy Conway in 1932. Jimmy is being threatened by hoods who want him to stop a strike. Jimmy is saved by Noodles and the gang and takes his first reluctant step toward corruption.

8. 1932, scene 116. Noodles runs toward a departing train on which the girl he loves, Deborah, is leaving New York, following a violent night with Noodles. Their eyes meet. Then "she lowers the window shade and cuts him out of her life.'' There is a cut to 1933, one year later, as Noodles enters Fat Moe's speakeasy, following, as we discover, a long period of drug-taking to forget Deborah.

9. 1933, scene 127. At a beach in Florida after Max has announced that he wants to rob a federal bank, Noodles looks at Carol, Max's girl, who lights a cigarette and stretches out in the sand. A plume of smoke ''issues up from the depths of a wicker chair,'' and we are in 1968, looking at an old Carol smoking in a nursing home. She then proceeds to tell Noodles, who has found her, that Max was mad, suffering from a brain disease, when he planned the bank robbery—that Max, in essence, committed suicide.

10. 1933, scene 127. Carol, concluding her tale to Noodles, says, ''If Max wasn't crazy, he soon wouldda been.'' There is a cut back to 1933, and we see a dialogueless sequence in which Max and Noodles, disguised as workmen, check out the federal bank.

11. 1933, scene 136. Noodles, who has just called the police so that he and the gang will be intercepted before they can commit the bank robbery, is confronted by Max, who angrily knocks Noodles unconscious after Noodles says Max is acting ''crazy!'' As the gun hits Noodles's head, there is a cut back to 1968 and Carol in an armchair at the rest home, saying, ''Max made fools of us, Noodles.''

12. 1968, scene 145. Noodles has been called to the home of U.S. Secretary of Commerce Bailey, who, he discovers, is really Max. The shootout in 1934 had been a hoax worked out with the syndicate and crooked cops. Bailey/Max, supported by the syndicate, has risen to his present position; but now he is under siege by a congressional committee, and Jimmy has brought word that he should shoot himself if he wants his son to live without threat. Max has brought Noodles to do the job. Max taunts him, pleads, points out that Max has spent his life with Noodles's former love, Deborah, that Max has robbed Noodles of his own life. Max gives Noodles a gun. Noodles looks at it and ''images of the past rise up.'' Scene 146 consists of a series of composite images from 1923 to 1933, including Max arriving in the new neighborhood as a boy and the image of a disfigured corpse on the street, a corpse which was supposed to be Max but we now know was not. We cut back to 1968 and Noodles looking up from the gun.

13. 1968, scene 147. Noodles refuses to kill Max, refuses, in fact, to admit Bailey *is* Max, refuses to acknowledge that his (Noodles's) life has been wasted. He leaves Max and goes into the street, where he appears to see Max being killed in the shadows behind a garbage truck. The reflectors of the truck glow "like two fiery eyes" and change into the lights of an old Ford. The people in the car are dressed in 1930s costume. Noodles of 1968 realizes he is not back in time, but firmly in 1968 where some rich people are going to a costume party. Noodles turns a corner and steps into 1933, Chinatown. It is the night Prohibition ended, the night Max and the gang were supposedly killed. Noodles goes to the opium den and gets a pipe. According to the final line of the script, "The smoke is harsh and kind of cleansing. It wipes out memories, strife, mistakes . . . and Time."

Before we move to an examination of each of these transitions in the script, it is important to point out that, within each of the narrative sections, there are also jumps in time. The three period jumps focused upon are those involving movement forward or backward of at least one year within the history of the story. Gennette differentiates between historical and story time. Historical time is the actual time transpired for an action to take place; story time is what we see of the history on the screen. Thus, in one sense, *Once upon a Time in America* takes about forty-five years of historical time. In the film, we see approximately three hours of that forty-five years. The ratio of what is left out to what is presented is nearly astronomical. Within each narrative block of time (for example, the twenty-two scenes in 1933 at the start of the film), there are brief movements forward in time (an hour, day, etc.). In addition, there are parallel actions—scenes which, although we see them in tandem, apparently take place at the same time. These are certainly not peculiar to this film and as techniques were well established by Griffith and others by 1912. However, those jumps of hours or even days or weeks that are unspecified are not foregrounded in the process of presenting information in *Once upon a Time*. In other words, in these cases no narrative device, visual metaphor, or optical effect is used that pushes to the foreground the idea that we are seeing a leap in time that we are to recognize as such. Those smaller leaps of time are presented as part of the "invisible" process of making a film. They are nonforegrounded ellipses. They are historical time covered in zero amount of narrative time. The ellipsis is usually in the form of a cut; the historical time between two shots is not recognized until information is given to us within the second shot to let us know that time has passed. For example, we can usually see that space has changed without dialogue to tell us.

Thus, we are going to deal only with those leaps of a year or more. As the Figure 2.1 shows, most of the leaps are of at least ten years. From scene 34 to scene 35, there is a leap of forty-five years. A similar leap occurs between scene 145 and scene 146. We might note that these two longest leaps are approximately twenty minutes into the film and twenty minutes before the film ends, respectively. They form part of the bookending process that begins and ends in 1934.

Now to the transitions.

1. Transition one, the train passing to reveal Noodles now old, establishes the motif of time change and space continuity. The cues we get to changes in time are, in most cases in the film, contextual; that is, the characters look older or younger, and their clothes are in keeping with the altered period, as are the cultural artifacts. In this transition, the automobiles are the first indication of change in time, followed by our seeing the aged Noodles. Thirty-four years have passed during the movement of that train. It is an ellipsis in Noodles's life that will not be covered in the film and will be referred to only obliquely. It is if no time visually has passed in Noodles's life, but he has aged. The time has had no meaning; and, indeed, at the end of the film, this is essentially what Noodles will tell Max in their final confrontation in 1968. This is a theme to which we will return throughout the film. Noodles has, essentially, died in 1933, whether figuratively in an opium dream or lost somewhere in the vast West of the American myth. He has done nothing for thirty-four years but live with his guilt and memories—memories and guilt with which he has come to terms.

2. The first major leap into the past—forty-four years—comes in the second transition, when the old Noodles looks down through the transom at Deborah dancing. He is the old man as voyeur. The viewer, who shares his point of view, is vicarious voyeur. It is a nostalgic voyeurism, a voyeurism of the past and the secret spying on a young girl. This leap into the memory of the past is through remembrance of the woman, the girl, the anima.

3. Transition three is conventional; it has no visual foregrounding of process. It is a straight cut—a leap of but one year. In transition eight, there is also a straight unforegrounded cut which, we discover through dialogue, covers an ellipsis of one year. Thus, the shorter ellipses, one year, are indicated by straight cuts that require exposition. In transition three, we find immediately that the gang of boys is doing well, that it has taken over the small empire of its defeated enemy.

4. Transition four involves a leap forward in time of forty-four years, handled by a Biblical reference etched in stone. Both the prison and the tomb have the same inscription from Isaiah. The prison and the tomb are both, in a sense, cessations of time. The inscriptions refer to the actions of persons just before their time ceases. There is a possibility that the inscription on the tomb has been placed there by Max as a clue to Noodles, a further pulling in of the line that will draw Noodles to the moment when he must decide if he will acknowledge his mistake and take revenge by killing Max. The primary problem with this explanation of intentionality on Max's part is that there is no sign given in the 1924 scene that Max or anyone else has seen the inscription. It is the camera that has seen the inscription and the audience that has been led to the transition that will leap forty-four years of historical time. Is the image part of Noodles's fantasy? Is the whole tale, bookended by the opium scene, an opium dream by Noodles?—A dream in which what he projects as a wasted life will be justified in the future, in which, in fantasy, he will discover that he did not betray his friends at all but was, himself, the tragic victim who becomes the tragic hero?

A problem with this, though it is a possibility favored by the director, Leone,[3] is that the period information in 1968 is contextually specific. In a novel, the illusion might well carry. In the film, we see television, 1968 automobiles, 1968 clothing, a Frisbee, etc. The information is not a distortion alone, but if it is an opium fantasy, then it is the fantasy of a seer. Alternatively, we can, as many have suggested, assume we have moved into the realm of imaginative projection. Thus, such questions are not reasonable; the testing of known data is not relevant. That seems to me a rather weak argument for accepting a seen future as possibly existing in the imagination of a character. We might also argue that we are dealing with a problem of convention. The fantasy of the future will lose the context of assumed naturalism of that future (which is, in this case, 1968, our past) which deviates from our experience of that world. Simply put, we have a sense of what existed in 1968. Were that to be confounded in a projection clearly seen as fantasy from 1933, it would change the genre of perception. Note, for example, the odd sensation of

---

[3] "And it this unrealistic vein that interests me most, the vein of the fable, though a fable for our own times and told in our own terms. And, above all, the aspects of hallucination, or a dream-journey, induced by the opium with which the film begins and ends, like a haven and a refuge."

This quote is taken from the note given to the author and other members of the writing and production staff by Leone as mentioned at the bottom of page 48.

examining the ''future'' in a film that is now past. *Just Imagine, Things to Come,* and *The Time Machine*—all three predict a future that did not come to be, but that was in the realm of science fiction. What, as in the case of *Once upon a Time in America,* do we do if we do not want to deal with the assumption of how the future will look to someone fantasizing in 1933?

5. Transition five moves from the hand grasping the Frisbee (1968) to Max's hand grabbing Noodles's suitcase, the same suitcase he had in 1933. An action continues from one time frame to another. Again we are reminded of an ellipse. We see none of Noodles's time in prison, as we see none of Noodles's time in exile. It is, in addition, the hand of Max bridging the time from 1968 to 1933, as we will find that it is the hand of Max that has manipulated the present—for it is always Max's function in the film to manipulate the *present.* It is Max who controls the gang in 1923–24, Max who sets Noodles up and dupes him in 1933–34, Max who recalls Noodles and brings him to be the executioner. However, it is Noodles who controls the *past.* Once the deed is done, the event over, Noodles converts it to his own nostalgia. Each period can be seen by Noodles as a nostalgic quest for family. In 1923–24, we see Noodles's real family only once. It is a scene of confrontation and rejection, immediately after which Noodles makes friends with Max, with both scenes using a stolen watch as the central binding image. The watch, clearly a reference to stolen time/real time, reappears prominently in the final confrontation between Max and Noodles in 1968. The 1924 episodes end with Noodles being taken from his family/gang and imprisoned. Time is taken from him.

In 1933–34, Noodles fears absorption of the gang/pseudofamily into the broader syndicate, which is also referred to as ''family.'' He fails to convince Max not to lead the gang into the broader syndicate/family; and the 1934 sequence ends with Noodles's exile in the West, alone. In the 1968 sequence, Noodles is called back and keeps meeting memories of the lost family/gang until he comes in contact with Max, who tells him his entire life has been an illusion. But Noodles prefers to hold the illusion rather than engage in the reality of betrayal and waste. The 1968 sequence ends with the apparent death of Max—once again the loss of family. Also worth noting is that, in their first encounter with the police in 1924 after Noodles has walked out on his real family following a fight, Noodles and Max pretend to a policeman that they are literally related, that Noodles is Max's uncle. Throughout the film, Noodles is referred to as "Uncle," his familial position—not the leader, not at the center, but affectionately at the side in the shadow of Max the leader, father, madman, betrayer, friend, stealer of women.

6. Transition six comes immediately after a major argument between Max and Noodles, the one in which Noodles complains that Max did not tell him the real goal of their job, the syndicate assignment of assassination. Noodles drives the car into the water; and we pick up the image of the steam shovel and the debris, debris in the water that carries over to 1968 and is then dredged up and looked at. The debris that begins in 1934, figuratively, with the betrayal by Max, is not brought out until 1968.

7. Transition seven involves Noodles looking at Jimmy on television. The old man in the present looks at a face from the past. As the voyeur had looked through the transom at the girl, we/he now look/s at the public face on television and the memory of that face in an earlier time. Jimmy's line that leads into the jump back to 1933, "If mistakes have been made in this situation, don't look at us," is a cliché that at the same time refers to "looking" at him. The leap back gives us a look at him and how, at least to Noodles, Jimmy became corrupted.

8. Transition eight, discussed earlier, is a straight, and not a symbolic, cut in one sense. The scene cut to is not directly related by information within it to the shot before of Deborah pulling down the train window shade. However, the pulling down of the shade is a termination, a literal optical effect, a metaphoric wipe. The literariness of the image is obvious. She doesn't want to look at him and doesn't want him looking at her.

9. Transition nine is a specific allusion to the fantasy nature of the tale. It is a plume of smoke that carries us from 1933 to 1968; and, as the smoke clears, it is Max's woman, Carol, who has aged. The shattering of time comes in 1933, when Max announces that he plans to rob the bank, and in 1968, when Carol tells Noodles for the first time that Max was literally mad or about to become so.

10. The motif of madness and fantasy is most evident in transition ten and the scene into which it leads. Carol says, "If Max wasn't crazy, he soon wouldda' been." We then see an essentially silent scene of disguise in which Noodles and Max check out the bank. The madness of the image is ours and Noodles's after we have been informed by Carol of Max's madness.

11. Transition eleven comes when Max knocks Noodles out and goes to his supposed "suicide." As the gun hits Noodles, time flies, and we go back to 1968; with the blow to the head, reference to madness, and sense of his own betrayal, Noodles awakens in 1968 to Carol saying, "Max made fools of us, Noodles." The transition does not relieve Noodles; the blow is not cathartic. He awakens from it to further guilt, although he is, in one sense, a man who has not only learned to live with his guilt, but to accept it. The transition is ironic, also. Noodles has to be hit on the head but still doesn't know that Carol's words can mean more than they seem, that she is a kind of Cassandra to whom he will not listen, cannot listen. She does not know that Max's trick went far beyond his madness, that he was not committing suicide but found a way out of the family for which Noodles sacrificed his life. The clues are there for Noodles to pick up, but he does not yet grasp them.

12. Transition twelve, the most elusive of the time transitions in the film, comes when Max in 1968 tells Noodles that he, Max, has stolen Noodles's past. It is at this point that Noodles "sees," and we see composite images from 1923–24 and 1933–34 which both sustained Noodles and filled him with guilt and remorse. As contradictory and painful as the images are, they have given Noodles a sense of meaning in time. In a simple sense, his life (selected meaningful time experiences) flashes before his eyes; and he decides that the story as he has fashioned and imagined it is more important than the history that Max urges him to accept.

13. Transition thirteen, the final transition in the film, is in many ways the most problematic. It begins with that false move back to 1933 in which the 1968 Noodles sees the old car and people in old costumes. He seems to have leapt back in time without a direct narrative connection. He is and we are disconcerted by the old Noodles in the fantasy of 1933–34. Is Max now dead? Did all this happen? A turn of a corner, the matching of two shots, and the linking of two times without overt ellipses or devices brings Noodles back to the 1930s, back to the opium den. Past/present/future merge, and we see Noodles for the last time— at the moment when his opium fantasy wiped out or transformed the painful experience of the death of his family/gang. (The film not only begins and ends in 1933–34, giving support to the importance of that time segment; but a breakdown of story time in the script shows that approximately 63 percent of the film takes place in 1933–34, while 23 percent takes place in 1923–24 and 14 percent takes place in 1968.)

A final point worth noting again is that the film never comes to the audience's present or an approximation of it. There is no historical present for the audience. The closest we come to the assumed ''now'' of the viewer is 1968. The entire film, therefore, is set in the past. There is no assumed present.

Noodles begins and ends alone, friendless, womanless, with no family—only memories and time, which, ultimately, may be all that any of us have. *Once upon a Time in America,* for all of its allusion to fantasy and fairy tale, suggests that the power of the fairy tale, the myth, the fantasy, is to bring the viewer and Noodles to an ultimate reality, that the fairy-tale beginning of ''Once upon a time'' really means that what we have is a truth about all tales and conclusions and the vanity of believing that we have anything beyond our imagination and mythology.

Criticism of the Analysis

Any analysis that tends to focus upon one aspect of a told and experienced tale is a reduction and distortion of that tale. The focus upon time in this article suggests somehow that time is a more important issue than, for example, space or archetype or politics or history or psychology.

At the same time, one can argue that, by focusing upon one strand and unraveling it, we may, with patience, come to the center of the ball, instead of flying from loose end to loose end and never getting below the surface. That is, essentially, the structuralist argument, which I find useful, although I know a film is not a ball of string and there is no guarantee that I am actually following the string to a real center rather than imagining a journey and then, like Noodles, reporting this imagination instead of a journey itself.

I realize, also, that my analysis of time is informed by my interest in archetypal criticism and Jungian analysis. Underlying my supposedly objectified analysis of what ''is there'' is a commitment to a tradition of understanding which encompasses not only Jung, but also Joseph Campbell, Heinrich Zimmer, and the rudiments of Buddhism.

I have attempted to use the tools of structural analysis to explore an interest in archetype. I have also, as I've pointed out earlier, chosen to ignore a great deal that might well be part of even an archetypal analysis. I have given little attention to the role of women in this film; I have barely mentioned Eve, who could be seen as the guiding anima who runs through the film, and have said little about Deborah, the idealization of the female that Noodles pursues and never attains. Even Carol, the whore/witch who can lead Noodles to enlightenment, is dealt with only minimally in this analysis. Unmentioned are Peggy, an earth-mother figure for the gang, and the other members of the gang/family itself, Patsy, Cockeye, and Fat Moe—the erratic spirit, the trickster, and the loyal brother. I have concentrated upon the issue of time in relationship to the traditional confrontation of male rivals, an archetypal image that draws me and, as Campbell, among others, has pointed out, is a dominant one in our mythological thought.

Thus, this examination of time in *Once upon a Time in America* is not *the* meaning of the film, but *a* meaning of the film, which, to make the argument as circular as the film I have discussed, is all we can ever hope for and also, finally, may be quite enough.

4
COMPARATIVE FORMS
The Samurai Film and the Western

In a Japanese samurai film, a samurai (SAM-oo-wry), or ronin (ROW-nin), can, with ease, defeat fifteen or twenty opponents at a time with his dazzling swordplay. The samurai also can face a gun and defeat it with his sword. He can perform these feats even if he is totally blind or has only one eye and one hand. He is equally successful when his opponent can fly or make himself disappear.

The jidai-geki (JEH-die-GE-key), or Japanese period film, especially the modern samurai film, deals with myth in a way that American Westerns cannot attempt because of different national needs, conventions, and historical film traditions. The American Western can stretch its plot and action to the limits of possibility—but not beyond this point, or the audience will not accept it and will not be satisfied with the film. A samurai film, however, must go beyond the limitations of acceptable possibility if it is to meet the expectations of its audience.

An exploration of how conventions work within samurai films and what functions, artistic or social, they serve can help the American viewer understand the samurai genre. Comparing and contrasting samurai films with Westerns can give added insight into the seemingly related—but also quite different—forms. One contemporary popular series of samurai films involves a one-armed, one-eyed samurai. In the first film of the series, *Tange Sazen Hien Iai-Giri (The Secret of the Urn),* director Hideo Gosha presents the story of a ronin who kills a spy, a "man" endowed with the powers of flying and invisibility. In the battle, the ronin loses an eye. This disfigurement is offensive to his sensei (SEN-see), or master, because it is a permanent symbol of his having been hurt by a nonsamurai. The master orders the right hand and arm of the samurai to be cut off. The samurai accepts this decision and goes off alone, later partly redeeming himself by protecting a valuable urn belonging to the clan from which he has been expelled. He cannot return to the clan; but he can, at the end, go off into further adventures, battling evil and searching for a master who will want him.

In samurai films since World War II, there has been a tradition of physical deformity. It flows through the films as a pulsing motif, sometimes crucial to the action and the hero, sometimes in the background. The hero's deformity is always the result of disgrace or defeat. It is then the responsibility of the deformed warrior to survive with dignity and to triumph over his loss, while accepting the physical toll it has taken. Critics have said that World War II and the searing horror of the atomic bomb haunt the samurai film (as they have also influenced the so-called American film noir) and give it many of its modern conventions.

There are two series of Japanese samurai films (with at least ten features in each series) dealing with warriors who are blind but who are experts with their swords. Blind instruments of justice, each warrior has the duty to rectify evil in Japan. (In addition, one of these films was the "inspiration" for a 1971 Italian Western, *Blindman*.) One of the two series, directed by Kimiyoski Yasuda, deals with a blind swordsman; the other series, directed by Kirokazu Ichimura, deals with the exploits of a blind swords*woman*. Both blind warriors are seen wandering through Japan in the chaos after the breakup of the clan system of the later nineteenth century. The majority of samurai films are set in a period of upheaval and of searching for spiritual direction and leadership, a sort of period that—probably not coincidentally—corresponds with the era of the American West drawn upon for most Westerns.

Another recurring motif in samurai films involves an almost mystical aversion to guns. In *Yojimbo*[1] (1961), directed by Akira Kurosawa, the samurai, played by Toshiro Mifune, faces a gunman and defeats him with a knife and a sword. The true samurai disdains the gun, which he sees as a symbol of encroaching industrialization, a manifestation of the

---

[1] I have chosen throughout this chapter to use the names of the Japanese films as they are best known in the United States. Thus some films, such as *Yojimbo* (which roughly translates as "Bodyguard"), retain their Japanese names, but others, such as *The Seven Samurai*, do not.

nonmythical and antitraditional, and an embodiment of the impersonal mechanization of war. This disdain of guns by the samurai is strikingly presented in Kurosawa's *The Seven Samurai* (1954), in which the bravest samurai and the peasant imposter who mimics him are shot in the film.

The samurai hero can be killed by the gun. All four samurai killed in *The Seven Samurai* are felled by gunfire. Bullets take Mifune's life in both Masaki Kobayashi's *Samurai Rebellion* (1967) and Kihachi Okamoto's *Red Lion* (1968), and again, strangely enough, in a recent Western, *Red Sun* (1972), a hodgepodge compendium of imitation Sergio Leone and misunderstood samurai films in which the warrior's death requires a rain of bullets far beyond that required to bring down an ordinary mortal.

Several other elements of samurai films should be mentioned to convey an understanding of the genre. First, while a duel does not take place in all films in the genre, the samurai frequently is forced into swordplay with another samurai who is not evil but whose master is on a different side. This kind of duel takes place in such films as Masahiro Shinoda's *Ibun Sarutobi Jasuke,* Hiroshi Inagaki's *Nachbuse,* Akijiro Umezu's *Hissatsu,* and Kihachi Okamoto's *Daibosatus Toge.* Regardless of who wins such a duel, both samurai are honorable. These duels, unlike showdowns in Westerns, are always fought in private, usually in a vast, open field.

Another important convention in samurai films is the use of a combination of legend and complex history. A Japanese audience seems to be aware of a myriad number of relationships as soon as it hears a familiar date or name. An American audience may be able to make certain assumptions about Jesse James, Billy the Kid, Wyatt Earp, and, perhaps, a few dozen others who lived or were reported to have lived between 1830 to 1915; but a samurai film presupposes a knowledge of hundreds of fictional and real characters over a period of hundreds of years.

As with the Western genre, it must be emphasized that, while there are conventions to be built upon in the samurai film, individual directors can make use of them for a wide variety of purposes. The diversity of their use in the samurai film is as great as the differences among the films of such directors of Westerns as John Ford, Henry King, Howard Hawks, Henry Hathaway, Budd Boetticher, and Sam Peckinpah.

Even with their variations in the use of the genre, however, the Japanese directors retain a horror of guns, reflecting a belief in military pride based on individual honor, not technology; they also retain the conviction that a historic tradition exists from which to draw strength and pride. The major Japanese samurai film directors all deal with the battle between obligation and human feeling, the contention between duty and inclination. These seem to be conflicts and needs that are shared by the Japanese directors and their audiences and without which the jidai-geki cannot be understood.

Attempts by directors of Westerns to make use of the samurai genre result in an interesting clash of cultures. Britain's Terence Young, in *Red Sun*, deals most directly with the idea of the samurai in a Western setting, but he fails completely to deal with the samurai as any more than a cliché. Condescension is displayed toward the samurai, who is viewed as a simple-minded man, determined, honorable, and in tune with nature.

Andrew Sarris, in *The American Cinema* (1968), points out that Spencer Tracy's defeat of Ernest Borgnine in *Bad Day at Black Rock* (1954) through the use of karate is like Mifune's swordplay in *Yojimbo*. The similarity goes far beyond Kurosawa's films, however. John Sturges, who directed *Bad Day at Black Rock* as well as *The Magnificent Seven* (1960), based on *The Seven Samurai*, was almost certainly familiar with samurai films. *Black Rock*, which clearly appears to be a transported samurai film, was released in 1955, five years before *Yojimbo*, but well after broad distribution of samurai films in the United States. Such films as Kurosawa's *Rashomon* (1950), *The Seven Samurai* (1954), and *Men Who Tread on the Tiger's Tail* (1945), Kenji Mizoguchi's *Ugetsu Monogatari* (1953), and Teinosuke Kinugasa's *Gate of Hell* (1954) were known in the United States before 1955.

In the Sturges film, Spencer Tracy comes to an isolated desert town shortly after World War II. Like so many samurai, he is deformed by battle and has only one arm. He also is without a ''master'' (a career soldier, he has been discharged from the army because of his wound) and is disillusioned. Tracy arrives in Black Rock to deliver a medal, belonging to a dead Japanese-American soldier, to the soldier's father, who lives near the town.

Tracy's overcoming of the villains involves his being true to Japanese samurai tradition. He never uses a gun. Instead, his weapon—by necessity—is a sort of combination of judo and karate, a sword substitute. In the final showdown, he defeats rifle-armed Robert Ryan with, ironically, an improvised bomb.

There is, however, a crucial difference between Tracy and a samurai hero. Tracy is very much interested in preserving his own life. He *wants* to bring about justice, but he will escape without providing it if he must and can. Duty to a cause is the guiding principle for a samurai. The samurai dedicates himself to tradition. Death is not relevant; it is, in fact, ennobling if it comes in the service of one's lord. The Western hero has a great sense of self; the samurai has a great sense of subordination of self.

A gunman in a Western arrives and acts because he needs money, is bored, seeks new adventure, and/or is driven by a desire for revenge. The end of the West is before him, and he knows it. The Westerner's moment in history is passing. He is filled with resignation and nostalgia, the realization that he must make way for "law and order," for "civilization." The gunman is basically alone. If he has a sidekick, as in Anthony Mann's *Bend of the River* (1951) or Howard Hawks's *Rio Bravo* (1958), the sidekick is both a helper and a responsibility who hampers the gunman and makes him vulnerable. The gunman is trapped into doing good deeds, an entrapment he would rather avoid but that he stoically accepts because his self-image is at stake. As Robert Warshow points out (in his essay "The Westerner" in *The Immediate Experience,* Doubleday, 1962), this image is of prime importance.

In Don Siegel's *Coogan's Bluff* (1968), Lee J. Cobb, angry at Clint Eastwood's insistence that he must continue to pursue the prisoner who has escaped him, says sarcastically and wearily, "I know, a man's got to do what a man's got to do." The need for the gunman to redeem his honor and his name is both a cliché and a valid ideal.

The samurai often shares with the gunman a drive for revenge; but it is always revenge for a wrong committed against his clan, his religion, or his country—never for a personal act, like Henry Fonda's revenge in *The Return of Frank James* (1940), Arthur Kennedy's in *Rancho Notorious* (1952), or James Stewart's in the Anthony Mann Westerns, especially *The Naked Spur* (1952) and *The Man from Laramie* (1955). The samurai is not a lone wolf. He is an artist, a minor nobleman with a distinct social role of which he is well aware. His reason for existence is closely tied to society. If he is alone, it is not by choice. He needs a master who can guide him in bringing justice to Japan.

The ways in which Sturges and Kurosawa see and present their ideas and feelings visually reflect their divergent attitudes toward their protagonists and their society. In *Yojimbo,* for example, characters move and change position, reflecting an awareness of each character's status

The Magnificent Seven.

The Seven Samuarai.

and relationship to others. Heroes and villains are shown as part of a whole. Sturges, too, sets up tableaux, especially outdoors, in which the relationship of the characters is emphasized, but the result is quite different. In *Black Rock,* the visual emphasis is on the isolation of individuals, their differences. In one scene, early in the film, the members of the group in town responsible for the murder face Tracy across a railroad track. They are far apart, relatively small, dark outlines against the sun and distant wilderness. Sturges's characters, both heroic and evil, are alone—separated and frightened. Some are better at masking their fear than others; but all feel it, as do characters in most of the Westerns of the past twenty-five years. Kurosawa's people are frightened, too (except for the samurai); but they are together, part of the same tradition, aware of a social role they can fill even if they choose not to do so.

Although Sturges and Kurosawa have basic, personal differences in the way they work within their respective genres, they have sufficient consistency in their use of conventions to make their films valuable in discussing the variations in similar motifs. Since both have used the same story to make a film, the comparisons are particularly striking.

The Magnificent Seven offers more contrasts between the conventions of the contemporary Western and of the samurai film. The Western gunman is fast. There are degrees of speed, different ways to wear the holster, but speed—more than accuracy—is the mark of the man. In *The Magnificent Seven,* Yul Brynner, the leader of the "good" gunmen, tests the speed of novice Horst Buchholz by telling him to clap his hands together as quickly as he can. Buchholz does; but, before his hands come together, Brynner has drawn his gun and inserted it between them. Buchholz tries to prove himself by doing the same thing, but he knows he cannot. He is humiliated because he has failed to pass the test of speed.

There is no *art* in the action of a fast draw, however; it requires only a steady hand and practice—lots of practice. A recurring convention in Westerns has the gunman going off by himself to practice. He is discovered practicing by a girl who wants to get close to him or a young man who wants to emulate him. The gunman makes a speech about how unglamorous it is to be a gunman, how hard one has to work at it. The desire for control, power, and self-respect goads him. The gunman is almost never proud of being a gunman, while the samurai is always proud to be a samurai. It is interesting that the violent American culture hero should be ashamed of his historical being and the violent Japanese culture hero should be fiercely proud of his historical past.

We almost never see a samurai practicing; we know that he has mastered his art. To a samurai, regardless of the individual interpretations of the director, a sword is more than just a weapon. The warrior shares his knowledge of tradition and self-esteem with his opponents and the audience. We watch him for his technique in much the way an audience is supposed to watch a bullfight. Villains in a samurai film seldom attack in groups—or even pairs. They come on singly, acknowledging that they are participating in a ritual, an affirmation of ability and not a sociological showdown. The blood that flows in color and scope in Daisuke Ito's *The Ambitious* (1967) rivals that of Sam Peckinpah's *The Wild Bunch* (1969) or *The Getaway* (1973), but the intention is quite different. Peckinpah wants us to be appalled; Ito wants us to accept the bloodletting as part of a form.

The artistry of the swordsman is emphasized in Kihachi Okamoto's *Samurai Assassin* (1969), the ads for which proudly told Japanese audiences that Mifune displayed and introduced "ten new techniques of swordsmanship more powerful and speedier than in previous samurai pictures." A samurai never considers that his profession might be ignoble. Such a confession would be equivalent to that of a cardinal renouncing the Roman Catholic church.

In *The Magnificent Seven*, the gunmen help the peasants because they have nothing better to do—nothing to lose; the odds are a challenge, and there is a chance to use their guns before they must resign themselves to becoming "store clerks." One gunman, played by Brad Dexter, sustains himself with the hope of buried treasure. Another, played by Robert Vaughn, wants to hide from his fear. At first, only the leader, Brynner, is truly moved by the peasants' plight; but he makes it clear that he, too, is trying to forestall the moment when he will have to put his gun away.

In *The Seven Samurai*, the ronin never discuss money or self. They all join the group to fall in with a new leader, a cause. The samurai played by Takashi Shimura accepts the role of temporary sensei out of a sense of social responsibility.

The establishing sequences introducing the leaders in the American and Japanese films point out a primary difference between the genres. Brynner, obviously a gunman, with holster strapped low, clothes tight, agrees to drive a dead Indian to Boot Hill in a hearse, dramatically lights a cigar, and proceeds up the hill. In the brief shootout, Brynner easily outshoots two of the town toughs, intentionally wounding rather than killing them, and forces them to back down. The town applauds his bravery (and that of Steve McQueen, who backs him up). Brynner is the hero of the moment and has proved himself to the audience.

Shimura, in contrast, is fiftyish, decidedly unhandsome, and apparently undistinguished. He proves himself and his right to act as a surrogate sensei by laying his sword aside, cutting off his hair (which is braided samurai fashion), and pretending he is a priest so that he can rescue a baby who is held captive by a knife-wielding madman.

In the Sturges film, the final battle is a test of the gunman's individual courage, a proving of his manhood. "Nobody gives me my gun and tells me to run," James Coburn announces. The Americans also come to the conclusion that the peasants are better off than they are, that a home and family are better than what they have, that farming is better than rootlessness.

The samurai, in contrast, are less defined as individuals; they are less spectacular in their statements and actions, and they never indicate a need to prove their courage or manhood. They do their job and accept what happens to them. They show feeling for and intimacy with the farmers, but the samurai never consider that they might be like them. The samurai are above the farmers in class—and wish to be, just as the farmers also clearly wish them to be. In a Western, the gunfighter is lonely, a man nobly apart from others. The samurai's individualism, in contrast, is usually underplayed (except in the work of some recent directors who are torn between group affirmation and feelings of self).

At the end of both *The Magnificent Seven* and *The Seven Samurai,* the leaders announce, "It is not we, but rather the farmers who have won. It is they who always win." For Brynner, this is an announcement of regret, defeat, and almost bitter acknowledgment that he represents a proud but dying part of American history, while the farmer is solid, enduring, and good. For Shimura, the statement is one of humility, sadness, and pride. His words are not of regret and have no bitterness; his sadness is not self-pity, but the sadness of a passing tradition represented in the beauty of the graves of the dead samurai, at which Shimura gazes.

Readings on Samurai Films

Books

Anderson, Joseph L. and Donald Richie. *The Japanese Film: Art and Industry.* Rutland, Vermont: Charles E. Tuttle, 1968.

Richie, Donald. *The Films of Akira Kurosawa.* Berkeley and Los Angeles: University of California Press, 1965.

Periodicals

Anderson, Joseph L. "Japanese Swordfighters and American Gunfighters." *Cinema Journal,* Spring, 1973.

Croizer, Ralph C. "Beyond East and West: The American Western and the Rise of Chinese Swordplay Movies." *Journal of Popular Film,* Summer, 1972.

Schrader, Paul. "Yakuza-Eiga." *Film Comment,* January, 1974.

5
COMPARATIVE FORMS

The Kung Fu Film and the Dance Musical

An understanding of Kung Fu films depends on our acceptance of them as violent myths and also as almost musical displays. The essence of the Kung Fu film is performance. Bruce Lee is the Fred Astaire of Kung Fu films. To make such statements implies a way of understanding the Kung Fu films. They can be viewed in two distinct, yet related, manners.

On one hand, Kung Fu films are films of performance, very much like Astaire or Gene Kelly musicals; many even have a separate choreographer for the battle scenes. In the Kung Fu film, as in the dance musical, we see the solo number, the ingenue number, chorus numbers, and dancing duos. Also, as in such musicals, the narrative of the film, while important, is a formalized manner of getting to and leading into the numbers. That this is not idle fancy can be seen in (a) the way in which the battles are staged and (b) the reactions of audiences to them. The battles are often prepared for by an establishing shot, a long shot showing the stage or "arena" in which the performance will take place. The obstacles and items to be used are also shown. Audiences accept these battles as performance by responding to the agility and grace of the performer. There is also the equivalence of the bow at the end of a number in the form of a medium shot or close-up of the protagonist waiting for applause, which he frequently gets from the audience.

The performer even has props, like Fred Astaire's cane and hat. The prop can be a rough staff *(Fists of Fury; Duel of the Iron Fists; Deadly China Doll)* or a rather strange double club connected with chains, called nunchukas *(The Chinese Connection; Enter the Dragon; Sacred Knives of Vengeance).* When the Kung Fu protagonist uses these devices, they become part of a skilled performance, similar to the way Astaire or Kelly might twirl his cane or flip his hat.

The call is, clearly, for identification with the protagonist; and the identification depends upon the myth of skill. For the American audience toward whom the dance musicals were directed, the skill was based upon dexterity, agility, and charm. The skilled performer was ambitious, got his chance, and made it to the top. Fred Astaire was, thus, a middle-class identification figure: a self-made, socially accepted success.

Bruce Lee is more clearly a ghetto figure, whose skill and agility are devoted, not to social success, but to the execution of his skills to earn audience respect and destruction of his enemies. In both cases, the dancer and the martial arts performer (Gene Kelly, Fred Astaire, Chuck Norris, Bruce Lee) are recognized outside the film as professionals in their art.

Another similarity between Kung Fu and dance films, especially those of Fred Astaire, includes the way Kung Fu battle sequences are shot. Generally, the protagonist is shown in full body. The more skillful the performer (and Lee appears to be the most skillful), the more of the total performance we see without cutting away to other angles or close ups. In a Bazinian sense, our acceptance of the myth is based to a great degree upon our belief that the performer is actually doing these things.

The strength of Kung Fu films for black urban audiences is clear by the choice of theaters in which such films are shown. *Variety* statistics for show dates in 1973 indicate that Kung Fu films are consistently strong box office in the downtown theaters drawing overwhelmingly black audiences in Chicago (the Oriental, the Woods), Detroit (the Adams, the Grand Circus), and Washington. (See *Variety,* November 14, 1973, or December 26, 1973.)

It doesn't matter that, in practice, to attain the Kung Fu hero's skill would require endless patience and practice if it even were achievable. Certainly, no amount of practice would teach a young viewer to fly as the Kung Fu hero often does. (In films like *Fearless Fighters* and *The Chinese Professionals,* in fact, almost all these skills are superhuman.) However, identification is so strong that the myth often persists into the private life of the viewer. The number of black youths who practice pseudo–Kung Fu is strikingly evident on urban street corners. By the same token the young man of the 1930s could not simply rise and start dancing in his room or on the deck of a ship as well as Fred Astaire did.

There are even particular movements like dance steps in Kung Fu films. These steps involve kicks, turns, and elbow throws. One might at this point argue a qualitative difference between the dance and the Kung Fu performance. Such distinction is based upon taste and tradition rather than upon an attempt to understand Kung Fu films by indeed accepting them as acrobatic or ballroom entertainment as the performances of Astaire were presented to a great degree.

A primary difficulty reviewers, critics, and some adults have in dealing with Kung Fu films is that their performance is based upon violence—destruction and death—not musical expression. Somehow, it is assumed that concentration on these objects of human fear is too serious to handle in a mythic form, or at least too serious to be handled with any reference to the skill and grace of the person performing the killing, regardless of his motivation within the film. This never seems to be raised as an issue when discussing the conclusions of *Richard III, Macbeth,* or *Hamlet,* however. In contrast, the context of popular entertainment is somehow seen as an unfit arena for dealing with such concerns.

However, if we wish to examine the Kung Fu films as potential expressions of some mythic relationship to the ghetto viewer, the imposition of a moral posture gets in the way of our understanding of the genre and also negates the possibility that valid creation can take place within it.

An analogy to Kung Fu films in terms of performance can be seen in the samurai and judo films of Japan, which are somewhat more directly related to violence as expression than is the musical. Certainly, few films can claim as bloody a battlefield as that which exists at the end of Kurosawa's *Yojimbo* or *The Seven Samurai.* In those films, and in the mass of samurai films, our admiration is directed toward the individual who can destroy hundreds of foes with his sword. However, the samurai is a middle-class figure in attitude, costume, and action. His deeds are motivated by an interest in the greater common good. The same is true of the judo expert. In films like Kurosawa's *Judo Saga,* the emphasis is on controlling one's skill—using it defensively for social good and never for individual revenge or attainment.

The Kung Fu hero, however, is invariably a lower-class working fig-

Fred Astaire in *The Sky's the Limit*.

Bruce Lee in *The Chinese Connection*.

ure who has no extended interest in society. His motives are all personal or familial; and the tools available to him are never guns and seldom swords (which are a class above him) but, instead, his own body and, perhaps, a club, a shaft, or a crude, blunt weapon.

The samurai and judo expert's grace depends upon their interaction with their foes, who are performing part of a total ritual that both sides accept; the Kung Fu hero has his own ritual, for which there are few rules and which allows for no mutual respect between adversaries. This dichotomy is most evident in *The Chinese Connection* and *The Screaming Tiger,* which deal directly with the conflict between the Kung Fu hero and the Japanese judo and samurai representatives; these latter are presented as arrogant, vain, and easily destroyed by the Kung Fu hero.

In one sense, Kung Fu as manifested in the films is simply graceful, dirty fighting. This is another distinction in kind and ethic from more traditional combat. It is radically different, for example, from the polite ritual of a samurai film or from American genre films until the 1960s. In American genre films, one confronts his enemy face to face and obeys certain rules, such as no hitting below the belt. But these are traditional American middle-class rules, which the ghetto viewer has probably had difficulty accepting as valid. Survival, according to rhetoric of the recent past, is a matter of dirty fighting and staying alive, no matter what you must do. The Kung Fu hero elevates this principle to an ''art.'' It becomes graceful to engage in dirty fighting. Not only is it graceful; there is a ritual pattern to it. Dirty fighting can be the means of righting mythic wrongs. It can be a respectable and admirable form of reaction to social ills and environment. The Kung Fu hero is not simply kicking his opponent in the face; he is doing it with grace and skill. It is a ballet of violence.

Another important aspect of Kung Fu violence is that it allows dignity to the small protagonist. One need not be Clint Eastwood or Jim Brown, and few ghetto kids are. Bruce Lee, and others, by their size and nationality, are metaphors for the downtrodden. The Hong Kong Chinese laborer is certainly a disdained member of society from Japan to Europe and has never been considered hero material before.

Elements of the possibility of such grace through violence in the persona of the small, agile man can be seen in Edward G. Robinson or James Cagney in the early 1930s. Such films and stars were especially popular with children of an Irish/Jewish urban lower class as are the Kung Fu films with black children.

There is at least one specific reference to presentation of graceful performance as violence in American film that might be mentioned here. In Vincente Minnelli's *Designing Woman* (1957), an issue normally raised by Kung Fu films is handled in an American context. Gregory Peck is a tough sports reporter surrounded by huge boxers. He is in love with Lauren Bacall, a designer, who is friendly with a number of "artsy" people, including a small, effete male ballet dancer. At one point in the film, Peck is attacked by a gang of "mugs" and, surprisingly, is rescued by the little ballet dancer who performs with leaps, kicks, and studied grace. It is, indeed, a Kung Fu performance in an American film by a ballet dancer, the unity of Bruce Lee and Gene Kelly directed by Minnelli. However, there is a major difference. The ballet dancer has affirmed upper-class art and ballet as a functional motif. Peck's respect for him after the display of his essentially dirty but graceful style is a rapport with conventional art. In the recent Kung Fu films, the respect is a result of lower-class, not upper-class, affirmation.

The plots of Kung Fu films are also important. Invariably, the stories deal with a lower-class figure who at first contains his Kung Fu skill. He makes the attempt to be a respectable working-class ghetto resident. He allows others, usually his relatives, to fight the initial battles, because he wants to get along, because he has vowed to follow the acceptable route of behavior.

His resolve disappears when his family is attacked and destroyed and he sees that being a good worker and loyal citizen has ruined him. His family is almost always destroyed by the man who employs the Kung Fu hero. If the man does not employ him, the man is at least powerful enough to control the city or town where the action takes place. The destruction of the family releases the Kung Fu hero. All that the ghetto figure has is his body, his job, and his family. He rips off his shirt *(Fists of Fury; The Big Boss; Duel of the Iron Fists)*, tastes his own blood after being wounded *(Enter the Dragon)*, displays great anguish, and proceeds to use his skill to get through the bureaucratic masses of underlings, who are like the creatures who confronted Theseus in the maze, having different skills and requiring different displays of grace and skill by the protagonist.

The minor villains always include one large or extremely powerful individual (such as the Russian in *The Chinese Connection*), a large group of skilled Kung Fu fighters *(Fists of Fury;* or *The Queen Boxer)*, and/or an individual who can handle a particular weapon which the protagonist always takes from him and uses or discards (*The Chinese Connection; Duel of the Iron Fists*). The final villain himself is always an older man, a father figure as clearly out of mythological consideration as Cronus or Seth, and the Kung Fu hero is just as clearly a mythical extension of Zeus or Horus. Such mythical patterns also reflect psychological conflicts that are universal—the conflict of generations, the Oedipal situation, etc. The father figure is always: rich—a worthwhile symbolic adversary for a ghetto hero; lecherous—a dirty old man; and quite skillful. There is some implication, indeed, that he may be a self-made ghetto figure who has profited by betrayal of his origins—a terrible father who, like Cronus, has gobbled up most of his children and must be destroyed by the last of them.

An important convention of the Kung Fu film is the handling of the final confrontation with the fatherlike villian. The fight is long and the combatants, equal. It is invariably settled in slow motion. Both parties leap high into the air toward each other and meet. When they come to earth, the protagonist is torn and bloody—but alive. The father figure is defeated and dead.

When viewed in this sense, the films are remarkably "moral" and unrevolutionary. They are films of revenge taken for destruction of one's family. The terrible villain is always destroyed for his conventional evils, which range from lechery and drinking to oppression of the lower classes. The films also frequently end with the protagonist about to be led off by police officers to face his punishment for having violated the law.

The law itself, as in American gangster films of the 1930s, is almost nonexistent in Kung Fu films. These are not films of law, but of myth; we are dealing with basic issues of life, meaning, and family. The fantasy resolution for a ghetto kid is not through the law. The fantasy is one of being able to right the wrongs of one's personal frustration through one's own limited ability. It is not surprising that films that deal with the skillful handling of wrongs done to one's immediate family should be particularly popular among black American youths. This does not, however, mean that the myths and their execution do not have a broader appeal to all those who feel the same restrictions and helplessness and who admire the performance.

Kung Fu films are remarkably intense. The percentage of time taken in battle and combat parallels the time taken in actual dance and song in a Fred Astaire musical; however, the time taken in battle in Kung Fu film is much greater than in so-called violent films, from gangster pictures to Italian Westerns, although the latter come closer. Only by realizing that the scenes of violence are at the core of the meaning and appreciation of these films can one perceive their real skill in presentation and performance and their possible meaning to an audience. In *Duel of the Iron Fists,* for example, there is not even a resolution. The film ends in the midst of yet another battle, with the hero still proving his skill. *The Chinese Connection* ends with Bruce Lee frozen in a leap toward a line of men with rifles.

To dismiss these films as "junk," as the Italian Westerns were dismissed several years ago, is to fail to deal with their potential merit. That merit may, indeed, vary. All Kung Fu films are not alike in quality, as all Westerns are not; but to even begin to come to an understanding of which are the good ones requires a willingness to understand genre.

Readings on Kung Fu Films

Books

Lee, Linda. *Bruce Lee: The Man Only I Know.* New York: Warner Paperback Library, 1975.

Mintz, Marilyn D. *The Martial Arts Film.* New York: A. S. Barnes, 1978.

Periodicals

Hyatt, Richard. "Haeee! Gung Fu Movies: A Primer." *Take One* 3, no. 12.

Jameson, Richard. "Something to Do with Death." *Film Comment,* March, 1973.

Stuart, Alex. "Chinese Chequers." *Films and Filming,* October, 1973.

6
LITERARY ADAPTATION

The Killers—Hemingway, Film Noir, and the Terror of Daylight

There have been two films based on Ernest Hemingway's short story "The Killers." An examination of the short story and the two films from a genre viewpoint is particularly interesting, because each version represents popular art, with an author of merit using the same basic material for narrative. All three versions were made as entertainment. All, I believe, are expressions of significance in genre study.

It is revealing to examine how a popular artist changes and adapts a basic story to meet his own needs and those of his society. The three versions were done approximately twenty years apart—a span during which significant cultural and historical changes took place. Hemingway's short story appeared in *Scribner's* magazine in 1927. The Mark Hellinger–produced, Robert Siodmak–directed film was released in 1946. Don Siegel's film came out in 1964. Both films were made for Universal Studios; and both, officially, are called *Ernest Hemingway's The Killers.*

Hemingway

Hemingway's story is brief, direct, and unexplained. It is left to the reader to understand what has happened and what the story means. The killers themselves are, I believe, intentionally portrayed as figures from pulp fiction. They wear derby hats, exhibit hard-boiled sarcasm, and posture and perform for themselves and the people they terrorize. Inter-

estingly, Carlos Baker, the Hemingway critic and biographer, has
called Hemingway's story and the novel *Little Caesar,* by W. R.
Burnett (on which the film of the same title was based), the only
enduring works about American gangsters.

Hemingway's two killers, Al and Max, suddenly appear in a diner,
much as Edward G. Robinson and Douglas Fairbanks appear at the start
of *Little Caesar.* Hemingway's Al and Max are gross, confident, cold,
lawless extensions of the big city. They display a cheap, fascinating
amorality that has no fear of law or man.

It should be noted that Hemingway's story was published just a few
months before the advent of the first commercial sound film. The killers
were not, therefore, posturing to imitate what they had seen in films.
The gangster of silent film days was radically different from what he
became with the appearance of *Little Caesar* (see chapter 2). The silent
gangster films, as mentioned earlier, were basically romances, with little or no ironically tragic figure. Even a film so advanced in many ways
as Josef von Sternberg's *Underworld,* which appeared the same year as
Hemingway's story, presented the gangster as a social symbol redeemed by self-sacrificing romanticism.

Hemingway's story, however, finds its meaning not in the killers or
even in the victim, Swede, whom they have come to kill. The focus of
the story is Nick Adams, the boy in the diner—the boy at the core of the
series of initiation stories by Hemingway. Nick watches the drama un-
fold and is powerless to save Swede. Both the killers and Swede accept
their roles as assassins and victim. Nick can only watch in confused
amazement. He doesn't know what is happening. The only explanation
Swede gives him is, "I got in wrong." Roles and fate are accepted by
killers and victim alike. Nick is exposed to life as a Greek tragedy. The
small town is not safe. No one is safe from fate; and no one can do anything about it except face it with dignity, as Swede does.

At the end of the story, Nick can only run—to try to evade the initiation experience. The last lines of the story are:

> "I'm going to get out of this town," Nick said.
> "Yes," George said. "That's a good thing to do."
> "I can't stand to think about him waiting in the room and knowing
> he's going to get it. It's too damned awful."
> "Well," said George, "you better not think about it."

To "think about it," for Hemingway, is to lose confidence in the beliefs of self-determination, good and evil, that had sustained you. As Antoine de St. Exupery said about horror, which is what Nick encounters, you don't feel it when you experience it. It becomes horror when it has passed and you have time to think about it. Nick's horror is in the realization, through the experience of watching it happen, that Swede's way of facing fate is the only possible response. It is a harsh code to absorb and accept, and yet it is the one Hemingway frequently returned to in his work.

The visual elements of Hemingway's descriptions help to sustain our acceptance of the sense of reality of the action. In a story of only a few pages, Hemingway inserts the information that the boardinghouse in which Swede lives is not owned by Mrs. Bell, who runs it, but by a Mrs. Hirsh. Sam, the cook, fingers the corner of his mouth when the gag is removed; and the killers arrange the people in the back of the diner as if, as Hemingway says, they were setting up a photo.

The Film Noir

Hemingway sold the film rights of his short story to Mark Hellinger, a journalist, film producer, and screenwriter, who had worked on such Warner Brothers films as *High Sierra* and *The Roaring Twenties*. Hellinger wanted a young director he knew, named Don Siegel, to do the film adaptation of the Hemingway story, but Siegel was under contract to Warner Brothers and was not free to take the assignment.

Hellinger then turned to a German-born director, Robert Siodmak. Andrew Sarris (in *The American Cinema)* indicated his belief that Siodmak's direction in the 1940s was indistinguishable from that of Jules Dassin in *Brute Force* and *Naked City*. One possible reason for the similarity may be that both of the Dassin films mentioned were produced by Hellinger, as was Siodmak's version of *The Killers*. The similarity might lie in the fact that Hellinger wanted a particular dark atmosphere, an atmosphere that had its roots in German expressionism and that was manifested in heavy shadows and artificial, controlled shooting on sets instead of on location. The films of this cycle also were notable for the relatively unambiguous nature of the characters portrayed in them.

Siodmak was known as an "atmosphere" director, one who liked working on sets with controlled lighting and striking camera angles. Siodmak films, both before and after *The Killers,* are characteristically dark expressions featuring nonheroes who are bigger than life. *The Killers,* too, reflected this atmosphere. Other similar films included

Phantom Lady, The Spiral Staircase, The Dark Mirror, Cry of the City, and *The File on Thelma Jordan.*

Siodmak was a master of this style, called the film noir, which emerged as the postwar feeling of pessimism affected various genres. The film noir, based on a literary genre that emerged a decade earlier in the novels of Dashiell Hammett, James Cain, and others, usually centered around a hardboiled American cop, detective, or insurance man who finds himself in a sick society—going into its darkest corners, ferreting out corruption. The evil often engulfs or destroys him (if he falls victim to greed or, more often, to a corrupt temptress); alternatively, he becomes cynically self-satisfied. The greatest threat to the film noir hero is not his male antagonist but a Medea figure, who can draw him by her witchlike powers into evil.

The film noir brought to the forefront of popular culture the nonheroic hero. Humphrey Bogart as Sam Spade in John Huston's version of Dashiell Hammett's *The Maltese Falcon* (1941) signaled the emergence of the new genre. The Huston film appeared at the start of World War II; so the form and its dark, nonheroic hero soon were submerged in the affirmation of win-the-war patriotism. After World War II, the nonhero reemerged, romanticized, in the character Humphrey Bogart played in Huston's *Key Largo.*

Heroes of the film noir, the genre that really began around 1944, were not Hollywood glamour figures; many of the directors who did their finest work during this period were not big-name American directors, but Europeans, mostly Germans, who had a heritage of the dark, controlled studio pessimism of German expressionism. The German directors (or European directors trained in prewar Germany), most of whom did their best work in the period of film noir or emerged at that time as noteworthy directors, included Siodmak, Edward Dmytryk (*Murder, My Sweet; Cornered; Till the End of Time; Crossfire*), Fritz Lang (*The Big Heat; The Woman in the Window; Scarlet Street*), Billy Wilder (*Double Indemnity; The Lost Weekend; Ace in the Hole; Sunset Boulevard*), Curtis Bernhardt (*Conflict; A Stolen Life; Possessed; High Wall*), Rudolph Mate (*The Dark Past; Union Station; No Sad Songs for Me; D.O.A*), John Brahm (*The Lodger; Hangover Square; Guest in the House; The Locket; The Brasher Doubloon*), and Jean Negulesco (*The Mask of Dimitrios; The Conspirators; Three Strangers; Nobody Lives Forever; Deep Valley; Roadhouse;* and *Johnny Belinda*).

The titles of the films of the period reflected their pessimism, with words like *darkness, cry, night, sidewalk, goodbye, farewell,* and *death.* The titles are as uniformly dark and ominous as the lighting and tone of the films. The films revealed a stream of American doubt, submerged during World War II, which then reemerged with the atomic bomb; the doubt reflected pessimism about the future following the death of Franklin Roosevelt, who had become a popular mythic father figure, and the prospect of an endless cold war and all its implications.

The overground big-budget "A" pictures reflected this pessimism and fear to a great degree, but it was the mass of slightly lower-budgeted genre films that most strongly plucked at the national conscience and played on fear. It was these "B" movies that made the films of the period memorable and identifiable examples of film noir.

The heroes of the films were as offbeat and cynical as the pessimism of the films merited. At the same time, however, they displayed a romantic heroism, a streak of knightly valor, stemming from the constant belief of American popular culture that a good man can somehow hold the world together, right wrongs, and reaffirm existence. It was a concept adopted from the hard-boiled fiction of the 1920s, in which Hemingway's writing, certainly *The Killers,* was central. Like the fiction of Hemingway, Hammett, James Cain, Raymond Chandler, William Irish (Cornell Woolrich), and others, the films displayed the pull between pessimism (and omens of darkness) and the eternal hope of American individualism.

The offbeat heroes included such actors as Bogart, who became a real star only in the 1940s, John Garfield (*The Breaking Point; The Fallen Sparrow; Nobody Lives Forever; The Postman Always Rings Twice; Body and Soul*), Edmond O'Brien (*The Web; The Killers; White Heat; D.O.A.; Man in the Dark*); Mark Stevens (*The Dark Corner; The Street with No Name; Cry Vengeance*), and Dick Powell (*Murder, My Sweet; Cornered; Johnny O'Clock; To the Ends of the Earth*).

Hellinger-Siodmak's *The Killers* was one of the first of the cynical postwar films noir, the first post-A-bomb example of the mode.

The opening of the film is like the Hemingway story, but there are important differences:

- The total sequence is done indoors. Even the outdoor approach to the diner is on a set, which gives an oppressive, film noir air quite different from the intentionally pulp-fiction atmosphere of the story.
- The killers are not, as in Hemingway, comic-serious poseurs. They

are deadly serious, with no overtones of irony about the way they see themselves or we see them.

- Nick Adams is not the focus of the incident in the film. In fact, we do not even see Nick's reaction after he visits Swede. The camera does not move to him or seek him out. Attention and focus shift from the killers to Swede and rest only briefly upon Nick, Sam (the cook), and George (the owner of the diner).
- Swede is more explicit about his death being part of an act in the past. "I did something wrong once," is his comment, not "I got in wrong," as we see in the short story.
- We see Swede killed. The horror is not left to the imagination; it is explicit. The screenplay called for the killing to be handled "a la Siodmak"—displaying shadows, a restricted setting, a horror from the past in action, and our viewing *of* that horror, not just a hint of it.

One central character in the film is the insurance agent, played by Edmond O'Brien. He is an archetypal film noir protagonist: the mystery nags him. He is driven by his desire to understand, to get the story straight, to sort out the mystery of Swede's death, to understand the past. Understanding the dark past and making some sense of it are essential to the film noir hero.

O'Brien masks his quest for understanding behind the pragmatic statement that he is really out to save money for the insurance company for which he works. He never discusses his reason for the zeal with which he attacks the problem, however; and at one point, his boss tells him that, even if he solves the mystery, it will do the company no good, because the loss has already been figured into the future, computed. In spite of the knowledge that his search will have no fiscal meaning, O'Brien goes on to risk life and job to get to the truth.

As in most films noir, the world is black and confused. It is up to O'Brien—a man with no family as far as we know, no background, a valued lone investigator—to make sense of the unknown. But Hemingway's emphasis was upon the acceptance of hopelessness with dignity, a hopelessness that need not and possibly cannot be understood. In the films noir in general and *The Killers* in particular, the need to get the story straight is compulsive. Not knowing is not acceptable; dignity is not sufficient. Man must understand, must run through life getting to the heart of the blackness.

O'Brien is the modern man, the determined—often, frightened—

man. Just before he bursts in upon the killer Dum-Dum, who he knows is searching the Swede's room, O'Brien is shown alone, his defenses down, hesitating about whether to plunge in to face the past in the room of death. Behind his cynicism and wisecracking in public is a private fear.

In contrast is the other central figure of the film, the Swede, played by Burt Lancaster. Another major element of films noir, one adopted from the German expressionistic tradition, is the idea of the doppelganger, or double—the hero's reverse image, with whom he must come to terms. In films noir, the double often represents the lost past. This is true in *The Killers,* in which Lancaster dies early in the film and is seen only in the flashback stories told to O'Brien, who increasingly identifies with him.

Swede is a silent, slightly stupid man of honor out of the past (*Out of the Past* is the title of one well-known film noir). He is an anachronism, with his roots in ideas of self-respect and dignity. He is a boxer, proud that he never has been knocked out in the ring, who willingly takes the rap and goes to jail for his girl. Both of these gestures are seen by his colleagues as foolish. Swede is very much a Hemingway hero, but O'Brien is very much a film noir hero. Swede dies because he has no place in the dark world of the late 1940s. O'Brien, the man of this period of darkness, gets revenge for Swede; he relives Swede's experiences through flashback, befriends his friends, makes enemies of his enemies, and is attracted by the girl who destroyed Swede. But O'Brien is a step ahead of them. His cynicism and caution, his lack of trust in humanity, save him and reaffirm him as the man of his time. It is his, O'Brien's, world. He is his company's best investigator. Even the police do what he tells them to do.

In the course of his probing into the past, as in most films noir, O'Brien leaves a trail of death behind him. In the end, however, he succeeds: he understands the mystery of the darkness, a mystery that the viewer of the late 1940s could not understand in his own dark world away from the screen and theater. O'Brien evens the score, gets a cynical weekend off, and then, we know, will be back to ferreting out more of the unending ills of society.

Another important aspect of the film noir is manifest in Siodmak's *The Killers.* There is no character change, and none is intended. Layers are peeled away to reveal a rotten core of betrayal. Doom prevails in words, lighting, music, and characterizations. Colfax, Lubinsky, the manager, Charleston, Blinky, Dum-Dum—all are expressions of an un-

changing cynical response through which O'Brien must plow and survive. The killers themselves, like Swede, are anachronisms. They are
too straightforward. The death of Al and Max is also inevitable; they are
as doomed as the monsters in the horror films of the 1940s.

The visual aura of the film is striking as an example of film noir.
Everything is indoors, even the street scenes, with the exception of one
robbery. The feeling of control, constriction, darkness is extended into
individual camera shots. The shot of Nick coming to warn Swede that
the killers are on their way appears to have been filmed with one shot of
Nick's run through the alley and a pan in the room to meet him coming
through the door. The shot demonstrates remarkable camera control,
which reflects the thematic need in the film to control and, at the same
time, demonstrates visually that, within the context of the film, there is
no essential difference between the darkness of the outside and that of
the inside.

The Terror of Daylight

Ten years after the Hellinger-Siodmak film was released, the film
noir style had disappeared. There was a new audience sensibility to be
considered, a new national fear and reaction to be explored. The Siegel-
directed version of *The Killers* was, significantly, intended to be a feature for television. Because of President John Kennedy's assassination,
however, it was pulled from television showing and was opened in Europe. Gradually, over the years following its release in 1964, it has
picked up a reputation and a following.

The Siegel film is similar to the 1946 Hellinger-Siodmak film noir
version in many ways, reflecting the elements of noir which persisted.
Siegel wanted to reduce the comparison of the two versions by calling
his film *Johnny North;* but the studio, which owned the rights to the use
of Hemingway's name with the story, refused.

Among the similarities of the 1964 version to the earlier film are the
following:

- The flashback technique of getting to the mystery is used.
- The woman still is seen as the betrayer; she double-crosses the victim
  and the investigator.
- The investigation is undertaken because someone is trying to under-
  stand, again, why the victim didn't run.
- The victim is an athlete, a man of action who cannot control the du-

plicity of society with his animal ability and his American sense of traditional fairness and sportsmanship.

The differences between the films are major ones, which lie at the core of Siegel's sensibility and that of many films of the 1960s:

- The Hemingway opening, instead of being used as a referent to open the film, is only vaguely evident in the brutal beginning. The killers are not talkative; they do not pose; they are businesslike, official.
- The killer, not the investigator, is the central figure.
- Darkness does not prevail: the film is in color, is bright; death and fear come in the daylight, in the most matter-of-fact locations.
- Much of the film is shot outdoors on location instead of in a studio.
- The evil of the film is not as clearly defined as it was in the earlier film; it is not as easy to say who is "good" and who is "bad." There is even some sympathy shown for Browning (Ronald Reagan), who betrays the athlete.

By 1964, into the cold war, after the president's death, literature and film were dealing with men who had fallen back into corporate identification for protection against the confusion of the world. The films of the period increasingly dealt with the fight to salvage self-respect and identity, to find some meaningful values in the face of the corporate onslaught and the fear of "1984," of overpopulation, and of mass society. In 1964–65, these concerns were evident in such diverse films as: *The Killers; Dr. Strangelove; Kiss Me, Stupid; Fail Safe; The Naked Kiss; These Are the Damned, Darling; King Rat; A Thousand Clowns; The Loved One; Mickey One;* and even Jerry Lewis's *The Patsy.*

In *The Killers*, Lee Marvin investigates the victim's death, just as O'Brien did, but Marvin—a brutal man, unlike the gentle O'Brien figure—is clearly not a hero in either the Hemingway or film noir sense. He is a brutal murderer, a man who has set his world in order and is disturbed by the actions of a man who did not conform to the way he had decided people should who face the horror of death. Marvin is a man in control of his feelings—a modern corporate killer with an attache case, a nice suit, and sunglasses.

Marvin is an automatic man, disturbed by the confusing actions of the victim. He seeks the money that the unraveling of the mystery will bring him, as O'Brien sought the money for his company; but Marvin keeps talking about *why* a man would die like that—without running, without fear.

Marvin does what O'Brien did; but he gains information not by friendliness and guile, but by force, the tool of his time. He is an American protagonist of the era: violent and controlled. He is a central figure but certainly not a hero and barely a protagonist; perhaps he is better described as an *an*tagonist.

He relives John Cassavetes's experiences, as the victim, but Marvin's elán is violent. His threat to the predatory woman (Angie Dickinson) indicates that, like O'Brien, he trusts no one. But, in the Siegel film, the threat is played as a love scene; violence and passion are consciously equated. Marvin's threat of death is almost a kiss. He is not a hero worthy of survival, as O'Brien had been. Like Cassavetes, Marvin is eventually betrayed by the woman and dies from the betrayal—but he exacts revenge for both.

As with other films of this period, time pulses throughout; the fear of death and destruction are central. "I haven't got the time," Charlie (Marvin) tells his victims who want to talk. The theme of the film is the song "Too Little Time." Charlie is fifty-three; he feels his age and knows that anything can happen in a violent world in which leaders are assassinated and murder takes place on the streets. Charlie, like Swede, has a code, however; and in that code lies his only merit: Charlie is a man of his word. It is a bizarre word, but it is the only thing one has left in the world of violence.

In contrast, his partner, Clu Gulager, is young and not driven. He is an untroubled professional, uncontrolled, undisciplined, in contrast to Charlie's coolness. Charlie has become an almost unconscious instrument of vengeance. He never kills without a reason—to extract revenge or to gain money. There is no apparent joy in his job; it is simply a job. Gulager represents the unknown variable, the death that can spring out without reason.

Like Charlie-the-killer, man must create a code of behavior. There are no heroes. There is no behavior pattern to rely on. There is no way to define good and evil. The question becomes one of self-understanding. Siegel's film explores concepts of good and evil and questions the value of defining morality, leading the way for such films as *Bonnie and Clyde, The Dirty Dozen, The Wild Bunch, McCabe and Mrs. Miller, The French Connection,* and a host of other films that used the horror of violence to question basic American concepts (see chapter 8).

Hemingway's definition of courage as "grace under pressure and in face of death" is unacceptable in the Siegel film, as is the Hellinger-

Lee Marvin in *The Killers.*

Siodmak film noir view that the cynical hero can go through the black world and salvage a vestige of light. The world is not like that. Death is by day in *The Killers* of 1964. There is no solace in light.

The colors and lighting in the 1964 film are bright, uniform, flashing, modern, cold. The atmosphere does not inform us; the world simply *is*. Violence defines it. The world is multilayered and deceptive. Marvin cuts through it with violence, as do *Bonnie and Clyde, McCabe,* Dustin Hoffman in *Straw Dogs,* Burt Reynolds and Jon Voight in *Deliverance,* and Steve McQueen in *The Getaway,* to reveal the amorality of existence and the fragility of accepted codes of behavior and of hope.

The images of the 1964 film are large, looming, screen-filling. The guns of the Siegel film are silent; death is seen in close-up, not in medium or long shots. Death in Siegel's film is horror, not an expressionistic dream or a literary allegory, as in the films noir. Violence and fear must be lived with. As the Indian says in William Saroyan's play *The Time of Your Life,* there may be no sidewalk outside the saloon. The world may be gone. We can never be sure of anything in a world in which real heroes are killed by madmen and a car can fly around a corner to kill a man on the way to the drugstore. ''There is no foundation up and down the line,'' says Saroyan's Indian. The Siegel film, like others that have followed it to the present day, dealt with the problem of stripping away postures—including those of business and economic security—to reveal the shallowness of modern existence, which has no foundation in love or morality—and which desperately needs one. ''The Killers,'' the story Ernest Hemingway wrote in 1927, has been the source of both personal and cultural expression in three distinct decades and by three distinctive artists.

Table 6.1

Selected American Literary Works and Their Adaptations in Film*

Literary Work	Adaptation in Film	Year	Director	Stars
To Have and Have Not, novel by Ernest Hemingway	*To Have and Have Not*	1944	Howard Hawks	Humphrey Bogart
	The Breaking Point	1951	Michael Curtiz	John Garfield
	The Gun Runners	1958	Don Siegel	Audie Murphy
The Front Page, play by Ben Hecht and Charles MacArthur	*The Front Page*	1930	Lewis Milestone	Pat O'Brien
	His Girl Friday	1940	Howard Hawks	Rosalind Russell
	The Front Page	1974	Billy Wilder	Jack Lemmon
Farewell, My Lovely, novel by Raymond Chandler	*The Falcon Takes Over*	1942	Irving Reis	George Sanders
	Murder, My Sweet	1944	Edward Dmytryk	Dick Powell
	Farewell, My Lovely	1975	Dick Richards	Robert Mitchum
The Postman Always Rings Twice, novel by James M. Cain	*The Postman Always Rings Twice*	1946	Tay Garnett	John Garfield, Lana Turner
	The Postman Always Rings Twice	1981	Bob Rafelson	Jack Nicholson, Jessica Lange
The Body Snatchers, novel by Jack Finney	*Invasion of the Body Snatchers*	1956	Don Siegel	Kevin McCarthy, Dana Wynter
	Invasion of the Body Snatchers	1975	Philip Kaufman	Donald Sutherland
High Sierra, novel by W. R. Burnett	*High Sierra*	1941	Raoul Walsh	Humphrey Bogart
	Colorado Territory	1949	Raoul Walsh	Joel McCrea
	I Died a Thousand Times	1955	Stuart Heisler	Jack Palance
An American Tragedy, novel by Theodore Dreiser	*An American Tragedy*	1931	Josef Von Sternberg	Phillips Holmes
	A Place in the Sun	1951	George Stevens	Montgomery Clift, Elizabeth Taylor
The Maltese Falcon, novel by Dashiell Hammett	*The Maltese Falcon*	1931	Roy del Ruth	Ricardo Cortez
	Satan Met a Lady	1936	William Dieterle	Warren Williams
	The Maltese Falcon	1941	John Huston	Humphrey Bogart
I, the Jury, novel by Mickey Spillane	*I, the Jury*	1953	Harry Essex	Biff Elliot
	I, the Jury	1982	Richard Heffron	Armand Assante

*There have been many examples of adaptation and remakes of such adaptations. This brief list includes films and original works that are relatively easy to find.

Table 6.2
Key Films Noir

Film	Year	Director	Principal Actors
Affair in Trinidad	1952	Vincent Sherman	Rita Hayworth, Glenn Ford
All My Sons	1948	Irving Reis	Edward G. Robinson, Burt Lancaster
Angel Face	1953	Otto Preminger	Robert Mitchum, Jean Simmons
Attack	1957	Robert Aldrich	Jack Palance, Lee Marvin
The Big Carnival (Ace in the Hole)	1951	Billy Wilder	Kirk Douglas, Jan Sterling
The Big Clock	1947	John Farrow	Ray Milland, Charles Laughton
The Big Heat	1953	Fritz Lang	Glenn Ford, Gloria Grahame
The Big Sleep	1946	Howard Hawks	Humphrey Bogart, Lauren Bacall
The Blue Dahlia	1946	George Marshall	Alan Ladd, William Bendix
Body and Soul	1947	Robert Rossen	John Garfield
Boomerang	1947	Elia Kazan	Dana Andrews, Jane Wyatt
Border Incident	1949	Anthony Mann	Ricardo Montalban, George Murphy
The Breaking Point	1951	Michael Curtiz	John Garfield, Patricia Neal
Brute Force	1947	Jules Dassin	Burt Lancaster, Hume Cronyn
Call Northside 777	1948	Henry Hathaway	James Stewart, Richard Conte
Champion	1949	Mark Robson	Kirk Douglas, Arthur Kennedy
Clash by Night	1952	Fritz Lang	Barbara Stanwyck, Paul Douglas
Confidential Agent	1945	Herman Shumlin	Charles Boyer
Conflict	1945	Curtis Bernhardt	Humphrey Bogart, Alexis Smith
Criss Cross	1948	Robert Siodmak	Burt Lancaster, Yvonne DeCarlo
The Dark Corner	1946	Henry Hathaway	Mark Stevens, Lucille Ball
The Dark Mirror	1946	Robert Siodmak	Olivia de Havilland
Dark Passage	1947	Delmer Daves	Humphrey Bogart
Dead Reckoning	1947	John Cromwell	Humphrey Bogart
Detour	1946	Edgar G. Ulmer	Tom Neal, Ann Savage
D.O.A.	1950	Rudolph Mate	Edmond O'Brien
Don't Bother to Knock	1952	Roy Baker	Richard Widmark, Marilyn Monroe
Double Indemnity	1944	Billy Wilder	Fred MacMurray, Barbara Stanwyck
The Enforcer	1951	Bretaigne Windust	Humphrey Bogart
Fallen Angel	1946	Otto Preminger	Alice Faye, Dana Andrews
The File on Thelma Jordan	1949	Robert Siodmak	Barbara Stanwyck
Force of Evil	1948	Abraham Polonsky	John Garfield, Thomas Gomez
Fourteen Hours	1951	Henry Hathaway	Richard Basehart, Paul Douglas
Gilda	1946	Charles Vidor	Rita Hayworth, Glenn Ford
Gun Crazy	1950	Joseph H. Lewis	John Dall, Peggy Cummins

Table 6.2 (Continued)
Key Films Noir

Film	Year	Director	Principal Actors
Hangover Square	1944	John Brahm	Laird Cregar, Linda Darnell
He Walked by Night	1948	Alfred Werker	Richard Basehart
High Noon	1952	Fred Zinnemann	Gary Cooper, Grace Kelly
High Wall	1948	Curtis Bernhardt	Robert Taylor, Audrey Totter
House of Strangers	1950	Joseph L. Mankiewicz	Edward G. Robinson, Richard Conte
Human Desire	1954	Fritz Lang	Glenn Ford, Gloria Grahame
I Walk Alone	1947	Byron Haskin	Burt Lancaster, Kirk Douglas
In a Lonely Place	1950	Nicholas Ray	Humphrey Bogart, Gloria Grahame
Ivy	1947	Sam Wood	Joan Fontaine, Patric Knowles
Johnny O'Clock	1947	Robert Rossen	Dick Powell, Evelyn Keyes
Key Largo	1948	John Huston	Humphrey Bogart, Lauren Bacall
Kiss of Death	1947	Henry Hathaway	Victor Mature, Richard Widmark
Kiss the Blood Off My Hands	1948	Norman Foster	Burt Lancaster, Joan Fontaine
The Lady from Shanghai	1947	Orson Welles	Rita Hayworth, Orson Welles
The Lady in the Lake	1946	Robert Montgomery	Robert Montgomery, Audrey Totter
Laura	1944	Otto Preminger	Dana Andrews, Gene Tierney
The Lawless	1950	Joseph Losey	MacDonald Carey
The Locket	1946	John Brahm	Laraine Day, Brian Aherne
The Lodger	1944	John Brahm	Laird Cregar, George Sanders
The Long Night	1947	Anatole Litvak	John Barrymore, Jr., Preston Foster
The Lost Weekend	1945	Billy Wilder	Ray Milland
Love Letters	1945	William Dieterle	Jennifer Jones, Joseph Cotten
The Man with the Golden Arm	1956	Otto Preminger	Frank Sinatra, Kim Novak
The Mask of Dimitrios	1944	Jean Negulesco	Zachary Scott, Peter Lorre
Ministry of Fear	1944	Fritz Lang	Ray Milland
Murder, My Sweet	1944	Edward Dmytryk	Dick Powell, Claire Trevor
Naked City	1948	Jules Dassin	Barry Fitzgerald, Howard Duff
The Narrow Margin	1951	Richard Fleischer	Charles McGraw, Marie Windsor
Niagara	1952	Henry Hathaway	Marilyn Monroe, Joseph Cotten
Night in the City	1950	Jules Dassin	Richard Widmark
Nightmare Alley	1947	Edmund Goulding	Tyrone Power, Joan Blondell
99 River Street	1953	Phil Karlson	John Payne
No Way Out	1950	Joseph L. Mankiewicz	Richard Widmark
Nocturne	1946	Edward L. Marin	George Raft
Notorious	1946	Alfred Hitchcock	Cary Grant, Ingrid Bergman

Table 6.2 (Continued)
Key Films Noir

Film	Year	Director	Principal Actors
On Dangerous Ground	1952	Nicholas Ray	Robert Ryan, Ida Lupino
On the Waterfront	1954	Elia Kazan	Marlon Brando, Eva Marie Saint
Out of the Past	1947	Jacques Tourneur	Robert Mitchum, Kirk Douglas
Panic in the Streets	1950	Elia Kazan	Richard Widmark, Paul Douglas
The Paradine Case	1947	Alfred Hitchcock	Gregory Peck, Alida Valli
Phantom Lady	1944	Robert Siodmak	Ella Raines, Franchot Tone
The Phoenix City Story	1955	Phil Karlson	Richard Kiley
Pickup on South Street	1953	Samuel Fuller	Richard Widmark, Jean Peters
Pitfall	1948	André de Toth	Dick Powell, Lisbeth Scott
Port of New York	1949	Laslo Benedek	Scott Brady, Yul Brynner
The Postman Always Rings Twice	1946	Tay Garnett	John Garfield, Lana Turner
The Prowler	1950	Joseph Losey	Van Heflin, Evelyn Keyes
Pursued	1947	Raoul Walsh	Teresa Wright, Robert Mitchum
Pushover	1954	Richard Quine	Fred MacMurray, Kim Novak
The Red House	1947	Delmer Daves	Edward G. Robinson
Ride the Pink Horse	1947	Robert Montgomery	Robert Montgomery
Roadhouse	1948	Jean Negulesco	Cornel Wilde, Richard Widmark
Rope	1948	Alfred Hitchcock	James Stewart, Farley Granger
Ruthless	1948	Edgar G. Ulmer	Zachary Scott, Louis Hayward
Saboteur	1942	Alfred Hitchcock	Robert Cummings, Bonita Granville
Scarlet Street	1945	Fritz Lang	Edward G. Robinson, Joan Bennett
The Secret Beyond the Door	1948	Fritz Lang	Joan Bennett, Michael Redgrave
The Set-Up	1949	Robert Wise	Robert Ryan, Audrey Totter
Side Street	1958	Anthony Mann	Farley Granger
Sleep My Love	1948	Douglas Sirk	Claudette Colbert, Robert Cummings
The Sniper	1952	Edward Dmytryk	Adolphe Menjou
So Dark the Night	1946	Joseph H. Lewis	Steven Gerdy
So Evil My Love	1948	Lewis Allen	Ray Milland, Ann Todd
Somewhere in the Night	1946	Joseph L. Mankiewicz	John Hodiak, Nancy Guild
Sorry, Wrong Number	1948	Anatole Litvak	Barbara Stanwyck, Burt Lancaster
The Spiral Staircase	1945	Robert Siodmak	Dorothy McGuire, George Brent
The Steel Helmet	1951	Samuel Fuller	Gene Evans
The Strange Love of Martha Ivers	1946	Lewis Milestone	Barbara Stanwyck, Kirk Douglas
The Stranger	1946	Orson Welles and Norman Foster	Edward G. Robinson, Orson Welles

Table 6.2 (Continued)
Key Films Noir

Film	Year	Director	Principal Actors
Strangers on a Train	1951	Alfred Hitchcock	Farley Granger
Sudden Fear	1953	David Miller	Joan Crawford
Suddenly	1954	Lewis Allen	Frank Sinatra
Sunset Boulevard	1950	Billy Wilder	William Holden, Gloria Swanson
The Suspect	1944	Robert Siodmak	Charles Laughton, Ella Raines
They Live by Night	1947	Nicholas Ray	Farley Granger, Cathy O'Donnell
Thieves' Highway	1949	Jules Dassin	Richard Conte, Lee J. Cobb
T-Men	1947	Anthony Mann	Dennis O'Keefe
Too Late for Tears	1949	Bryon Haskin	Dick Powell, Lisbeth Scott
Touch of Evil	1957	Orson Welles	Charlton Heston, Janet Leigh
Union Station	1950	Rudolph Mate	William Holden, Barry Fitzgerald
Where the Sidewalk Ends	1950	Otto Preminger	Dana Andrews, Gene Tierney
Whirlpool	1950	Otto Preminger	Gene Tierney, Jose Ferrer
White Heat	1949	Raoul Walsh	James Cagney, Virginia Mayo
The Window	1948	Ted Tetzlaff	Bobby Driscoll, Barbara Hale
The Woman in the Window	1944	Fritz Lang	Edward G. Robinson, Joan Bennett
The Woman on the Beach	1947	Jean Renoir	Joan Bennett, Robert Ryan

Readings on Film Noir

Books

Alloway, Lawrence. *Violent America: The Movies 1946–1964.* New York: Museum of Modern Art, 1971.

Hirsch, Foster. *The Dark Side of the Screen: Film Noir.* San Diego: A. S. Barnes, 1981.

Kaplan, E. Ann, editor. *Women in Film Noir.* Revised edition. London: BFI Publishing, 1980.

Place, J. A., and L. S. Peterson. "Some Visual Motifs of Film Noir." In *Movies and Methods,* edited by Bill Nichols. Berkeley and Los Angeles: University of California Press, 1976.

Periodicals

Durgnat, Raymond. "The Family Tree of Film Noir." *Cinema,* no. 6 and 7, August 1970.

Porfiro, Robert G. "No Way Out: Existential Motifs in the Film Noir." *Sight and Sound:* 45, no.4 (Autumn, 1976), pp. 212–17.

Schrader, Paul. "Notes of Film Noir." *Film Comment,* Spring, 1970.

7
LITERARY ADAPTATION
The Treasure of the Sierra Madre—Novel into Film

B. Traven's 1935 novel *The Treasure of the Sierra Madre* presented a great challenge for John Huston, who both wrote the screenplay and directed the film adaptation of 1948. Like Traven's other work, including *The Death Ship* (1934) and *The Bridge in the Jungle* (1938), *Treasure* is a fantastic, hyperbolic, nightmarish saga, far from a naturalistic novel. And Traven's language is strange, to say the least—he shifts between grammatical and ungrammatical, formal and colloquial seemingly on whim.

Upon first reading, the dialogue might appear to be "undeliverable." For example, here is the gold-hatted bandit's angry outburst when Curtin, one of the trio of prospectors, challenges him to prove he is a federal officer:

> Badges, to god-damn hell with badges! We have no badges. In fact, we don't need badges. I don't have to show you any stinking badges, you goddamned cabron and ching tu madre. Come out of there from that hole of yours. I have to speak to you.

—Or earlier, when the old man, Howard, ridicules his two partners, Dobbs and Curtin, for not recognizing the gold on which they are standing:

> Well, tell my old gra'mother. I have burdened myself with a couple of fine lodgers, two very elegant bedfellers who kick at the first drop of my

rain and crawl under mother's petticoat when thunder rumbles. My, my, what great prospectors a driller and a tool-dresser can make! Drilling a hole with a half a hundred Mexican peons around to lend you hands and feet! I still can do that after a two days' spree you bet. Two guys reading in the magazines about crossing a lazy river up in Alaska and now going prospecting on their own.

In both speeches, the changeable style is that of the tall tale rather than the ''realistic'' novel. Note the arbitrariness of Traven's choices. Gold Hat's switch to the formalities of ''We have no badges'' and ''I have to speak with you,'' contrasts with the crudities of the rest of his outburst. In Howard's monologue, there is no rationale for his contraction in the word ''gra'mother'' and his lack of contraction elsewhere nor for the combination of standard English and dialect in ''elegant bedfellers''—a formulation not repeated. And so forth.

But it was probably this weird dialogue that attracted John Huston to the novel in the first place. A teller of tall tales himself, an accomplished writer and lover of the bizarre, Huston took on the same challenge in his later adaptation of *The Man Who Would Be King* (1975). He retained the very dialogue from Kipling's story that was most difficult and idiosyncratic; e.g., the encounter in Kipling's office when Dravot and Peachy discuss their trip and pact. As for *Treasure,* Huston explained the appeal in 1947:

> Traven's unique, a combination of Conrad and Dreiser, if you can imagine such a thing. His people speak no known language—or an English, at any rate, like none I've ever heard. I don't believe he's German, as rumored, for his style hasn't that German exactness; more like the north countries, possibly Sweden. But he's a powerful writer; when you read him, you really take a beating [Philip K. Schever, ''Huston Aided on Location by Army Life,'' *Los Angeles Times,* June 29, 1947, p.1].

Huston asked to meet with Traven during the shooting of *Treasure* in Mexico; but the reluctant author, who obsessively guarded his identity, promised nothing. However, waiting at the Reforma Hotel in Mexico City one morning was a thin little man with gray hair. He handed Huston a card introducing himself as H. Croves, translator from Acapulco. He carried a note from Traven indicating that Croves was the novelist's representative. Convinced that Croves was actually the shy author himself, Huston hired him as a technical advisor. Croves was present for all the Mexican shooting; and, indeed, he made many suggestions that

Huston accepted. As "Hal Croves" told Judy Stone in an unprecedented 1966 interview:

I, Croves, came and visited John Huston and he asked me questions about certain details. I said, "Here, present it this way." He agreed. He was even applauding. "Great ideas, Mr. Croves!" "The ideas I gave you are according to the sense of Traven because we talked it over months ago. . . . I know exactly what is on his mind." I worked so well with John Huston that he even put me on the payroll of Warner Brothers [Judy Stone, *The Mystery of B. Traven* (Los Altos, Calif.: William Katmann, 1977].

Interestingly, Croves's major quarrel with Huston was over the casting of Walter Huston as Howard, in what became an Academy Award–winning performance. He told Judy Stone:

I said, "John, he is your father, but not the type." Traven wrote about a man so old he can't even stand on his feet any more but he still has the dream of gold, gold, gold, gold and the gold goes away. Lewis Stone would have been the right type in my idea and I'm sure Traven's. I admit that Walter Huston was great. He deserved the Oscar he received. Lewis Stone would not have been so good. Only he was more like the character Traven had in mind [Judy Stone, *Mystery of B. Traven*].

Setting

Both novel and film open in the town of Tampico, but Traven devotes a number of pages to the Hotel Oso Negro and its inhabitants, "the scum of five continents," who somehow function and protect themselves in a kind of Lumpenproletariat utopia:

The girls were safer here than in any hotel which makes a fuss about its moral standing. The women were never molested by men coming in drunk. By the unwritten law of the hotel and of the men who lived here any man who tried to harm one of the girls would have been dead at sunrise. . . .

It rarely happened that anything was stolen. . . . A thief in this hotel was never afraid of the police or jail. He was only afraid—terribly afraid—of the beating he would receive if he were found out. . . . [A] score of guests . . . would take the thief into one of the shacks and there preach him a sermon that would make such an excellent impression on his mind and body that for the next seven days he could not move a finger or an eyelid without moaning. These sermons proved so effective that the hotel could guarantee that no theft would recur inside of two months to come.

Huston's film includes two relatively brief sequences in the hotel, but he describes none of the inhabitants except Howard. Clearly, Huston's concerns are not with the social organization of the hotel, but only with the protagonists who have bedded down there. (Although Traven's ''Bolshevik'' sympathies are felt in the novel—as in the passage above—the author of *Treasure* refrains from presenting doctrinaire political positions. True, Traven is antigold and vehemently anticlerical; but what he does believe in is never articulated except by inference. Nor is political ideology expressed directly in the movie, despite the levels of allegory about ''greed.'' So perhaps Huston is faithful to the book?)

Plot Changes

There is a sequence early in the novel in which Dobbs and a man named Moulton journey into the jungle to find jobs at an oil camp. They are joined by a cowardly Indian. At one point, the trio spend a mad night in a tree, convinced that ''a great cat, a tiger, a huge tiger, a *tigre real,* one of the biggest in the jungle'' is after them. The morning proves that the tiger was a burro, ''an ordinary ass tied to a tree by a long lasso,'' and Dobbs angrily claims that he knew it all the time. This comic quest is a prelude to the longer, absurd quest later in the novel. Dobbs, Moulton, and the Indian do not find work and are forced to return to Tampico. John Huston skips past this segment. He combines Moulton with Traven's character Curtin (Tim Holt), introduced later, and gets quickly to the primary relationship with the other partners, Dobbs (Humphrey Bogart) and Howard (Walter Huston).

In the novel, after Curtin and Dobbs have been cheated out of their wages by Pat McCormick, they corner Pat in a bar and make him pay, without resorting to battle; in the film, a brutal fight takes place with Pat (Barton MacLane) nearly beating up the two partially drunk partners. The tables are turned midway, however; and Pat, bleeding and unable to see, pays the men while prone on the floor. Huston's interest in the fisticuffs supersedes Traven's desire for showing Pat as an exploiting capitalist: Huston admires Pat's courage in fighting two adversaries, and he also uses the fight to bring Dobbs and Curtin closer together.

Narrative Technique

Traven often interrupts the narrative for extended parables—always obliquely connected to the main plot. There are three especially lengthy tales, two told by Howard and one by Lacaud (called Cody in the film and played by Bruce Bennett), the stranger who tries to become a partner with the trio in the mountains.

Howard's first story is about a prospector friend of his, forced to return to a once-prosperous mine to help greedy neighbors get more gold. The second expedition proves a disaster. The point of the story for Howard is that he will know when he has enough gold. Curtin scoffs at the tale: "I don't see any curse on gold." Dobbs deceives himself: "I sure would be satisfied with a certain sum, take it and go away to settle in a pretty little town and let others quarrel." Director John Huston leaves the story out of the film.

In Howard's second parable, a doctor cures the blind son of an Indian chief and is rewarded with a silver mine. When he is murdered by Indian miners he has hired at slave wages, his wife take over. She "disappears" after accepting the hospitality of the regional viceroy, who steals the silver. This tale anticipates Howard's behavior later in *Treasure* when he helps cure an Indian leader's son. Howard leaves the Indian village behind to search for Dobbs. He departs without riches, only "the very best horse his host had. . . ." In Huston's movie, Howard acts as honorably as he does in Traven's book, but he needs no parable to motivate his charity.

The third story in the novel takes up all of chapter 12 and is offered by Lacaud, although told in the third-person authorial voice. (This is the most uncanny digression in the novel, for this tale is spun for many pages while bandits are climbing the mountain to attack the prospectors. As usual for B. Traven, not even impending death takes precedence over a good yarn.) Lacaud offers a vivid episode about how the same bandits robbed a train, murdering countless women and children. For the film, John Huston uses the thread of Lacaud's story but places the train robbery in the present tense instead of flashback and makes it less violent (only four passengers are murdered, and these events occur off screen). He also situates the sequence earlier in the film and offers his principal characters as participants in the events; in Traven's version they only heard the story. Dobbs, Curtin, and Howard are passengers on that train, helping to fight off bandits; and there they get their first glimpse of Gold Hat (Alfonso Bedoya), who later kills Dobbs. (As in his adaptation of Dashiell Hammett's novel by the same name, *The Maltese Falcon* (1941), where Huston excised Sam Spade's important existen-

Above and below: Humphrey Bogart with Walter Huston and Tim Holt in *The Treasure of Sierra Madre*.

tial digression concerning "Flitcraft," Huston here shuns important material because it is difficult to incorporate visually into the film without recourse to flashbacks or a complex chronology.)

Characters and Characterizations

In Huston's film, Gold Hat becomes an archetypal, fairy-tale villain, encountered three magical times—on the train, at the campsite, and when he murders Dobbs. (Gold Hat is not one of the trio who kills Dobbs in the novel.) In a brilliant example of transposition, Huston took the "I don't have to show you any stinkin' badges" line, uttered as part of a long exchange between the bandits and prospectors at the campsite, and shifted it to much later, the frightening moment before Dobbs dies. It is the last thing that Gold Hat says (and defiantly) before setting his men on Dobbs.

As for Lacaud, he introduces himself, quite inscrutably, in the novel as "Lacaud. Robert W. Lacaud, Phoenix, Arizona; Tech, Pasadena," and that is all that is ever learned about his past. He is half mad, ultimately harmless; and he is finally left behind to work the mine after the others move onward. In Huston's film, Cody/Lacaud is not crazy. He becomes a genuine menace to the original trio by threatening to reveal the existence of the gold unless he is accepted as a member of the partnership—and the three men vote to shoot him. Their decision is never carried out, because Cody is murdered by the bandits at the campsite. (At this point, Huston attaches a scene that offers more details about Cody. Howard and Curtin search the dead man's belongings. They read his personal letter aloud and discover from his wallet that Cody had a fruit orchard in Texas and left behind a wife and child. This sentimental sequence has been criticized as a lapse in tone for Huston's tough movie.)

Both Traven and Huston loved Howard. It is no accident that John Huston picked his father to play the delightful role. And it is interesting to notice how Traven's own eccentric writing style in the narrative passages (and in his philosophical sections) sounds so similar to the dialogue he put in Howard's mouth. It seems fair to conclude that Howard is Traven's surrogate—just as papa Walter becomes the surrogate for son John.

Traven and Huston also had an affection for Dobbs. Though he is frequently recalled as a moral brute and a madman, Dobbs is a highly contradictory character in both works, until his crack-up. He is initially generous with his cash, willing to share it and put up extra money to finance the trip. Later, Dobbs is the one who helps Howard repair the "wounded" mountain. And though Dobbs succumbs to the disease of gold, he is not viewed as evil by Travel or Huston or, for that matter, by Howard, who says—in his last comment on Dobbs in the novel— "Dobbs has lost his head so completely that he can't use it any longer." (In the movie, Dobbs's mental deterioration is shown by his regression to animalism: his clothes fall apart, his beard grows, and his body moves closer to the ground. Several times, Bogart straightens himself to reveal his shell of humanness, only to crouch forward moments later. Twice in the film, Dobbs reacts irrationally—and thus, ironically—to charges that he is less than human. When Dobbs believes Curtin has called him a "hog" about money, he throws away the gold Curtin offers him to prove he is a civilized human. Later, when Curtin implies that Dobbs is "uncivilized," Dobbs hits him.)

The friendship of men is explored seriously by Huston. The film offers a constant reorganization of the three partners in a single frame. (Often one partner appears in the foreground with the activity of the others behind him.) The word "partner" is repeated frequently by each, a condition not so evident in the novel. But sometimes the three-way relationship is seen skeptically. For example, when the three decide to become mining partners at the hotel, Dobbs and Curtin shake hands. Huston shows only their clasped hands in the frame, with Howard's head placed between them, glancing uncertainly from one to the other. (How do we know whether to believe these often self-deceived protagonists?—When one of Huston's characters lies down, he generally speaks more honestly than when he is standing—an allusion to couch, dream, confession.)

Denouement

In the novel, Curtin says nothing about returning to the United States. It is quite probable that he will accept Howard's offer and join him as an assistant medicine man. (He will remain an emigré in Mexico, just as B. Traven had done.) The book ends with Howard getting on his horse. "No sooner was he seated in the saddle than the Indians shouted, whipped their ponies into action, and hurried back home." The last word is "home," and the implication is of resolution and potential peace.

Huston's film ends more ironically. The partnership is dissolved; and Curtin will sell the burros and head for Texas and an uncertain future, although with a visit planned to Cody's ranch and widow. Curtin has gained wisdom and experience; and Howard, an Indian kingdom. But Huston summarizes the quest for wealth in the last shot of the film: an empty gold bag blowing on the thorns of a desert cactus.

Cinematic Adaptation—a Footnote

Interestingly enough, B. Traven's novel contains a number of specific references to movies; but all such references are deleted in Huston's film version. For example, in the novel, Dobbs and Howard discuss taking their money and starting a movie house in Tampico, with Howard as business manager and Dobbs as artistic manager. At the end, Curtin and Howard discuss and reject this idea. Perhaps a grocery store would be cheaper.

In the siege by the bandits, one of the miners wishes that he were in a movie so he could be rescued. This, indeed, happens. When the bandits suddenly vanish, Howard thinks they have really left, explaining, ''They would have to be awfully good movie actors to play a trick like that so perfectly.'' Finally, there is Dobbs's dread moment of epiphany as the three tramps are about to jump him:

> It flashed through his mind that he had seen many a movie in which the hero was trapped in a situation like this. But he realized at the same time that he could not remember one single picture in which the producer had not done his utmost to help the trapped hero out again to save the girl from the clutches of a bunch of villains. Before he could think of any of the tricks he had seen in the pictures by which the hero finally escaped, he felt, with a strange bitterness in his mouth, that his situation was real. And whatever is real is different. No smart film-producer was on hand to open the trap with a good trick.

8
HISTORICAL PERSPECTIVE

The White-Hot Violence of the 1970s

As an example of critical bias overwhelming thoughtful analysis, one might examine the reaction to the recurrent issue of violence in American films. Violence exists on the screen; the audience responds with shouts and encouragement for the violence; the critic is moved by the violence . . . therefore, the violence is evil and encourages violent behavior.

Whether film violence does carry over into action has been under consideration since the Payne Fund studies, privately funded examinations of various features of the media, carried out at the University of Chicago in the 1930s. Psychologists and social scientists still have not answered the question.

The point I wish to emphasize is not that violence on the screen has no effect, but that the degree and nature of this effect are by no means as certain as many critics assume. Some social scientists have kept alive the possibility that Aristotle's concept of catharsis is in effect in violence on the screen: that to see the act is, in some way, to purge the viewer of the need for violence (or sex). And in some way, the viewing of the violence in an aesthetic context contributes to one's understanding of the action. These social scientists argue further that if one has a predisposition to commit acts of violence, it is ipso facto not created by the violence on screen. It might be liberated by exposure to such violence, but it might also be liberated by something else—an argument, or the witnessing of an accident, perhaps. The social scientists add, however, that viewing of filmed violence, even for such a person, might have a cathartic, aesthetic effect.

It is difficult, if not fruitless, to argue either way. The moral argument, however, might best be understood or mitigated by exploring the content of the films involved rather than by responding in cultural isolation and fear. Although I am in favor of almost total freedom of depiction on the screen, I cannot help feeling that film violence can—somehow—have a negative effect on behavior, or, at least, produce this effect in a sufficient number of cases to make it a valid consideration. Such considerations involve us, not in an analysis of the films and the situation, however, but with our morality and cultural identification.

Before moving to my analysis of the content of violence in American films, I wish to refute, or attempt to refute, two crucial and basic assumptions concerning film violence—subjects that must be dealt with in a genre examination.

1. Violence itself has become a genre, very simple-minded but very potent.

2. There is an audience that desires no context but violence—that will, given a visible excuse, drag any film down to its level and make watching the movie an extremely nervous experience for everyone else.

Concerning the first assumption, to see films simply as exercises in violence, and to call this violence "genre," is to dilute the value of the concept of genre in content analysis and to ascribe to violence a weight of meaning that it does not have. Violence, in films such as *Straw Dogs*, *Bloody Mama*, *The Grissom Gang*, *The Getaway*, *Bonnie and Clyde*, and others to be cited later, is a motif—a primary motif—but just that, one of a number of elements that must be considered and understood in examining the films. Thus *The French Connection* and *Dirty Harry*, considered generically, have their roots in what might be called the "police" film. This genre incorporates decades of depiction in literature (going back to the fiction of Emile Gabouri and Edgar Allan Poe, if one wishes) in such diversified films as William Wyler's *Detective Story*, Akira Kurosawa's *Stray Dog* and *High and Low*, Gordon Douglas's *The Detective*, Rudolph Mate's *Union Station*, Jules Dassin's *Naked City*, William Keighley's *G-Men* and *Bullets or Ballots*, Anthony Mann's *T-Men*, and in television series such as *M-Squad*, *Dragnet*, *Ironside*, *Felony Squad*, *Kojak*, and others. That violence is being employed as a motif in this genre merits analysis; but violence taken out of context, or elevated to become the main consideration of an analysis, is thus served up to moral condemnation without any understanding of the work or works involved.

Concerning the second assumption, there are several points to consider. First, if there actually is an audience that desires no context but violence, it has always had an opportunity to view films that cater to it. The extravaganzas of the 1950s and 1960s—Stanley Kubrick's *Spartacus,* for example—were often keyed to scenes of violence or sadism. This tendency also existed before 1950 in the films of Cecil B. de Mille and his imitators. Today's critics might consider how the earlier audience found its violence in the religious/historical film, which met with a broad acceptance—and provided exactly what the society of that time found appealing in the tying of violence and sadism to religion and spectacle. The consideration presents itself that this earlier violence met a social need by providing substitute victims. It is possible that such films of violence and death were presenting a displaced ritual. The media are increasingly serving the function of tradition. Violence and its audience are not new. Today's film violence, however, is not tied to a socially accepted tradition of religion or history. We should consider whether presentations of violence in the 1970s and 1980s are really so far removed from the old depictions and their meaning.

As for the critic's response to the audience whose enjoyment of violence both frightens him and makes the watching of the movie an extremely nerve-wracking experience for others—it is possible that what the critic witnesses in such audience reaction is the inability of the audience to absorb what they are seeing and to grasp exactly what it means. Although this is not always the case, the viewing of violence in films like *The Wild Bunch, Dirty Harry, Shaft,* and *Slaughter* can cause the audience to howl and laugh and *encourage* the protagonist—but these reactions are *clearly psychological.* Viewers cannot cope with the blatant statement of violence or deal with the stark horror of it, and so they distort what they see. According to Leon Festinger, dissonance takes place and the viewers work to create resonance, but the picture—the image—won't let them; it makes them nervous, challenges them.

The critic, because of background and training, often reacts consciously to violence and, perhaps, sees it for the statement of repulsion that it probably is in the films being reviewed. That others in the audience cannot handle the film on the same plane does not mean that they are not being affected by it; it simply may mean that their defenses are stronger than the critic's.

To maintain that audiences are dragging the film down to their own level is patently absurd. Each of us has a unique reaction to a film. Audiences can convert or distort the meaning of the film and its images to force the film to conform to their own preconceptions and ritual needs, but there is no reason the "mob response" must cause critics to respond in the same way. For me, the very fact that audiences responded with howls of laughter—nervous, confused laughter—in seeing *The Wild Bunch* (and the Northwestern University student audience responded with much more apparent enjoyment than did the predominantly black audience the night the film opened in Chicago) confirmed in me the feeling that the violence was too much, had gone too far. To hear the audience unable to respond, as I did, with resignation and pain affirmed for me that my feelings were indeed true and that they were trying to find their own way of dealing with the violence.

As to what the films themselves are saying, we must turn to analysis. The violence in films such as *The Wild Bunch, Beach Red, The French Connection, Dirty Harry, Wrath of God, Straw Dogs, Soldier Blue, Little Big Man, The Wild Angels, Night of the Living Dead, Scorpio,* and the Italian Westerns has arisen in a historical context. Violence on film has flowed in the United States since the assassinations of Dr. Martin Luther King, Jr., the Kennedys, and Malcolm X., in spite of a crackdown on violence in television and on film. An examination of the films of that time—Siegel's *The Killers,* Blake Edwards' *Gunn,* and Buzz Kulik's *Warning Shot* are good examples—shows that violence was much less graphic before than after the assassinations.

When the attempted moratorium on violence broke down, and Lyndon Johnson and Richard Nixon served out their presidencies, there existed in the United States, both in literature and in news coverage, a feeling of impending chaos along with a lack of firm belief in leadership—the credibility gap. In other words, the loss of belief in the invulnerability of our leaders has probably influenced us to put less emotional stock in them.

American values of the 1950s, shaken by the revealed corruption of Sen. Joseph R. McCarthy and further by the Korean War, held on through the belief that salvation lay in democratic response, in working together within the system. These beliefs did not die, but they were being questioned and sometimes attacked (and to a great extent, still are) by the communications media which, themselves, are reflecting national feelings and concerns, just as did the German films of 1919 to 1935 or the patriotic documentaries of England during World War II.

In the films of violence under consideration, there are many consistencies which make a tentative quantitative assessment worthy of consideration; such an assessment, it seems to me, is essential to a broad understanding of films produced during a specific period. Generalizing from one or two examples has been a common problem for both social science research and film criticism.

The following are some tentative observations of content of the late-1960s/early-1970s white-hot violence film.

- The protagonist is often a male who finds himself alone and in need of defining himself, or proving himself, through an act or acts of violence.
- The protagonist, as in most adventure tales, may be in his position out of choice or by chance (the former is the case in *Dirty Harry, The French Connection,* and *Beach Red;* the latter, in *Straw Dogs* and *The Wild Bunch*); but, when the physical challenge comes, he not only accepts it but welcomes it.
- The protagonist, like the hard-boiled detective and the Western hero, must learn to exist without love as long as he is committed to his action of protective violence. Dirty Harry, Popeye, Wilde (in *Beach Red*), the members of *The Wild Bunch* (except for Angel), and George Peppard in *The Groundstar Conspiracy* all know this from the start. Dustin Hoffman, in both *Little Big Man* and *Straw Dogs,* learns it during the course of the film, as does Alain Delon in *Scorpio.*
- Sex, if it exists at all—and it frequently does not for the protagonist in any normal way (*Dirty Harry; Day of the Jackal; The French Connection; The Groundstar Conspiracy,* and *A Clockwork Orange*)—is rapid, informal, and uninvolved.
- The law is insufficient to help a man when the time comes for him to prove himself. The law in *The Wild Bunch* is ineffective in the form of the cavalry and malevolent in the form of the railroad detectives; the law in *Straw Dogs* is a one-armed squire who dies as the violence begins; the law in *Charley Varrick, Dirty Harry, Billy Jack, The French Connection,* and *The Godfather* is restrictive and not present when the protagonist has to face the evil manifestation of chaos and violence.

- The films are large, brightly colored, filled with the exaggeration of blood. They are bigger than life even when (as in *The St. Valentine's Day Massacre* and *Dillinger*) they purport to be the true depiction of real events. The films, in fact, elevate their all-too-often-flawed protagonists to an almost mythical position.
- The protagonists are imperfect, though heroic. They reflect the real tensions of the mass audience and allow the viewer to emerge vicariously with the protagonist into some kind of heroic light—providing a way to find self-respect. This is true in *Dirty Harry* and *The French Connection*, in which the protagonists are bigoted policemen. The ambiguity at the end of *The French Connection*, while it creates a level of possible symbolic significance with which we might quarrel, does demonstrate a clear understanding of this tendency of the viewer to identify with the chief character by calling into question the success and failure of the protagonist. Our identification is questioned, though it had been nurtured throughout the film.
- The lighting in the films is always stark. Objects and people are in clear relief. Nuances of lighting generally do not exist. The image is clear, crisp, almost comic-strip simple (which often makes it very beautiful) in style.

It is possible to extract additional motifs and consistencies to elaborate a quantitative analysis of white-hot-violence films, but I would like to return to a consideration of these motifs in light of the genre's historical context.

The protagonist, who finds a clear-cut situation in which to define himself physically through acts of violence, can be seen as enacting a ritual to replace the fact that social man cannot so define himself in his own society. Our society is too complex, the issues themselves are too complex, and opportunities for meaningful physical expression seldom arise; when they do, they are often ambiguous. Wars no longer are well-defined affairs that a nation must win or lose. In the white-hot-violence films, issues invariably are clearly defined, evil is evident, and we want to see its destruction. Ambiguity is reduced; ritual reenactment is produced. In one sense, the films of violence do become simpler, presenting an inverted picture of people's feelings about their complex position in society. To state that the social need being met and clarified in these films is thus invalid, however, is to ascribe to film art a need to be overtly complex. Complexity is not an objective criterion for aesthetic

Dustin Hoffman in *Straw Dogs*.

Fay Dunaway in *Bonnie and Clyde*.

validity. In theory, at least, works that present the most overtly simple content often are considered archetypes—those films that are the most aesthetically valid (such as primitive art or the animation of Norman McLaren) and the most difficult to produce.

The fact that the protagonist is not at odds with society in these films of violence is, I believe, a reflection of the individual's desire to retain the value and reassurance of social symbols and ritual behavior. That one must ultimately act on one's own is not necessarily a rejection of society; it is simply the affirmation of one's ability to be important, to hold social structure together, to reaffirm the value of social structure. Whether we choose to see Dirty Harry as a fascist (ultimately, he throws away his badge because he has been unable to work within the system of the society he wishes to protect) or in the context of other Siegel-directed films (as the culmination of a series of heroes constantly being forced to face and destroy an increasingly abstract and evil version of one's own antisocial drives) is not at issue. The issue is that *Dirty Harry* is a work of popular art that, of necessity, reflects its time.

Love, for example, is tenuous in a society that can be destroyed by a bomb in a few minutes or in which the person willing to put himself (or herself) on the line for love might be murdered either by a fanatic es-pousing a mythical cause (*A Clockwork Orange*) or by a chance maniac (*Dirty Harry; Bloody Mama; The Dirty Dozen*). Again, love in the 1970s is a reflection of its time, a time in which social and political posi-tions are unclear, in which socially and culturally defined roles are be-ing questioned. The mass hero, the bigot hero, the profane hero—each one represents the extensions of one's hopes, the part of the mass viewer that, if it were able, would step out and put the world back into shape.

The violence the protagonist must display during the film is a reflec-tion of the need of the viewer to *destroy* before the world can be made clean. The very lighting of the films indicates their need to be stark, clean statements, as opposed to the films noir. Any ambiguity in the film—at least conscious ambiguity—would reflect upon the dream of the viewer, and the image on the screen would cease to represent a clear mythic approach (the villain in *Dirty Harry* doesn't even have a name).

One might carry the concept of mythic heroism even further. The very fact that the heroes are flawed reminds us of the classical flaws in the heroes of mythology; one's vulnerability, like that of Achilles, Christ, or Daedalus, renders one potentially tragic. The emergence of the common man as hero, the common man transformed into heroism, is not simply a manifestation of film. One might see in television's Archie Bunker the comical *other* side of the coin.

Individual variations of violence within the general context of white-hot-violence films determine the creative contribution of any given film. If one receives, from the death of Bonnie and Clyde or the Grissom Gang, only a vicarious pleasure in destruction and blood, or an affirmation that violence is condoned, one is missing the point—or a number of points—about the content of the film. That the death of Bonnie and Clyde is shown to take place so slowly reflects upon the sadness of their attempt to be greater than others, to force the world to make sense for them—a task in which they never succeeded.

By the same token, to say that the violent deaths in *Straw Dogs* simply affirm a belief in violence as a way of forcing life into some kind of ultimate meaning is to ignore the fact that the act of violence is, throughout the film (from the first images of children in the graveyard to the expressionistic exaggeration of the church party), clearly part of a personal ritual of affirmation for David. In fact, David's affirmative stand is an extension of the Western Hero's essence in style.

The thematic unification of all the films of violence is an attempt by the individual to return style (excellence or originality) to life as a means of affirming one's personal existence. Style might, in the past, have been confirmed through religious ritual, a business hierarchy, the American dream (Ned Buntline to Horatio Alger to Harold Lloyd to Jerry Lewis), the various genres. Such an affirmation is still possible; but, in films of violence, an act of individual self-reliance and self-assurance, in spite of the consequences, is at the heart of comprehension. This violence, the presentation of exaggeration of physical response, is an attempt by persons to redefine their position and meaning in society through the traditional forms of the media.

The content of the films of violence—and their relationship to the traditional forms on which they are based—appear to be a variation of affirmation of American individualism and free enterprise, which has always had within it the possibility of the individual emerging as too powerful a force. We are not dealing, however, with the potential of Plato's benevolent dictator turning out to be not so benevolent or with Dr. Caligari turning out (as he did in G. W. Pabst's *The Last Ten Days*) to be Hitler, but with the traditional American mythic hero who is forced to reaffirm personal values among the confused and confusing challenges of the contemporary world. Film violence has proved to be an altered but durable concern clearly reflecting our time. Previous cycles of physical violence in film have led to the emergence of their counterpart—the physical hero viewed as a comic or ironic figure—as an easing of the social tension created by the alienation that the protagonist represents in more recent films, such as *48 Hours* or *Vice Squad*.

Table 8.1
Key White-Hot-Violence Films

Film	Year	Director	Principal Actors
Ambushers, The	1967	Henry Levin	Dean Martin
Barquero	1970	Gordon Douglas	Lee Van Cleef
Beguiled, The	1971	Don Siegel	Clint Eastwood
Billy Jack	1971	Tom Laughlin	Tom Laughlin
Bloody Mama	1970	Roger Corman	Shelley Winters
Boston Strangler, The	1968	Richard Fleischer	Tony Curtis
Brotherhood, The	1968	Martin Ritt	Kirk Douglas
Catch 22	1969	Mike Nichols	Alan Arkin
Coogan's Bluff	1968	Don Siegel	Clint Eastwood
Dandy in Aspic, A	1968	Anthony Mann	Laurence Harvey
Day of the Jackal	1973	Fred Zinnemann	Edward Fox
Death of a Gunfighter	1969	Robert Totten and Don Siegel (under pseudonym Allen Smithee)	Richard Widmark
Detective, The	1968	Gordon Douglas	Frank Sinatra
Dirty Dozen, The	1966	Robert Aldrich	Lee Marvin
Dirty Harry	1972	Don Siegel	Clint Eastwood
Easy Rider	1969	Dennis Hopper	Peter Fonda
French Connection, The	1972	William Friedkin	Gene Hackman
Groundstar Conspiracy, The	1973	Lamont Johnson	George Peppard
Gunn	1967	Blake Edwards	Craig Stevens
Hannie Caulder	1972	Burt Kennedy	Raquel Welch
Hard Contract	1969	S. Lee Pogosin	James Coburn
Harper	1966	Jack Smight	Paul Newman
High Plains Drifter	1973	Clint Eastwood	Clint Eastwood
Hombre	1966	Martin Ritt	Paul Newman
In Like Flint	1967	Gordon Douglas	James Coburn
Kelly's Heroes	1970	Brian Hutton	Clint Eastwood
Killers, The	1964	Don Siegel	Lee Marvin
Klute	1972	Alan Pakula	Jane Fonda
Kremlin Letters, The	1970	John Huston	Patrick O'Neil
Lady in Cement	1968	Gordon Douglas	Frank Sinatra
Lawman	1971	Michael Winner	Burt Lancaster

Table 8.1 *(Continued)*
Key White-Hot-Violence Films

Film	Year	Director	Principal Actors
Light at the Edge of the World, The	1970	Kevin Billington	Kirk Douglas
Little Murders	1971	Alan Arkin	Elliott Gould
McCabe and Mrs. Miller	1971	Robert Altman	Warren Beatty
Man Called Horse, A	1969	Elliot Silverstein	Richard Harris
Murphy's War	1971	Peter Yates	Peter O'Toole
Nevada Smith	1966	Henry Hathaway	Steve McQueen
One Hundred Rifles	1969	Tom Gries	Jim Brown
Our Man Flint	1966	Daniel Mann	James Coburn
Patton	1969	Franklin Schaffner	George C. Scott
Point Blank	1967	John Boorman	Lee Marvin
Pretty Poison	1968	Noel Black	Anthony Perkins
Rio Conchos	1964	Gordon Douglas	Richard Boone
Riot	1968	Buzz Kulik	Gene Hackman
St. Valentine's Day Massacre, The	1967	Roger Corman	Jason Robards, Jr.
Scorpio	1973	Michael Winner	Burt Lancaster
Secret Invasion, The	1964	Roger Corman	Stewart Granger
Shaft	1971	Henry Hathaway	Richard Roundtree
Stalking Moon, The	1968	Robert Mulligan	Gregory Peck
Straw Dogs	1971	Sam Peckinpah	Dustin Hoffman
Traveling Executioner, The	1970	Jack Smight	Stacey Keach
Two Mules for Sister Sara	1969	Don Siegel	Clint Eastwood
Ulzana's Raid	1972	Robert Aldrich	Burt Lancaster
Valdez Is Coming	1971	Edwin Sherin	Burt Lancaster
Von Richthofen and Brown	1972	Roger Corman	Don Stroud
Wild Bunch, The	1969	Sam Peckinpah	William Holden
Willie Boy	1970	Abraham Polonsky	Robert Redford
Wrecking Crew, The	1968	Phil Karlson	Dean Martin

117

9
PSYCHOLOGICAL PERSPECTIVE

Horror and Science Fiction

But in man, the "animal being" (which lives in him as his instinctual psyche) may become dangerous if it is not recognized and integrated in life. Man is the only creature with the power to control instinct by his own will, but he is also able to suppress, distort, and wound it—and an animal, to speak metaphorically, is never so wild and dangerous as when it is wounded. Suppressed instincts can gain control of man; they can even destroy him.

The familiar dream in which the dreamer is pursued by an animal nearly always indicates that an instinct has been split off from the consciousness and ought to be (or is trying to be) readmitted and integrated into life. The more dangerous the behavior of the animal in the dream, the more unconscious is the primitive and instinctual soul of the dreamer, and the more imperative is its integration into his life if some irreparable evil is to be forestalled.

> —Aniela Jaffe, "Symbolism in the Visual Arts," in *Man and His Symbols,* edited by Carl G. Jung

Horror and science-fiction films are very much like shared dreams. In one sense, the horror film is a cathartic nightmare and the science fiction film, an uneasy dream of prophecy. In the past, these shared dreams were in the form of myth and folktale. The stories of Gilgamesh and the monster Humbaba, Perseus and the Gorgon, Beowulf and Grendel, St.

George and the Dragon, and hundreds of other stories are horror tales complete with monsters. In the past, these tales had religious meaning; they were perpetuated to turn into allegory those aspects of fear that the individual could handle in no other way. More recently, Jungian analysts have argued that these works and others are archetypal, symbolic, and manifestations of a shared unconscious.

Thus, horror and science-fiction films can be viewed, in one sense, as mythic presentations of universal concerns and fears. If a particular film or type of film continues to draw audiences, its claim as a meaningful work is reinforced. As with dreams, it is not necessary that the viewer who responds to the work be consciously aware of its meaning to him. It is not the responsibility of the individual viewer, any more than it is the responsibility of the individual creator, to find the meaning of the myth or dream. It is the critic's duty to take whatever tools of psychological or mythical information he or she can absorb and understand and to apply them to the film of horror and science fiction, in an effort better to understand what it is on the screen to which the audience is responding. Although some elements of horror film and science fiction overlap and both are, in content, outgrowths of literature, myth, and religion, it is possible to examine horror and science fiction separately and to identify their differences.

The Horror Film

Horror films are overwhelmingly concerned with the fear of death and the loss of identity in modern society. The method most often used in films to explore these themes is, not to confront the idea of death as such, but to cast the question in symbolic or dream form—to present the work as questioning the meaning of life.

In film after film, we find, for example, the essentially immortal monster—the werewolf, the created being, the zombie, the witch, the superanimal. Until recently in American films, the immortal creature was not seen as being affirmed, or content, in its immortality; immortality was clearly a curse from which the tormented creature sought release. In many of the films, the creature is acutely aware of what its immortality costs—its cost to him is alienation from the human world. The wolf man is acutely aware of this aloneness; he is pained because he constantly finds love but knows that he is doomed to destroy or outlive the love object. The motif of immortality as loneliness is a recurrent one: the Frankenstein monster is agonized (in the earliest films in the series) by his realization that he is, indeed, not a man; he, too, is alone; in the later Universal horror films, such as *The House of Frankenstein,* the vampire seeks a cure for his immortality; the mummy is a slow, resolute vision of ghastly, cursed immortality who comes to claim the film's heroine, reminding her and us of the fragility of life and the inevitability of being claimed by the past.

The immortality of the monster is linked closely to the fact that it must destroy others to continue living. To survive beyond your contemporaries is to drain them, to be a monster, to live off others, to diminish the meaning of lives. The curse of immortality is loss of feeling, being equated with the uncontrolled animal at one extreme (*The Wolf Man; King Kong; The Cat People; The Howling; An American Werewolf in London*) or the mindless continuum of the living dead or loss of identity at the other (*Invasion of the Body Snatchers; White Zombie; Night of the Living Dead; The Mephisto Waltz; The Possession of Joel Delaney*).

The parasite theme—of living off others—relates to another consideration of exactly what the ''monster'' represents in horror films. Many of the monster films in the genre play upon the horror of disease and its relationship to mortality. That we, as humans, look upon disease as horror can be seen in the fact that novels about disease traditionally have been novels of horror: Albert Camus's *The Plague,* Daniel Defoe's *Journal of the Plague Years,* and Reuben Merlis's *The Year of the Death.* Disease was, surely, the prime horror of human existence until recently; and today, in the form of cancer, it ranks in power perhaps only a little behind our fear of nuclear destruction.

The vampire tradition is clearly one that relates to disease. In Murnau's *Nosferatu,* we are told by the titles that the populace sees the unknown deaths as a disease. The image of the vampire is constantly equated with shots of crawling rats. The docking of the ship of death is the release of the rats, which symbolize disease for us both in reality and in literature.

The mark of the vampire, two small holes in the neck, is a disease mark evoking the image of pox. Frequently, after a visit by the vampire, the victim is attended by a physician who says the victim is suffering from an illness with distinct disease symptoms—anemia, eruptions (the two marks), lethargy. Often, we are told, as millions have been told by physicians for centuries, ''There is nothing I can do for her. We must keep her in bed and pray.'' The vampire is a physical symbol of a virus that destroys those we love, coming in the night while we are asleep. It is as if the vampire were the embodiment of that virus, the thing with which we cannot come to terms, the conversion of the unknown—death, disease—into a physical evil. We do not understand, cannot come to terms with, death and disease; but we can find solace in a horror film because these horrors are caused by a concrete, identifiable evil.

Occasionally, the disease as horror is very close to the surface of a film. Roger Corman's *The Masque of the Red Death,* like Edgar Allen Poe's story of the same name, is distinctly about the plague. It plays on the blood-red decor and personifies death as a masked stranger. The plague, however, is not evil in Corman's film; it simply *is.* In fact, the plague in the Corman film almost represents blind justice, for it takes the good and the evil alike, sparing only enough people to continue humanity's existence.

Whether or not they deal directly with fear of disease or death and mortality, the horror films share a common concern with fear of the unknown. In films about the devil and witches (*Day of Wrath; The Conquerer Worm; Rosemary's Baby; The Omen I, II,* and *III; The Exorcist I* and *II*), the issue is not whether the devil actually exists, but the degree to which our fear of human subordination to evil haunts us. In most films dealing with the devil, we are convinced that there is not a devil, that there are only evil people who use the fear of witchcraft and the power of the devil to control an ignorant populace and to gain their own evil ends. Remarkably often, the evil desired by the human villains of most horror films is sexual (most notably in *The Mephisto Waltz;* the vampire films of Britain's Hammer studio; *Mad Love; The Black Cat; The Unseen;* and *The Entity*).

The sexual object of the monster is, almost invariably, an altogether innocent victim. The sexual act frequently is consummated by the semi-human monster. This consummation taints the victim by confirming that total escape from horror is not possible and that society must be touched by death and evil.

That we have mixed reactions to the horror film's monster can be seen in the frequency with which some kind of schizophrenic trial is part of the horror. A recurrent motif of horror films is the struggle between good and evil within the individual—the recognition that it is not merely an external manifestation of evil we are seeing in the form of a monster, but something monstrous within ourselves. This motif is repeated over and over in horror films; but its prototype can be seen in all the myths of good and evil brothers, the Biblical conflict between Cain and Abel, and the doppelganger concept in literature and the film noir. Robert Louis Stevenson's *Dr. Jekyll and Mr. Hyde* has been made into a film at least six times. Each time, this story of split personality is filmed with the same actor playing both roles, both parts of himself. In Rouben Mamoulian's version, great pains are taken to have the transformation from Jekyll to Hyde take place before our eyes, to make us face the realization that we are seeing, not two men, but one—that the horror we see enacted in the film is also something potentially and inescapably within ourselves.

The horror of *Dr. Jekyll and Mr. Hyde* comes, not so much from the murders Hyde commits, but from the dawning realization in Jekyll that he cannot control his transformations, that he has no power to determine the times when one part of his personality will be dominant. The horror, in short, comes from Jekyll's loss of identity, his forced submission to the totally animal part of personality. This concern with loss of control is central to many horror films. The individual is carefully balanced between good and evil, an animated state and the condition of a zombie or robot.

As with *Dr. Jekyll and Mr. Hyde,* some horror films present the possibility of going toward, being forced into, or sympathizing with an animal state (*The Wolf Man; Island of Lost Souls; King Kong; Son of Kong; The Fly; The Creature from the Black Lagoon; The Cat People; The Ape Man; The Wolfen;* and *The Swamp Thing*); others, the possibility of being overcome by animal drives, destroyed by basic animal savagery (*Them; Night of the Lepus; Alligator; Jaws*). Other horror films deal with the possibility of sinking into total conformity to the point where one becomes simply a mindless pawn, has his or her identity stolen (*Invasion of the Body Snatchers; Night of the Living Dead; The Omega Man; It Came from Outer Space; White Zombie; I Walked with a Zombie; Isle of the Dead;* and *The Human Duplicators*).

Losing one's mind frequently is an overt theme of horror films set in mental hospitals (*Shock Corridor; Shock Treatment;* and *Asylum*). Other horror films deal with the mental patient who exhibits animal irrationality—giving reign to animal passions and destroying those who might stifle such unleased perversions (*Psycho; The Cat and the Canary; The Shuttered Room; Night Must Fall; Q; Halloween I* and *II*)— sometimes in a manner we fear to see in ourselves.

The horror film, especially when it deals with fear and mortality, is a film of interior darkness. Horror comes inside, into domestic sites or grotesque extensions of them. The dark, isolated castles are distortions of smaller homes, exotic versions of our own domestication. More recently, the horror has been brought closer to the surface in the domestic settings of city apartments and small farms of such films as *The Mephisto Waltz, Rosemary's Baby, The Other, The Exorcist, Night of the Living Dead, The Possession of Joel Delaney, Play Misty for Me,* and *Deadly Blessing.*

Graves and crypts seem constantly to be defiled in horror films. The actors (representing the audience) frequently are called upon to exhume a corpse, to find it missing, and to deal with the meaning of the body's disappearance—to view this possible resurrection as a horror, rather than as a Christ-like miracle. Such scenes of horror, reaction, and the release of evil in a crypt or grave occur in *White Zombie, The Murders in the Rue Morgue, Dracula, The Tomb of Ligeia, The Fall of the House of Usher, The Wolf Man, The Mummy,* and *Creepshow. Frankenstein,* however, is predicated upon the idea of the resurrection of a number of people's parts in the body of a single creature.

Compared to the means of death in other film genres, the horror film's visual context is striking. Gangsters use guns and thus remain distant. Period costume films involve other distancing devices—the bow and arrow, crossbow, spear, and catapult; even the sword is designed to keep combatants at a distance. In the horror film, however, the weapons of death are personal. Death is immediate, violent, bone-wrenching, bloodspilling. Fangs, claws, fingers, and axes are the means of death in a horror film; the tactile element of imagined physical horror is essential. Strangling is almost exclusively a motif of horror film, as is the bite. The animal nature of the attack and the fear of the meaning of animalism are the core of such personal weapons. In film after film, we hear actors say, ''It looks as if his throat's been torn out by an animal.'' Or, ''Don't look, miss. It's too horrible.'' The words conjure up visions of blood and defilement.

On the other hand, if the villain—the evil—represents loss of identity rather than sinking into the animal within, the weaponry's horror lies in its impersonality. In such films as *White Zombie, I Walked with a Zombie, Rosemary's Baby, The Other, Invasion of the Body Snatchers,* and *The Day Mars Invaded the Earth,* the victim apparently has not been physically harmed. He looks the same. He is, in one sense, ''alive.'' In another sense, although his body has not been defiled (as it might have

Kevin McCarthy in *Invasion of the Body Snatchers*.

Klaus Kinski and Isabelle Adjani in Werner Herzog's *Nosferatu The Vampire*.

been in an animalistic horror film), his mind and identity have been taken—a horror perhaps even more to be feared.

The true villains of many horror films are not the monsters, but the people who created them. Quite often the creator is a scientist who has taken unto himself the role of God, an affectation of which he is frequently accused by the other characters. In *Dr. Cyclops*, this God-like assumption of power is manifested by a scientist who shrinks his victims, reducing humanity visually to helplessness, and then towers over his victims like a god. The same shrinking of victim by scientist occurs in *The Devil Doll* and *The Puppet People*. Sometimes, the scientist-creator (he may simply be the locator, as in *King Kong*, and not a scientist at all) is basically a good person who is exploring the unknown, as any of us might if we had the opportunity. But whether or not he begins his studies with good intentions, he invariably is overcome by his fascination with the unknown. Having unleased the monster, the scientist-creator-explorer becomes its victim, for, after all, he is mortal like the rest of us.

Quite often, the villain-creator in American films is played by a European—Boris Karloff, Bela Lugosi, Claude Rains, Basil Rathbone—or by an American actor who affects a European accent or name (Vincent Price was the prime example). The villain represents what the American viewer sees as corruption in European society; that society's powerful tradition and intellectual superiority are inherent in the villain's evil. At the same time, however, the person who defeats the evil force often is a religious figure, also from the Old World. This religious savant faces and defeats the evil creature unleashed by thoughtless science and puts to rest the monster (*White Zombie; Dracula; Frankenstein*).

More recently, though, the aspect of horror has changed, and any kind of hope for the viewer has been withdrawn. Horror films of the recent past have, increasingly, been more pessimistic, more horribly confident that the dark side of our nature will triumph, that our worst fears must be faced, and that the evil within us simply cannot be destroyed or controlled. *The Other* ends with the triumph of the evil part of the schizoid personality: the old religious figure, the grandmother, has been defeated, and the family has been destroyed. The family in *The Mephisto Waltz* also is destroyed; those who have given in to the will of the devil, given in to their animal drives, have survived.

In *Rosemary's Baby*, the innocent girl (Mia Farrow) cannot deny her child, even though it is a creature of the devil. In this film, however, the old doctor (Ralph Bellamy) is not an affirmed religious figure, but a devil's advocate. And by film's end, Rosemary's home is destroyed and evil has triumphed.

In *The Murders in the Rue Morgue,* Herbert Lom continually rises from the grave to haunt Christine Kaufmann. The last image of the film is that of the girl sitting upright in bed, facing the spectre of his return after he has destroyed her family.

In many of these modern horror films, the religious weapons of earlier times—crucifixes abounded in horror films of the 1930s and 1940s—have been replaced by distortions of them, perversions of religion by the anti-God villain. The endings of the following films similarly affirm the need to face the dark shadow that cannot and perhaps should not be repressed: *Phantasm; Friday the 13th I, II,* and *III; Deadly Blessing;* Carpenter's *The Thing; The Howling;* and *The Omen I* and *II.*

Another variation of the horror film involves elements of science fiction, a primary outgrowth of which is that often there is no evil creator, no single personification of evil in the film. Instead, the evil is within society as a whole; society—the dead—threatens the single protagonist with death and taunts him with the certainty that he, too, will someday be like "them." The hero fights desperately to hold on to life, to escape the horror of being like "them"—the dead—as long as he can. Struggles are a distinct manifestation of the viewer's own struggle to ward off death as long as possible. In some films, the protagonist is permitted the dignity of dying, but only after he makes a sacrifice of himself for others—by giving up his life for the future, because he has faith in that future. The hero's death (as in *The Omega Man*) is a sacrifice, an acceptance of his belief that his own life and death are fruitless, because evil and death will triumph no matter what he does.

Night of the Living Dead is a particularly good example of how this fight for life can play upon the elements of the horror film. In this film, the dead suddenly rise one night and begin to consume the living. A small group of people, led by a black man known only as Ben, struggles to remain alive during the night by fighting off the living dead. Most of the film takes place at night, in a farmhouse. The siege upon the home is another recurrent, claustrophobic image of the horror film. The home is one's final sanctuary, the last place to take a stand. If one cannot hold onto one's home and family, one's life is, essentially, meaningless. This isolation and attack motif appears in such films as *Straw Dogs, The Omega Man, The Brain Eaters, The Birds, The Thing, The Amityville Horror, Zombie, Dawn of the Dead.*

In *Night of the Living Dead,* the people in the house under siege are typical Americans, the wholesome types who are triumphant and affirmed in most American films. In this film, however, all are destroyed by the creatures of death. The young lovers, the family, the heroine—all fall victim to the living dead. Ben, the hero, is killed by the gross and broadly comic sheriff's posse, which mistakes him for one of the living dead. Ben is a victim of the living.

The claustrophobic element of fear in *Night* is heightened by the increasing constriction of those in the house. Little by little, they are forced into more restricted areas with fewer options for escape. They retreat from outside to the house, then to a single room, and finally to the basement, which has only one way in or out.

During the course of the film (as in *Invasion of the Body Snatchers*), traditional ways of killing monsters are employed. The living dead are burned, stakes are driven through their bodies, and they are shot—all to no avail. The dead, both in this microcosm and in reality, outnumber the living. Traditional ways of getting rid of our fears are taken from us.

In *The Mephisto Waltz,* the evil of the witches moves out of their mansion and into a typical middle-class home, destroying it and triumphing over its inhabitants. The evil ones feed upon the family, take over their bodies, assume their identities, and corrupt the living heroine (Jacqueline Bisset) by convincing her that there is no way to beat the devil. One can only join him and profit from the association, giving in totally to the animal within, plagued by sexual desire and affirmation of life, yet fearing death.

In contrast, *King Kong* is a distinct tragedy. This earlier film demonstrates that there is no place in our society for the animal or, perhaps more accurately, that we fear the unleashing of the animal nature of humanity and realize that we must keep it carefully under control.

Kong is the animal unleashed in New York much as Mr. Hyde is the animal unleashed in London in *Dr. Jekyll and Mr. Hyde.* Kong is master of his own primitive, dangerous world, a place where man can go only under penalty of death. Humans cannot return, in the film, to their animal past—and survive. The prehistoric monsters of *King Kong* and *The Lost Continent* are reminders of the past to which we cannot return. Kong in New York is, however, doomed; the bestial manifestation of our own animal fears cannot remain chained. He is unleashed by passion—his love for a girl who, he believes, is being attacked by the flashbulb-popping reporters. She represents a civilization he cannot understand.

The horror of *Rosemary's Baby* (which is strikingly similar to the Val Lewton film, *The Seventh Victim*) is that the urban situation itself is not safe. Rosemary's baby, her husband, and herself are corrupted by inescapable evil. Her own home—like the homes in *Straw Dogs, The Omega Man, It's Alive, The Brood, Night of the Living Dead,* and *The Mephisto Waltz*—is no refuge. One of the most horrible moments in *Rosemary's Baby* is our discovery that a passageway leads from Rosemary's apartment directly into the neighboring apartment of a woman who practices witchcraft.

In *The Other,* however, the horror comes from a return to the idea of the split personality, the struggle between good and evil within the same body, the allegorical battle for possession of the soul. The boy is a Jekyll/Hyde, with Hyde triumphant; there is added horror in the fact that innocence has been corrupted. The child holds out no hope for his own future in society. He has destroyed his family and will continue to live as an uncontrolled animal with a cunning mask.

The Science-Fiction Film

In contrast to the horror film, the science-fiction film deals with fear of life and the future, not fear of death. (See ''The Imagination of Disaster,'' a fascinating analysis of the idea of impending disaster as a dominant theme in science fiction and horror, in Susan Sontag's *Against Interpretation,* New York: Dell, 1961.) There is a constant fear that man will *have* no future, that he will inevitably destroy himself through overpopulation (*ZPG; Soylent Green*), governmental conformity (*Fahrenheit 451*), pollution (*Silent Running*), or atomic catastrophe (*The Omega Man; The Last Woman on Earth; Five; The Last Man on Earth; Planet of the Apes;* and *The World, the Flesh and the Devil*). Often, the fear of the future is more abstract and represents our cultural feeling that we are destroying ourselves, losing control to the point where machines will take over and the scientist or superior intellect will turn us into slaves. This feeling can be seen in the many science-fiction films that deal with the attack upon humanity by superior beings from outer space (*It Came from Outer Space; The War of the Worlds*).

Science-fiction films frequently show humans in a new context, test them against the unknown—the anything-can-happen future, to see if they can survive the most extreme fantasies of their own minds. In *Planet of the Apes,* astronaut Charlton Heston finds himself in a future where he is forced to come to terms with his knowledge of being alone; essentially, the same situation prevails for Rod Taylor in *The Time Machine.* In both cases, the protagonist finds a docile, beautiful human whom he tries to "save" from the world of the future by taking her along with him. In the first *Planet of the Apes* film, the hero succeeds. In *Beneath the Planet of the Apes,* a sequel, he fails, as does the hero of *The Time Machine.*

Fear of the future is at the core of many science-fiction films. In spite of the defeats they experience, the hero and his audience usually are given some element of hope for the future—along with the warning that has been imparted (*The Day the Earth Stood Still; 2001: A Space Odyssey; This Island Earth; The Omega Man; Andromeda Strain; The Incredible Shrinking Man; Westworld*).

In *2001,* the viewer sees hope for humanity's future in the final moments of the film, when Keir Dullea waits to reenter the life cycle, to be born again as the embryonic man, to merge with the universe in the void of the future. In *The Day the Earth Stood Still* and *It Came from Outer Space,* there is a promise of return, some time in the future, by superior creatures who can help people restore order to their world before they destroy themselves. Space creatures who offer people solace and hope for the future invariably are capable of making themselves look like humans, of showing humans the scientist/God in humanity's own image.

Also recurrent in science-fiction films is the theme of humans being their own worst enemy. In *Fantastic Voyage,* in which a team of scientists is reduced to miniature size to enter a human body, the body's own defense mechanisms attack the intruders' miniature submarine. Metaphorically, in this and other science-fiction films, humanity is truly the enemy of humans. It is almost always individuals who have brought the potential destruction of the future down upon their own heads. It is humans who are responsible for pollution and atomic warfare. It is persons who must overcome their own animal emotions and fears if they are to survive as social beings.

Also in contrast to the horror film is the *distance* of the science-fiction locale. The story usually does not take place in our home or in an image of the past, but in spaceships, on other planets, in exotic locations beneath or above the earth, or in the future. The films are not dark; they are light, generally bright and vivid, sometimes almost too bright. Horror is a matter of the past—our fear of it and of becoming part of it. Science fiction frequently takes place in the bright daylight of the unknown future. Often there is no personified villain in science fiction; the villain is one's own self. This motif is most striking in *Forbidden Planet,* in which the movie monster turns out to be the id of a scientist who lives on the planet. When the scientist falls asleep, his inner evil is released—just as surely as Jekyll released Hyde—and then is turned into destructive energy.

In recent years, science-fiction films have become more hopeful. For instance, the union of Man and Machine becomes a positive force in *Star Trek: The Motion Picture.* In the sequel to that film, *The Wrath of Khan,* although the beloved Mr. Spock dies, his death is linked with the birth of a new world, a birth that renews Captain Kirk's energy and resolves his midlife crisis. And finally, in *E. T.*—the most financially successful film ever made—the power of love forms a bond between the human and the alien. Still, even these recent films, despite their hopeful endings, have elements of tragedy and despair. For example, Deckard and Rachel, the hero and the heroine of *Bladerunner,* survive the city to escape into pastoral splendor; but in that film what is left of civilization on this planet is presented as very dark and malevolent—full of brutality and corruption.

Science-Fiction—Horror Films

While there are major differences between them, horror and science-fiction films, as two genres dealing with aspects of the unknown, often overlap or play on considerations and elements of each other. Since World War II, the atomic bomb, and the first steps in space travel, there has been an increasing mixture of the two genres—to the point where it is descriptively accurate to speak of "science-fiction—horror films." Certainly *Invasion of the Body Snatchers, Forbidden Planet, Night of the Living Dead, The Blob, The Green Slime,* and *Alien* are examples of such combinations. In some cases, the meaning of the dual theme is that outer space does indeed hold images of horror for us, images reinforced by the potential destruction of nuclear weapons which, like space travel, are the creations of science.

The Fantasy Film

Although we will not explore in this book a third genre related to science fiction and horror, it is worthwhile to acknowledge the existence of the fantasy genre. The fantasy film contains elements of both horror and science fiction; but it is usually presented as a personal, dreamlike, childhood exploration of our less-than-conscious thoughts. Fantasy films almost always take on the form, or appearance, of a self-contained dream. Quite often, in fact, the fantasy is presented as a dream of one of the characters (*The Wizard of Oz; Under the Rainbow; The 5,000 Fingers of Dr. T; Alice in Wonderland; The Secret Life of Walter Mitty;* and *The Bluebird*). Invariably, the fantasy theme is one of reinforcement of the world outside the fantasy, an acceptance of the real world as a less interesting but safer place to be.

Readings on Horror and Science-Fiction Films

Books

Atkins, Thomas R., editor. *Science Fiction Films.* New York: Monarch Press, 1976.

Baxter, John. *Science Fiction in the Cinema.* London: A. Zwimmer; New York: A. S. Barnes, 1970.

Blair, Karin. *Meaning in Star Trek.* New York: Warner Books, 1977.

Brosnan, John. *Future Tense: The Cinema of Science Fiction.* New York: St. Martin's Press, 1979.

Butler, Ivan. *Horror in the Cinema.* South Brunswick, New Jersey: A. S. Barnes, 1979.

Derry, Charles. *Dark Dreams: A Psychological History of the Modern Horror Film.* South Brunswick: A. S. Barnes, 1977.

Dillard, R. H. W. "Even a Man Who Is Pure at Heart: Poetry and Danger in the Horror Film." In *Man and the Movies,* edited by W. R. Robinson. Baton Rouge: Louisiana State University Press, 1967.

Douglas, Drake (pseudonym). *Horror.* New York: Macmillan, 1966.

Dyer, Peter John. "The Roots of Horror." In *International Film Annual no. 3,* edited by William Whitebair. London: John Calder; New York: Taplinger, 1959.

Huss, Roy, and T. J. Ross, editors. *Focus on the Horror Film.* Englewood Cliffs, New Jersey: Prentice-Hall, 1972.

Hillman, James. *The Dream and the Underworld.* New York: Harper & Row, 1979.

Johnson, William, editor. *Focus on the Science Fiction Film.* Englewood Cliffs, New Jersey: Prentice-Hall, 1972.

Jones, Ernest. *On the Nightmare.* New York: Liveright, 1971.

Lenne, Gerard. *Le cinema fantastique et ses mythologies.* Paris: Editions du Cerf, 1970.

McCarty, John. *Splatter Movies: Breaking the Last Taboo.* Albany: Fanta Co. Enterprises, 1981.

Pitts, Michael R. *Horror Film Stars.* Jefferson, North Carolina: McFarland, 1981.

Pohl, Frederik, and Frederik Pohl IV. *Science Fiction Studies in Film.* New York: Ace Books, 1981.

Prawer, S. S. *Caligari's Children: The Film as Tale of Terror.* New York: Oxford University Press, 1980.

Sobchack, Vivian Carol. *The Limits of Infinity: The American Science Fiction Film, 1950–75.* South Brunswick, New Jersey: A. S. Barnes, 1980.

Taylor, Al, and Sue Ray. *Making a Monster: The Creation of Screen Characters by the Great Makeup Artists.* New York: Crown, 1980.

Warren, Bill. *Keep Watching the Skies!: American Science Fiction Movies of the Fifties.* Jefferson, North Carolina: McFarland, 1982.

Periodicals

Cinefantastique. American magazine devoted to horror, science fiction, and fantasy films. Mailing address: P.O. Box 270, Oak Park, Illinois 60303.

Collins, Robert G. "Star Wars: The Pastiche of Myth and the Yearning for a Past Future." *Journal of Popular Culture* 11, no. 1 (Summer 1977), pp. 1–10.

Ellison, Harlan. "Three Faces of Fear: A Theory of Film Horror from the Works of Val Lewton." *Cinema* (U.S.A.) 3, no. 2 (March 1966), pp. 4–8, 13, 14.

Fantastic Films. American magazine devoted to horror, science fiction, and fantasy films. Mailing address: 21 West Elm Street, Chicago, Illinois 60610.

Franklin, H. Bruce. "Future Imperfect." *American Film* 8, no. 5 (March 1983), pp. 46–49, 75, 76.

Gordon, Andrew. "The Empire Strikes Back: Monsters from the Id." *Science Fiction Studies*, 7, part 3, no. 22 (November 1980), pp. 313–18.

Starlog. American magazine devoted mostly to science-fiction films. Mailing address: 475 Park Avenue South, New York, N.Y. 10016.

10
SOCIAL PERSPECTIVE

Comedy and Social Change

It is possible to identify two dominant modes in the comedy genre, in addition to situation comedy. First, there is the mode of the individual, the person out of keeping with the culture, the one whose comic adventures stem primarily from an inability to get along in society. Frequently, the individual wants very much to become a part of the society, but a combination of the person's own infantilism and society's indifference forestalls success, at least temporarily. This mode of comedy was, perhaps, most popular in the 1920s, with the emergence of American international confidence and concern over the individual's ability to get along in an increasingly complex society. Charlie Chaplin, Buster Keaton, Harold Lloyd, Stan Laurel and Oliver Hardy, Harry Langdon, and others reached their peak of popularity in this period of silent films before the depression. The mode continued in the films of Chaplin in the 1930s, Bob Hope in the 1940s, Danny Kaye in the 1950s, Jerry Lewis in the 1960s, Woody Allen in the 1970s, and Cheech and Chong in the 1980s.

The second mode of comedy emerged by the early 1930s, after having been latent in earlier films. This second mode was the man versus woman type. It first appeared in the 1930s, and continues to exist today. Most of these films are absurd depictions of the confrontation between a man and a woman, an interaction in which the defenses of the male are often exposed and ridiculed. One frequently hears these comedies called "screwball," indicating the manner of presentation rather than the meaning of the comedy. In most of these films, the woman is liberated in emotion, a bit zany, free-spirited, expressing logic of liberation that the male cannot handle. He is too rigidly tied to a system of work and assurance about the man's role in society. The comedies of Howard Hawks (*Bringing up Baby; Monkey Business; I Was a Male War Bride; His Girl Friday;* and *Twentieth Century*) are often cited as examples of the male versus female type of comedy, but the elements are not unique to Hawks's films; they are generic. The pattern is clear in William Wellman's *Roxie Hart* and *Nothing Sacred,* Raoul Walsh's *Me and My Gal,* Preston Sturges's *The Palm Beach Story,* George Cukor's *The Philadelphia Story* and *Pat and Mike,* W. S. Van Dyke's *It's a Wonderful World,* and Billy Wilder's *The Major and the Minor, Sabrina,* and *Kiss Me Stupid.*

Again, the pattern persists in more contemporary contexts in such films of the 1970s and early 1980s as *What's Up, Doc?, Paper Moon, Made for Each Other, The Main Event,* and *Best Friends. What's Up, Doc?* is a conscious updating of Hawks's earlier comedies with a number of interesting modifications, including the acceptance of the female protagonist (played by Barbra Streisand) as an aggressive, dominant figure in the relationship, without having to excuse her as eccentric or ridicule her for daring to dominate.

Made for Each Other also concerns the element of sexual dominance, but here it is treated as a physical issue with comic psychological connotations. The elements are the same, but the comedy derives directly from sexual issues recognized as problems by the protagonists. In the film, the audience is introduced to the two protagonists in vignettes of their growing up—comic vignettes that illustrate the psychological traumas that make the two what they are as loving, hating adults. From Joseph Bologna's point of view, lying in his crib, we see his parents quarrel over his name. Mother insists that he be called Gigi instead of Guido. Later, Mother tells him of the horrors of love and sacrifice in a bizarre religious story of plucking one's eyes out for a woman's love. The Oedipal allusion is clear. In another vignette, the child is shown surrounded in the bathtub by his mother and sisters, talking about how Gigi plays with himself. Gigi grows up to be a woman-destroyer, a man who cannot have a lasting relationship with a woman. The context of the vignettes and the film is broad and comic; the psychological elements are reduced to their simplest essentials to make them immediately recognizable and comic. Gigi meets Pandora (Renee Taylor) at a group therapy session, where everyone, including Pandora, reveals his or her problems and vulnerability. Pandora, as we know from her childhood vignettes, had a father who was unfaithful, indifferent, and traumatically embarrassing to his daughter. Her adult revenge is to live with a married Chinese artist, an action which causes her father to drop dead. She becomes a man-smotherer. She and Gigi are, obviously, *not* made for each other; yet they carry on a love/hate relationship and, in the end, decide to marry. The relationship between the two is essentially that of the man/woman films of the 1930s and 1940s; but, instead of the psychological interplay revolving upon a plot device—theft of a formula, need for disguise, false accusation, a job to do—the film deals directly with the sexual issue, bypassing metaphor.

The two dominant modes of comedy in American film were concerned with serious aspects of societal existence: (1) the human struggle to attain a satisfying role in society and (2) the archetypal struggle for supremacy and status between men and women. Perhaps one reason for the power of these two themes in American films is that both topics are difficult—maybe even impossible—for us to face and deal with unless we state them in a comic form. In short, it is ironic that a partial explanation for the laughter in the films may be that the only way many of us can deal with these subjects is to distance ourselves with laughter.

The individual comic in film probably reached a peak of American popularity in the period from 1918 to 1928, when comedy was devoured by a public facing the confusion of often depressing contemporary history somewhat inappropriately called the Roaring Twenties. The Great War had ended; the Treaty of Versailles had been rejected by the American people. Because the ''Red scares'' of the previous decade had carried through into this period, there existed a great fear of Russia and its revolution and a desire to retreat into isolationism (both of which were encouraged by the media). Possibly as a partial result of the Red scare—which combined with a middle- and upper-class fear that individual enterprise was in jeopardy from a mass revolution of the lower classes—the Ku Klux Klan began to rise as a spectre of repression. After the war, there had been a handful of Klan members; but by 1918 (coinciding with the rapidly growing migration of blacks to urban areas), the Klan had grown to 4 million members. *Birth of a Nation* was a popular manifestation of the fear that haunted many Americans. *Birth,* however, was not the only film to deal with the fear of a mass revolution. A number of pictures, including Wallace Worsley's *The Penalty* (1920), played heavily on that fear. In *The Penalty,* Lon Chaney is a legless madman who plans to unleash an army of anarchistic immigrants on America and take over. His vision is seen in a dream-reverie sequence, corresponding, perhaps, to the nightmares of millions who were afraid of losing their grip on prosperity.

Thus, the twenties were not *all* "roaring." There was, however, a taste for scandal. Warren Harding succeeded Woodrow Wilson in 1920; and, in spite of later reports condemning Harding for corruption, the public delighted in hearing risqué stories about the president. When Harding's administration was exposed, the newspapers and the public attacked the exposures more than they did Harding himself. Along with this presidential leadership figure, the American public had its "Apostle of the Self-Made Man," Henry Ford, the admired, ruthless businessman who launched a popular anti-Jewish propaganda program and later won an award from Hitler for his efforts.

When Harding died in office, amid rumors of his possible murder, the country turned to Calvin Coolidge. The peak of the so-called Roaring Twenties came, not under the administration of its logical exponent, Warren Harding, but under the cold and remote Coolidge who (with Henry Ford's enthusiastic agreement) said in a speech before the Society of American Newspaper Editors in Washington, D.C., on January 17, 1925, that "the chief business of the American people is business. This is a business country; it wants a business government. . . . The man who builds a factory builds a temple. . . . The man who works there worships there."

Comparisons between business and religion were common in politics and entertainment by the mid-1920s. As an antidote to the fear of revolution by the lower classes, there arose a myth that big business was the protector of the American worker. In addition, there was a resurgence of the idea of the self-made man, a concept that—consciously or not—was used to sustain the middle classes and contain the lower classes. The idea was buoyed up by prosperity. When Herbert Hoover was elected in 1928, at the peak of the economic boom, his campaign motto was "four more years of prosperity."

The myths that arose during this period of history are clearly shown in the popular culture of the era, particularly in the comedy films of the 1920s. Henry Ford is, perhaps, an almost archetypal figure in the era's comedy, although his name is seldom mentioned. The period of 1918 to

The waif (Paulette Goddard) helps Chaplin's Tramp remember the words to a song by writing them on his cuff in *Modern Times*.

Jerry Lewis and Marion Marshall in *The Stooge*.

1927 saw the rise of the automobile and the kingdom of Ford, the Michigan farmboy inventor who became the super self-made man. The automobile and its mechanisms frequently dominate the comic films of this period. They represent the ideas of possibility and aspiration and, at the same time, a fear that the mechanical is more important than the human, that the machine will replace man. Mack Sennett's comedies before 1919 were almost a love-hate affair with the automobile and the train. The machines, in fact, frequently took over in Sennett films and became the stars. The humans who were carried along by them often were incapable of control; they were merely victims of a machine that appeared to have come to life, to have a mind of its own. The result for the audience was embarrassment, and the release was laughter. After all, the films *were* comedies. Sennett's characters would always rise from the rubble, survive a five-story crash, barely miss a collision, or escape the onrushing train. The man merged with the machine, often becoming a part of an "automobile-centaur." However, the machine would be crushed, mutilated, exhausted after its frenzy; while the man—regardless of the height of the fall or the speed of the collision—would take a few wobbly steps, brush himself off, and walk away. These typical Sennett film elements became important in the work of other individuals who made comic films in the 1920s. It may be, however, that Sennett's decline came about because he did not realize that comedy had moved a step ahead as a genre—that the individual had to get out of the machine.

Another dominant myth that affected films made between 1918 and 1928 resulted from the rise of radio. The first regular broadcasts were in 1920. By 1922, there were 220 stations on the air. Radio personalities soon developed, and radio advertising became a social force. Economic prosperity and increased leisure for the middle classes led to an increasingly hedonistic advertising, which centered upon appeals to recapture youth and achieve sexual fulfillment. This pattern of advertising continues today and greatly affects the content of our films and media. In the 1920s, however, the desire to attain what the radio (and films) promised often was at the core of the films of Chaplin, Keaton, Langdon, Lloyd, and Laurel and Hardy. The comic character's desire to attain certain almost unattainable goods is often thwarted by his inadequacy, an inadequacy often shared by his audience.

Related to this desire for advertised goods was another myth of the "Jazz Age": that there was, supposedly, a "new morality." Women had won suffrage in 1920. There was a sudden, popular rebellion against Victorian conventions, a rebellion reinforced by radio advertising and films. Sexual freedom became a touchstone in literature and sophisticated film. This freedom, however, was largely an urban phenomenon. The country was clearly not united in its attitude toward liberation, and there existed a distinct moral schism—a division of attitude and stance on the issue. Quite often, the film audience can see the comic performer caught between two conflicting drives: his desire for (and affirmation of) sexual/moral freedom and the pull of his basic American conservatism.

Another important mythic element of the period came as a result of the Eighteenth Amendment (enacted in 1920) and the impact of Prohibition. Here, too, was a pull between conservatism's power and the new freedom. To an extent, Prohibition was carried over from wartime temperance and rural legislative control. The rise of Prohibition, which was generally considered restrictive, in urban settings at least, brought forth a new popular hero—the individual who stood up against an unjust law, the gangster who supplied the public with alcohol. Al Capone got his first big job in Chicago in 1920; the St. Valentine's Day Massacre took place in 1929. The film comedies of this period are filled with gangster figures who display a surface romanticism but who are actually in opposition to the individual (Harry Langdon's *Long Pants,* for example).

Another factor of the era was the rise of tabloid newspapers. These papers, most notably the *New York Daily News* and the Hearst chain, imitated the popular appeal of radio, often using sensationalism to bring about a so-called morally free society.

Sensational criminal cases of the 1920s and 1930s also were played upon: the Ruth Snyder execution; Richard Loeb and Nathan Leopold; the Nicola Sacco–Bartolomeo Vanzetti case; and the John T. Scopes trial. The sports figures who became most prominent, Jack Dempsey and Babe Ruth, were known as heroes with tainted backgrounds; their moral laxities only reflected the modern urban morality. In one sense, they were simply Henry Fords of the athletic world. Chaplin's boxing match with a Dempsey-like, corrupt fighter in *City Lights* is a play about the idea that one feels a bit guilty about admiring such a hero. In contrast to Ruth and Dempsey were Bobby Jones and Charles Lindbergh, clean-cut Americans of good morals. Again, the schism in American values was manifest in its heroes: Lindbergh was the strong, older, romantic hero; Dempsey, the more modern, morally tainted hero. The individual

comedian of the period often found himself caught between these opposing heroic postures. Chaplin's tainted acts, for example, are often
acclaimed by the characters in his films, while his heroic ventures often
result in his vilification.

There are a number of important similarities among the men who rose
to comic prominence in the films of this period. In many cases, these
similarities are central to each comedian's popularity in the genre.
Charlie Chaplin, Buster Keaton, Harry Langdon, and Stan Laurel all
developed their talent in the music hall, burlesque, and vaudeville. To
some extent, this was also true of Oliver Hardy, who appeared in min-
strel shows, and Harold Lloyd, who was a character actor on stage before entering film. This background also applies to certain more modern
comedians, including W. C. Fields, Bob Hope, Danny Kaye, and Jerry
Lewis.

Through the efforts of the comic individuals of the 1920s, a comedy
style featuring the personal performer emerged. Comedy in this mode
was not an ensemble effort. These men, who began the tradition of the
individual who is lost in society, were perfectly cast as slightly grotesque, downtrodden clowns, the butt of humor that often turned to
sympathy. They reflected, in their film performances, the man alone—
man against a chaotic, increasingly mass-oriented, mechanistic society.
These were the little men caught in the midst of baffling confusion,
wanting to be a part of their society, but unable to make it or live up to
the myths of strength, the self-made man, and sexual power that were at
the core of their times. They were, not coincidentally, little men in size.
Chaplin, Keaton, Langdon, and Laurel were—like the little actors who
became the stars of the gangster films of the early 1930s—very small
individuals. The more aggressive members of the comic genre, Oliver
Hardy and Harold Lloyd, were somewhat taller. Even the Marx Brothers, who were transitional comedy figures, were small in stature, as are
Woody Allen and Mel Brooks.

To further examine social change in America in relation to film comedies, we can study the work of major figures in comedy from 1914 to the
present. We can examine the implications of their work and their generic contributions. We can also study the ways in which the work of
pioneering individuals in film comedy—particularly Charlie Chaplin,
Buster Keaton, Harry Langdon, and Harold Lloyd—affected the work
of later figures such as Laurel and Hardy and the Marx Brothers as well
as such contemporary figures as Jerry Lewis, Mel Brooks, and Woody

Allen. We will examine these individuals as genre figures and not, as has so often been done, as comedians to be extolled or vilified depending upon one's contemporary response to their comedy.

Charlie Chaplin

Charlie Chaplin made 81 films, in only two of which (*A Woman of Paris,* 1923, and *A Countess from Hong Kong,* 1967) he did not star. He wrote, directed, edited, and composed music for his own films. In the 1920s, he was the most popular film personality in the world. His films of that period included *The Kid* (1920); *The Gold Rush* (1924); and *The Circus* (1928). Chaplin's style was distinct: there was little camera movement, as he saw and directed action in "scenes." After he filmed comic action scenes, there would be little cutting; the scene would often be filmed in just one take, similar to a live comedy performance. Adding to the idea of a performance was Chaplin's tendency to show the actor's whole body during a scene, much like the dance sequences performed in Fred Astaire's films. In addition, there is little cinematic flourish in Chaplin's films. This lack of special effects strengthens the film as a performance and gives the feeling that, when an action is shown, the danger or attack is real. Chaplin used no double. Theoretically, we become involved with the action as a continuum.

The humor in all Chaplin features is thematic, relating closely to the history and myths of the 1920s. Chaplin was very much a man of his time, and his films are a mixture of the era's sentimental feelings and violent action. The normal procedure in Chaplin's films is to present a social problem and then introduce Chaplin to wrestle with it as both comedy and sentimental romance.

The central concept of *The Circus* is that of the little man, Chaplin, who is pushed into someone else's role; he is rewarded for someone else's deeds, takes lumps for someone else's errors, and emerges from each experience a little stronger, but materially with less. The pace and danger of the film increase as Chaplin's identity crisis grows. First, Chaplin is confused with a pickpocket whom he follows into a house of mirrors. Even the viewer does not know which is the real Chaplin and which is the crook. Outside the fun house, Chaplin is forced (in a further thematic extension) to hide from the police, to pretend he is a dummy programed to strike another dummy—the crook. Thus, after a sequence in which Chaplin has had to make his way through a mirror image of self, he is forced to turn himself into a mechanistic creature, an automated dummy. He literally hides behind a mechanistic facade. Chaplin then is chased by the police directly into the center ring of the circus, where his comic actions become a microcosm of the entire film. Part of our enjoyment in watching Chaplin in the ring is knowing that the character is unaware of where he is, unaware of being watched and laughed at. Next, he finds himself on a treadmill getting nowhere, a comic image of Chaplin's inability to progress in any guise out of the circus-like existence. Again, it is the treadmill, a machine, which carries him and makes him helpless. The film continues to build on Chaplin's role as performer and unconscious clown—his pathos and, at the same time, performing ability.

In each of his films, Chaplin performs a number: a comic act in *The Circus,* a song in *Modern Times.* As Chaplin takes on the role of a clown in *The Circus,* he assumes that identity and merges his own with it. His life becomes more precarious, his identity more in question, to the point where he finds himself harassed by animals and chased onto a high wire. The film's comedy is closely related to the danger Chaplin is experiencing. It is especially poignant to realize that Chaplin has allowed himself to get into this danger because of his romantic love for the circus high-wire performer. She is very much the idealized figure of commercials, and her image lures Chaplin to near-death. As a high-wire artist, she is far above him; when he reaches her heights in the film, he is in maximum danger. The film opens, in fact, with the girl swinging slowly back and forth on her trapeze, an ethereal, unattainable figure. Several years ago, Chaplin added a sound track to the film, in which he sings a sad, romantic song about the girl whom we watch, slowly swinging.

The film is rich in identity problems, myths (not only those of the 1920s), and universal motifs. Throughout the film, for example, Chaplin is harassed by a donkey which chases him at moments when he seems to be in control. The donkey seems to be a serious contender for the girl's affections. The ass, as an animal, is very much a reminder of Chaplin's own animal wishes; it appears to ridicule him and to reduce him as a hero.

All of Chaplin's films show this unity of theme. In *City Lights,* the idea of illusion prevails: the core idea of the film is that things are not what they seem. Chaplin survives by accepting this fact and rebounding from the shock of each shattered illusion or by accepting the things that are not what they seem and using them anyway. At one point, he mistakes confetti for spaghetti but eats it nevertheless, ignoring the fact that it tastes nothing at all like the food he had expected. The idea that things are not at all what they seem is strongest in the human relationships in the film, however. Chaplin has rescued an alcoholic millionaire, clearly a self-made man, a Henry Ford who hides from the rigidity of his real world in drink. When he is drunk, the millionaire takes Charlie to his bosom and lavishes gifts and food on him. When he is sober, however, the man rejects Charlie and throws him out. Charlie quickly learns to accept these changes: to take advantage when the man is drunk, to accept defeat when he is sober. The sober American ''success'' is cruel, callous, inhuman; the released man is friendly. The man embodies the two warring aspects of society in the 1920s: on one level, he represents callous industrial conservatism and business pragmatism; on the other level, the morally loose, free but erratic middle-class American. The tramp, like his contemporaries, is caught between these levels; somewhat at the mercy of both, he is unable to identify comfortably with either.

Modern Times, released in 1936, clearly shows that the generic concern about mechanism and industrialization extended beyond the 1920s. All the jokes in this later film center around the dominance of the machine. The machines drive Chaplin mad. Each time he takes a tentative step toward coming to terms with the machines, he finds them to be monsters—as much in absurd control of human life as were Sennett's automobiles and, insidiously, controlling the human worker for the benefit of a business tycoon who sits in his office, constantly upping quotas and demanding more from the humans, who are treated like machines. Chaplin keeps trying to come to terms with the machines for the sake of love, for the girl he wishes to please. He wants to provide a home for her, but he cannot cope with the machine—or with his society. Chaplin's efforts, like those of many of the viewers who saw the film at the start of the Depression, are not sufficient. The monster has already taken over. People can only keep trying—and losing—in the battle with our ''modern times.''

Even the idea of domestic achievement is parodied in the film. The house Chaplin sets up for the girl and himself is fragile. It literally falls apart, just as members of households in the early days of the Depression feared their homes were figuratively falling apart.

The historical context is but one aspect of understanding Chaplin's

work in the comedy genre. Each film has another level, a more universal one that relates to basic psychological archetypes and often to mythic
ideas of romance. As Chaplin grew older, his overriding generic themes
grew darker. In *Monsieur Verdoux* (a 1947 film noir), for example, the
subject matter is death, and all humor in the film stems from the transi-
tory nature of life.

A return to Chaplin's films of the 1920s as generic pieces makes it
evident that the comedian presented his themes through melodramatic,
not modern, devices. Although this feeling is true of his films of the
1930s, too, it is strikingly presented in the 1920s films. Emotions are
extreme, open, and stylized—very much in contrast to the era's vogue
of societal cynicism. The films are replete with romantic images,
straight out of the pages of Victorian literature (as were the films of another sentimentalist, D. W. Griffith). The Victorian image presented a
clearer division between good and evil for the viewer, at least in terms
of his own concepts in popular culture. In Chaplin's films, there are
blind girls, street urchins, girls who have cruel fathers, poverty-
stricken girls, evil industrialists, and swaggering bullies. There is always a romantic princess of the lower classes who must be rescued by
the grotesque, yet romantic, figure of the tramp. He is called upon to
save lower-class virtue from the evil kings of modernity—robber barons
or industrialists who represent the nonromantic. Modern concerns are,
in these films, turned into fairy tales.

The tramp, however, is a grotesque little man, not a fairy-tale knight.
The world of the nonromantic is not so clearly overcome by the hero's
resolution and good intentions. The modern hero is not strong and brave
and true. He is willing, but his flesh and intellect are sometimes weak—
and the dragon is much more formidable when it is made of iron and
concrete.

Ultimately, Chaplin's films are romances that find the hero affirming
sentimental, rural American values when he can; finding himself drawn
to, but finally rejecting, the new morality and its promise of success;
and, generally, succeeding in rescuing the lower-class girl—all the
while recognizing his inability to be a part of society.

The Gold Rush is a startling exception to this pattern. In it, Chaplin
succeeds: he becomes wealthy, and he gets the girl. There are ironies
about the success, questions about whether or not his victory is
hollow—but a victory it is. For this reason, the film is by far the most

traditional of Chaplin's features and the closest he ever came to making a sincere heroic comedy.

Buster Keaton

Buster Keaton began making films about five years after Chaplin and made a total of 124 films during his career. Between 1923 and 1927, he made 10 features in his own studio. They are his best-known films. It is not surprising that Keaton, the performer who most symbolically illustrated the comic hero of the 1920s, should flourish only during that period, whereas Chaplin, Laurel and Hardy, and even Harold Lloyd could continue to make successful films into the 1930s.

In all of his films, until he actually moves, Keaton appears to be an inanimate object. There is no life to his face. He is like a machine at rest, a robot that, once set into motion, reminds us of how machinelike and Pavlovian we are. Keaton goes through the external movements of emotion and social aspiration but never reveals any internal enthusiasm or human feelings. The image of the treadmill, and the man who gets nowhere on it (which appeared in the films of Chaplin), are recurrent in Keaton's films.

In many ways, Keaton is a combination of man and machine (like Sennett's automobile-centaur), with each element at odds with the other in one body. This man-machine is a reflection of the 1920s' confusion between conservatism and mechanism on one hand and moral and physical freedom on the other. Chaplin usually seems in his films to be a few steps ahead of engulfment by the mechanism of American existence; Keaton's body, however, appears to be overcome by it. Keaton's way of running is a visual combination of two elements of man and machine— he accelerates, winds up, and changes pace and direction abruptly, beyond our human ability to do so.

The recurrent image in film after film of the 1920s is Keaton's need to master a machine if he is to survive and win the girl. In *The General,* the machine is a train; in *Steamboat Bill, Junior,* a steamboat; in *The Cameraman,* a camera; in *Sherlock Junior,* a movie projector, a car, and a motorcycle; and in *The Navigator,* a huge ship. The machines with which Keaton must come to terms are bizarre and oafish. He must not only come to terms with each of them, but must actually become part of them to help others. At one point in each film, he must juggle a number of pieces of mechanism at one time in order to save someone. Nowhere is this man-machine role clearer than in his merging with the steamboat at the end of *Steamboat Bill, Junior.* Although throughout each film he has trouble mastering the machine, by the time the actual crisis comes about, he suddenly is able to merge himself with the machine to save a life.

Women, for Keaton, are a hindrance to his mastery of the machine, because they bring in an element of emotion. This idea—that emotion and work cannot coexist—is very much a recurring American mythic element. It is still a common belief that the modern person must overcome emotion to succeed and that emotion shows weakness or is a feminine characteristic (a point that psychologist Carl Jung deals with as universal in his view that each man has within him feminine aspects, the anima, with which he must come to terms, just as women have a masculine aspect, the animus, with which they must do the same). In Keaton's films, women represent emotion, which is looked upon as being unpredictable. At one point in *The General,* the girl Keaton is saving almost burns down a bridge on which Keaton's train is standing. The act could isolate Keaton or lead to his death or capture. He saves himself and, in a moment of internal conflict, raises his fist to strike the girl and then pulls it back and kisses her instead. There is a similar bit of business in *The Navigator,* involving a girl and a bomb.

In his features, as well as in such shorts as *Cops,* Keaton's early inability to master the machine gets him into trouble with society and with the law, men in uniform. Keaton is not simply a little man trying to master the machine and become part of a mechanistic society. The machine and his society plague him into perpetual motion, into a treadmill chase in which he will be destroyed if he slows down, just as Chaplin almost is destroyed in *Modern Times.* Keaton is seldom attacked by one person, but by mobs—total societies—or plagued by massive disasters. In *The General,* he is pursued by an entire army; in *Cops,* by an entire police force; in *Seven Chances,* by hundreds of wedding-gown-clad, marriage-hungry women. If his society is not after him, or goading him, nature is. In *Steamboat Bill, Junior,* there is a terrible storm; at one point in *Seven Chances,* an avalanche of huge boulders; in *Balloonatic* and *Our Hospitality,* a waterfall.

Keaton escapes by luck, by determination (his head against the wind, in *Steamboat Bill, Junior,* is a perfect visual example), and, inevitably, by a mastery of the machine and the mob through his agility and invention.

One unusual characteristic found in Keaton's films, but not in those of other comic individuals, is a purposeful lack of identification with the person in the audience. Keaton, in his films, is under a camera-microscope. In one sense, he is a microscopic American—an amoeba on hinges, wearing a stone mask. Life in a Keaton film is more like a night-mare than the fantasy found in the films of other comic performers.

Chaplin, in his films of the 1920s, cannot decide whether he wants to be a part of society; and, when he tries to conform, he finds himself incapable more often than successful. Keaton, on the other hand, wants very much at all times to be accepted as a part of society, but he doesn't know how to go about gaining this acceptance. Inside Keaton's mechanical-man shell is a wild, emotional creature which struggles un-successfully to get out, but which is just successful enough to thwart the mechanical man's actions.

In some ways, Chaplin's tramp is a mixture of sentiment and vio-lence; his character is capable at one moment and defeated at the next. There are elements of both the adult and the child in the tramp, but he is essentially an adult character. He looks like an adult, though he is a clownish variation of adulthood; and he mocks the adult affectations of neat clothing, mustache-grooming, and genteel manners. The tramp is, essentially, a lower-class adult who mocks conventional responses and behavior.

Keaton is more the tortured adult who cannot merge emotion and façade. His machinelike façade is outside and fixed; his human emotion is within. Keaton is neither an adult nor a child but an uneasy example of one aspect of the human condition.

Harry Langdon

Harry Langdon, whose comedy, like Keaton's, certainly thrived only in the 1920s, was also disturbing on the child-man level. Langdon's ex-terior façade was totally childlike: he appeared to be a huge, white-powdered baby who couldn't button his coat properly or put his hat on straight. He constantly had a finger to his mouth. He was the total inno-cent, but with a disturbing difference, especially for the American audi-ence of the 1920s—for Langdon, like the viewer, was not a baby. He was over forty when he began making films, and he looked every year of his age. There is a grotesque aspect to the continuing innocence of Langdon in *The Strong Man* (1926) and *Long Pants* (1927), both di-rected by Frank Capra; *Three's a Crowd* (1927); *Heart Trouble* (1928); and *The Chaser* (1928).

His innocence, like that of his viewers and his country, was gone.

Clinging to lost innocence by clinging to a childish façade is grotesque, and disturbing, and sometimes comic. Langdon, in many ways, reminds one of Bette Davis in *Whatever Happened to Baby Jane?* Like Baby Jane, Langdon is a grotesque, pathetic, and sadly comic figure.

Langdon was a chubby Pierrot with a white moon-face and stark features. His clothes were babylike—little boots on turned-in feet, a squashed round hat that never fit snugly on his head. His outgrown jacket—reminding the viewer of his outgrown behavior—had six buttons, the top one of which was the only one Langdon buttoned, and always in the wrong buttonhole. He had a plump, small body. His arms were held stiff like a baby's and refused to remain flat at his sides. His hands were pudgy and clumsy.

Adding to the grotesquerie of innocence, Langdon was constantly being picked up and put down by equally grotesque mythical figures. In *The Strong Man,* for example, he is picked up and carried by both the strong man, a master/father figure, and the "floozy," a vamp/mother figure.

There is, because the comic is both middle-aged and a white-powdered baby at the same time, an eerie edge to Langdon's comedy, especially in his sexual encounters. His virtue—which is comic, considering his age—is constantly being saved. Chance, Right, and God are always on his side; Langdon always triumphs, but never by his own hand. A God-like fate always intervenes.

Langdon's innocence, perhaps like his viewer's clinging hope in American innocence during the confused age of the 1920s, often annoys and provokes the urban adult characters in his films who don't want to accept the manifestation of innocence in another adult. His innocence enrages other characters, by mocking them unconsciously or by provoking them into attacks in which they always lose. Something always protects this American grotesque, and that something usually is the myth, or hope, of innocence rewarded.

The plots of Langdon's early films underline the concerns of the viewer of the 1920s, as well as the conflict between the supposed American innocence and the harshness of existence its citizens were recognizing and cynically responding to. In *Tramp, Tramp, Tramp,* for example, Langdon wins the $25,000 needed to save his father's shoe factory. Without the luck of this innocent who is protected by fate, the capitalistic, self-made man would fall.

In *Long Pants,* the innocent—like the society in which he lives—

becomes sex conscious. The image of sexual fantasy in the film is a female gangster, an urban-hero/sex-object-in-one, who vamps the innocent. Langdon leaves his wife for the woman and leaves the woman only when he is finally forced to recognize that she is engaged in mayhem. He carries his fantasy of the sex-object/hero as far as he can, but ultimately he must reject it.

Chaplin's films display grave doubts about the American dream: whether it is possible for all to participate in it—and whether one should even try. Keaton's films indicate that there is no choice but to participate, but that participation is hard and often means the sacrifice of self to the machine. Langdon's films constantly affirm conservative American values, but their affirmation masks an uneasy tension. Langdon represents the meek who shall inherit the earth, but the final step of identifying with him is taken from us by virtue of his grotesquerie. The tension of society lies within his films. One major sector of America (including the viewer) wants this affirmation of conservative values; but there is a realization that, if it is attained, we no longer will be the innocents who deserved it.

In one sense, *The Strong Man* is a perfect example of the generic form for the Langdon character. The film has an intentionally biblical structure, a fundamentalist form that comes as much from director Frank Capra as from Langdon's character. The film opens and closes with a battle. In the opening battle, Langdon is defeated and becomes a spoil of war. Although the audience is told that Langdon is not an American but a Belgian, the viewer identifies with him and feels his loss. Langdon is, in a sense, a biblical slave to the strong man.

In America, Langdon is sustained by the hope of finding Mary Brown, with whom he corresponded during the war. When he can get away from the strong man, he searches for her; and he soon finds that everyone in the city wants to take advantage of him. Even the doorman at a hotel mocks him, and a floozy tries to lure him into her room to use him. The city is corrupt, and only chance saves him from it.

The second half of the film finds Langdon, with the strong man, in a lawless frontier town. By chance—or an act of God—he finds Mary Brown there. Like the girl in Chaplin's *City Lights,* she is blind—a sign of her own innocence, her inability to see the corruption around her.

Langdon is aware of no corruption. He seems unable to differentiate between good and evil until it is thrust upon him. When the strong man becomes drunk, Langdon is forced to go on in his place at the saloon, the town's center of corruption and vice. Langdon appears to be in control: he uses chance elements—including a hole in the floor—to give the impression that he is doing tricks. Then a clear biblical intrusion occurs. He sees the people of the town, the rural conservatives whom the blind girl represents, circling the saloon and calling God to bring down its walls. When the ruffians inside the saloon, who represent vice and corruption, abuse the conservative picketers, Langdon tries to appeal to their compassion. They have none and move forward to destroy him.

At this moment, God intervenes: a cannon on the stage, used by the strong man in his act, becomes Langdon's weapon against the crowd. He constantly fires, then hurriedly reloads just in time to stop another onslaught on the stage. The situation is both comic and nightmarish. It is up to this innocent on the stage, this clownish individual, to take on the responsibility for his entire society, to protect its innocence and conservatism.

In addition to the cannon, Langdon employs a huge stage drapery, which he hurls over the crowd attacking him. He swings above them, stands on top of them, destroys the entire building—fulfilling the townspeople's hope of bringing down the walls of Jericho. As soon as he has defeated the forces of evil, Langdon curls up in a fetal position and falls asleep on the stage.

The final images of the film are similarly revealing. Langdon has been made the town policeman. We see him in his uniform, over which he trips, being led by the blind girl. It is his brand of innocence on which the traditionalist must rely; but this innocence can be sustained only by the help of divine intervention.

Harold Lloyd

Certainly, the least grotesque and least consciously clownish comic individual of the 1920s was Harold Lloyd's "Glasses" character. He is the one who looks most like the film audience's interpretation of a middle-class man, and that is what Lloyd in his autobiography *An American Comedy* (New York: Longmans, 1928) says he intended in creating the character. The Lloyd character wants very much to be a part of society, to be a self-made man, to get the girl, to make friends, to be an urban, contemporary success. He invariably succeeds, but he also shows us, along the way, how gross and psychologically suspect social aspiration was in the 1920s—and still is today.

According to Lloyd's autobiography, the Glasses character had been in the back of Lloyd's mind for some time before he emerged on the screen. Lloyd had given much thought to a youthful character, possibly a boy, who could be carried through a series of college films as a comic Frank Merriwell. The idea of using minimal makeup and wearing the glasses came, according to Lloyd, after he saw a film in which a bespectacled person was forced to shed his docile nature and defeat a villain in hand-to-hand battle.

It is important at this point to note that Lloyd very consciously chose not to portray an antisocial character, a character at odds with society (as were those of Chaplin and Keaton). The Glasses character derived from Lloyd's own personality and background and reflected its creator's attitudes in comic terms as clearly as did the characters played by Chaplin and Keaton.

Conformity, conventional aspirations, zeal for life, a belief in self, a reflection of middle-class America—these were the building blocks Lloyd played with in his comedies. His love of the system with which he was dealing did not stifle his inventiveness or keep him from seeing problems that existed in the establishment. But, whereas the problems in a Chaplin film (and those of Keaton, too, to a great extent) stem from the evil, often one-dimensional, villains who represent the institutions of society, Lloyd's problems stem from the very real frustrations all people encounter. These common frustrations are expanded to Freudian proportions in a Lloyd film, but they remain familiar to the viewer. For Lloyd, such frustrations arise from the physical problems of urban existence. The daily task of getting up and getting to work (as in *Safety Last*) becomes a chore of monumental dimensions, as does getting a turkey home on the streetcar (*Hot Water*) or going for a ride with one's family (also in *Hot Water*). Added to these daily frustrations are the Glasses character's aspirations—his desire to succeed and his American determination—which are always rewarded, in spite of the fact that the character himself may not be physically or emotionally up to the challenge he faces (*The Freshman* and *Mad Wednesday* are perfect examples).

Although Lloyd's Glasses character had a variety of façades, ranging from farm boy to doctor to millionaire, all the film roles had something basic in common. ''I represented a certain group,'' said Lloyd. ''In my case, it was young people working at a vocation and always struggling against a bigger guy.'' The struggle, unlike Chaplin's, was always successful; Lloyd is always confident of his ultimate success—if he can just leap over one more social hurdle. The plot device is a reduction, *ad absurdum,* of the American dream.

The Lloyd character maintains eternal optimism, his belief that everything will work out if he just keeps at it. The Glasses character is an exaggeration of the American success dreams epitomized by such popular writers as Horatio Alger. The American audience recognized in Lloyd's Glasses character their own aspirations—simplified, reduced, and ridiculed at the same time they were lauded. The sadness in a film by Chaplin, Keaton, or even Harry Langdon could be absorbed and appreciated by the audience because there was no direct identification with the comic hero. The audience kept its distance and felt sorry for "the little fellow,'' as Chaplin called himself in his narration of *The Gold Rush.* Lloyd's Glasses character was not a "little fellow.'' To create an aura of sadness after convincing the audience to closely identify with the Glasses character would probably have alienated the viewers. Such sadness might cause embarrassment, which would cause resentment and destroy the consistent tone of satiric buoyancy of the American spirit.

Lloyd was quite aware of this quality of identification with his character. In *The Freshman,* there is a scene in which the Glasses character attempts to make friends at a college by buying ice cream cones for a few people. Soon, he is surrounded by hundreds of people, all of them wanting cones; as the camera pulls back and away from the scene, he is being swamped by students. His attempt to buy friends has failed. When Lloyd first shot the sequence, he strung it out to build up the joke, but he found that it didn't get laughs. "Finally,'' he wrote in his autobiography, "we analyzed it—the audience felt too sorry for the kid. They resented those students taking advantage of him the way they did. So, not until we cut it down did the things pull together.''

The direct identification factor was so important to Lloyd that he did his own stunts—and the stunts in a Lloyd picture were often quite dangerous. "It was not that I preferred to risk my neck,'' wrote Lloyd, "or that I was against using a double. It was simply the fact that a double's action did not look like mine or give off the same comic feeling.''

Lloyd capitalized on the danger of his stunts, however. He purposely included dangerous actions in his films, shot them to emphasize their danger, and publicized them well. In *Safety Last,* for example, the camera placement emphasizes the fact that Lloyd is, indeed, high up on a building; when he slips or dangles, the camera remains slightly above him and gives us the entire scene in a single take.

Through all the danger, Lloyd never allowed his character to take off his glasses—or to lose his identity. The glasses remain on even when the character goes swimming or when he plays football (in *The Freshman*).

Lloyd made two kinds of pictures: character comedies and thrill pictures. The thrill pictures all dealt in some way with the scaling of a building. They were ledge-hangers, as opposed to cliffhangers. The thrillers, or skyscraper pictures, were: *High and Dizzy* (1920); *Look Out Below* (1920); *Never Weaken* (1921); *Safety Last* (1923); *Feet First* (1930), a talking picture; and *Mad Wednesday* (also released as *The Sins of Harold Diddlebock*) (1947), which was directed by Preston Sturges.

Approximately one-fourth of *Safety Last* is devoted to the climb up the building. Before that sequence, Lloyd's character is established as a brash young country boy working as a clerk in a big-city department store. Audiences familiar with the Glasses character, as they were with Chaplin's little tramp, knew as soon as they saw Lloyd in the film that he was ambitious, resourceful, and willing to do almost anything to make a name for himself.

Early in the film, Lloyd realizes that he is going to be late for work. Being ambitious and afraid of facing the boss, he proceeds to make his way to work as rapidly as possible. The viewer begins to identify with Lloyd, for he knows exactly how Lloyd's character feels. Then, the exaggeration comes; but it is the kind of nightmarish exaggeration that confronts many urban dwellers. The streetcar is too crowded; the clerk can't find an inch of anything to hang onto. Finally, he lies down in the street, pretending to be sick or hit by a car. An ambulance arrives and loads him inside. As he passes the department store, however, Lloyd jumps out the rear of the ambulance and rushes to punch in on the time clock.

A short time later, Lloyd plucks up enough courage to see the boss. He pauses outside the door, torn between fear and ambition, hesitates, reaches out, changes his mind, turns in defeat, and, as the door accidentally begins to open, grabs it in desperation and gently closes it, his heart pounding.

The above scenes are typical of Lloyd's inventiveness. They are not simply comic bits, but serve as part of the building up of an individual character, as well as striking home some of the psychological traumas of American industrial life.

Not until the viewer of *Safety Last* is completely in sympathy with Lloyd's character does the film move on to its climax, the scaling of the skyscraper. Actually, Lloyd had shot these climbing scenes before he made the first part of the picture—even before he was sure of what events would actually take place during the main part of the film.

The danger sequence begins, not with Lloyd's choosing to climb the outside of the building, but with his agreeing to replace a friend who was to be paid for acting as a human fly. The friend is suddenly pursued by a policeman; Lloyd, fearful, but believing in the responsibilities of a friendship—and expecting his friend to replace him on the first floor— begins the upward climb. It is psychologically important that Lloyd does not climb the building because he wants to—it is always to help someone else; Lloyd is not a fool, but he is a good friend. At each floor, as Lloyd climbs, he is met by a new obstacle; his friend continues to pass by, inside the building, pursued by the policeman and urging Lloyd ever upward. That Lloyd's ascent of the skyscraper, in this and other films, is at least semiconsciously metaphorical seems quite likely. Ambition, friendship, and pride drive Lloyd upward just the same as they drive the viewer—and Lloyd, in other pictures—upward in business or social intercourse. The crowds watch from below, encouraging him and not worrying about the danger that increases with each upward step. The potential fall becomes increasingly frightening.

Lloyd encounters and overcomes a series of obstacles in his upward climb: pigeons, a tennis net, a painter's board, a clock, a mouse, and a weather gauge. Another obstacle is Lloyd's friend, who almost kills him while trying to help him. At one point, the friend drops a hose out of a window so that Lloyd can climb up; but, before the friend can tie it to anything, the policeman arrives, and the friend flees. Lloyd, not knowing that the hose is connected to nothing, struggles to grasp it; when he finally does and trusts his weight to it, his friend returns just in time to grab the end of the hose before it carries Lloyd to his death. In this scene, Lloyd has been established as a living, breathing human being—a comic, but a vulnerable person like you or me. We know we are viewing a movie, but we are carried away by the illusion that Lloyd is mortal.

The hero's mortality is an essential illusion if a film is to work. When Charlie Chaplin and Mack Swain totter into the cabin on the precipice (in *The Gold Rush*), we enjoy the joke, are taken up by the nightmare, but are not concerned that Chaplin might fall to his death. *We* are not the little man; we are just watching him. The same feeling is true when Keaton is shot down in *Balloonatic* and when the cannon turns and is aimed at him in *The General*. We are entertained, engaged, while waiting for the ingenuity of Keaton to save the day. Never for a moment do we really fear that Keaton will be blown to pieces. But we are, in a sense, within Harold Lloyd when he ascends a building or faces a bully or goes to a dance with his suit barely basted together.

The observations of the crowd in *Safety Last* as Lloyd climbs the building reveal that they are too distant physically and psychologically to understand his plight. When he becomes entangled in a tennis net, a woman, through a subtitle, suggests—as he struggles not to fall—that he get rid of the net because it might cause him trouble. Later, a mouse gets into Lloyd's pants and causes him to dance around madly on the ledge high above the onlookers; they, in turn, begin to applaud—assuming that he is dancing to show that he is unafraid. Lloyd carries the gag a step further by having his character remove his cap and smile at the crowd, to play to their expectations in spite of his own danger. The most famous obstacle in *Safety Last,* however, and the most famous scene in a Lloyd film, concerns a clock. Donald McCaffrey, in his book, *Four Great Comedians* (New Brunswick, N.J.: A. S. Barnes, 1968), describes the frightening comic sequence:

> His face becomes twisted with comic horror when the famous clock incident is enacted. He slips from the window and grasps frantically at the edge of the huge clock on the corner of the Bolton building that shows the time of 2:45. He cannot hold onto the edge of the clock but clutches the big hand and, horror of horrors, the hand moves with the weight to half past two. As Harold attempts to pull back by grabbing the small hand, the crowning blow of the incident occurs—the whole face of the clock springs outwards and down.

Our reaction of fear and laughter is, I believe, equivalent to the reaction we feel toward the handless clock of Ingmar Bergman in *Wild Strawberries*. Our reaction to the *Safety Last* sequence stems in part from Lloyd's clinging to that mechanical manifestation of the passage of time. It is Lloyd's own time on earth to which he is metaphorically clinging—and to which we react.

Safety Last is a comic nightmare that touches the core of human fear. *The Freshman* carries on this comic nightmare, but the later film's concern is not death as the final failure, but failure as the supreme embarrassment. The humor in the film derives from embarrassment, and embarrassment is a keystone of the Glasses character's effect on the audience. Failure is the worst defeat a Lloyd character can suffer—failure in rather conventional social terms. *The Freshman* examines the fear of failure that the audience shares with the Glasses character and plays on the viewer's embarrassment as Lloyd exposes his inner self so painfully (for us, not for him) in an effort to be liked and successful.

As the film opens, we see Lloyd in the collegiate dress of the twenties, a woolen turtleneck sweater and a beanie, conducting college cheers through a megaphone. The camera then shows us that he is displaying all this energy alone in his room. He has no friends, so he tries to buy them with ice cream cones. He dreams of girls and is so desperate for attention, and to be "in," that he willingly substitutes for the football team's tackling dummy.

Later, when he is the last player who has not been maimed during the big football game, he is sent in by the coach and—by luck—becomes a hero. But before this happens, the film audience views a scene that captures the comic genius of Harold Lloyd. Lloyd must go to a dance while wearing a suit held together with temporary stitches. His tailor accompanies him to the dance and hides, coming to his rescue as the suit starts to come apart. We are kept in comic suspense that Lloyd will suddenly become naked in the crowd, that he will be revealed in a Freudian nightmare of exposure. The embarrassment is excruciating and funny because it is so painful.

Such moments of embarrassment occur frequently, and just as meaningfully, in many Lloyd films. In *Hot Water* (1924), he is given a live turkey by his boss and is forced to take it home with him on the streetcar, under the critical eyes of his fellow passengers. In *Grandma's Boy*, he is forced to court a wealthy girl while wearing a hand-me-down suit that is several sizes too small. In *Movie Crazy* (1932), Lloyd accidentally puts on a magician's suit and is forced to pretend that he does not notice a plethora of birds, handkerchiefs, and rabbits that appear as he dances on a crowded floor. Such scenes are more than just comic; because of the audience's identification with the character, they are painfully embarrassing.

Individual comedy, which explores the position of individuals in relation to their society, continued into the sound era and to the present day. Chaplin, Keaton, and Lloyd continued to make films; but their dominance in comedy gave way to verbal individuals like W. C. Fields and Mae West, who were essentially monologuists of cynicism and comic embodiments of corruption. In the comedy of Fields and West, the conflict between urban and rural America, or conservatism and moral freedom, did not exist. The new comedians were totally urban and morally free. There was never any conflict or doubt in their characters. Their humor stemmed from their desire to participate completely in modern society and its corruptions—and, in Fields's case, to fail; in West's case, to succeed.

The individual comedians who have persisted in popularity have invariably dealt with the problems raised by the conflicting pulls of existence that we have explored. This approach also can be applied to the films of more modern comedians like Bob Hope or Danny Kaye. Hope's early films reflect society's almost hysterical response to the torments of existence in the 1940s, and Kaye shows a very Harold Lloyd-like desire to succeed in the 1950s. The comic individual of the 1960s, however, is Jerry Lewis.

Jerry Lewis

After making eighteen comedies with Dean Martin between 1949 and 1956, Jerry Lewis has appeared in twenty-seven more films without him. Eight of them were directed by Frank Tashlin, and Lewis has directed more than ten. The basis of understanding Lewis is understanding the persistence of the idea of split personality in his work, an idea that formed a core of the comic genre of the individual performer in the 1920s. Lewis, himself, in interviews and in his book *The Total Filmmaker,* refers to the two parts of his character as "The Kid" and "The Idiot."

In all of Jerry Lewis's films, there is a recurring theme that incorporates these two personalities. The Kid is alone, he is violently seeking love but is unlovable; he is able to cope with the world only by hiding, by retreating into the surreal, childish cartoon world of the Idiot. The Kid escapes from his sentimental, vulnerable personality by turning himself into a childish grotesque, by retreating into fantasy. This retreat is always in the form of disguise—seeking another personality to hide behind, a new personality that reveals the character's anxiety. Interestingly, children can respond immediately to Lewis on these levels, and French critics and their public also have appreciated Lewis's comedy, but American adults find it necessary to deny Lewis, to refuse to recognize that he is dealing with basic human concerns that have been at the core of this generic mode.

Of his multiple roles in his films, Lewis has said in *The Total Filmmaker,* "There's a schizo in all of us; and people are, in actual fact, double-faceted in personality—triple-faceted." Concerning his work, Lewis feels that "comedy is nothing more than a mirror we hold up to life. And people don't want that." Lewis has also said, of comedy of irresponsibility, that "most people cannot deal with identifying with that kind of humor, or with humor that breaks down the demeanor of the individual."

In a Lewis film, the character switches from the sentimental Kid to Idiot whenever frustration in a world of proper behavior leads the Kid to seek protection in the child's world of the dream, the Idiot world. There is usually little advance warning of the change. It is triggered by pain or frustration with which the sentimental human cannot cope. In each film, there is the Jerry character, the Kid, sometimes even called Jerry (as in *The Big Mouth*), who is vulnerable, who sees himself at times as romantic, and who deals with women on an almost maudlin, sentimental level. The Kid's world is well-defined; it is an idealized world of romance and pseudo-sophistication. He is desired or chased or pursued only for what he can give to others.

The Kid is unaware and naive, a sadly comic figure. He is confused by authority, and society's institutions refuse to respond to him. In *The Big Mouth,* he is frustrated by a telephone operator from whom he seeks help, by the police who ticket him when he calls for protection against murderers, and by the FBI man who offers him protection—only to be revealed as an escaped inmate from a mental institution. The Kid doesn't understand sexual innuendo either. To no avail, in *The Big Mouth,* does a girl carry on a lengthy discourse with him in his room, offering to "do my best to straighten you out."

In addition, when Lewis is the Kid, the world of violence is painful, and it is related, often strikingly so, to the conventions of reality. The execution of the underling by an Oriental villain in *The Big Mouth* is a scene of pure horror. When the character of the Kid is dominant, the camera movements in a Lewis film are elaborate, studied, and inventive. The almost 360-degree movement of the camera around Lewis and Janet Leigh on a couch, in *Three on a Couch,* ties the Kid to the constrictions of the "real" situations, just as it does in *The Big Mouth* when

Lewis is surrounded in his room by criminals who threaten him with death.

These scenes featuring the Kid are markedly different in handling, lighting, color, and character from the scenes showing the Idiot. Once he has retreated into the role of the Idiot, the Lewis character's psyche is revealed in cartoon structure. He can run up walls, change shape, be tortured, shot, or torn apart—and come together—in almost every film. The Idiot is marked by his perpetual motion, which is shown in his trademark, white tennis shoes. He frustrates society and his attackers, instead of being frustrated by them. The Idiot sequences are notable for Lewis's indestructability, again like that of the Sennett comics. It is as if, by falling back into his childlike dreams, he is protected by them. The cartoon dream state protects him, just as it did the Sennett characters in their cars. In *The Family Jewels,* the Idiot falls out of an airplane, disarms a giant torpedo, and escapes from exploding dynamite.

The comedy in the Idiot sequences is always extreme slapstick in style. In addition, the Idiot always resorts to disguise, hiding behind the façade of another identity like a child playing grown-up (most notably in *The Family Jewels, The Big Mouth, Which Way to the Front?* and *Hardly Working*). In *The Nutty Professor,* the film that deals most clearly with the ideas of retreat and schizophrenia, the grotesque professor—the surreal comic figure—retreats into the gross sentimental world of Buddy Love.

Invariably, in Lewis films, the final sequence shows Lewis taking the girl into his surreal world (the realm of the Idiot), the dream world in which one is constantly being chased but where one can survive and win. Generally, moreover, in the world of the Idiot, violence doesn't hurt. You can't really be hurt in the world of your dreams. At the same time, everything is so simple: the Lewis character in disguise is capable of gross sexual innuendo, the kind he cannot even understand as the Kid. He feels released as the Idiot and is far more likable than the sentimental Kid. Even the framing of the Idiot sequences—and the film's lighting and color—contributes to the cartoon character of the dream retreat. The close-ups are massive; the colors, stark, and blues and red predominate.

The Kid is part of the real world of commercialism and nonfeeling, as Lewis sees it. He is surrounded by images of commercialism—Pepsi signs, Continental Airlines, Firestone, issues of *Field and Stream,*

Colonel Sanders, Hilton hotels. This advertiser's haven is in sharp contrast to the Idiot's world of fantasy and images. The Kid allows himself to be absorbed totally into the surreal world, the child's dream world, where he can release himself from the tensions of the real world through the clowning of his second identity, the Idiot.

In the Kid's world, sound frustrates and embarrasses the Lewis character. A desk bell is painfully loud. A bite of an apple reverberates. The Idiot *uses* sound: he screams at his attackers and tricks them with verbal jokes. The narrator in the Kid section of a Lewis film is normalcy, adulthood. Moving into the world of the Idiot, the narrator is reduced to absurdity. Adult commentary is turned into meaningless gibberish, as it might be heard by a child.

In one important sense, Lewis's ideas also can be seen in the earlier films of two transitional comic figures, Stan Laurel and Oliver Hardy. For this reason, we'll go back again in time to consider this "team."

Laurel and Hardy

Laurel and Hardy did not become a film team until 1926, with *Putting Pants on Philip*. Together, they made silent shorts but no silent features. Laurel and Hardy are, in a way, extensions of the problems of individualism against society that had been brought out in the work of Chaplin, Lloyd, and Keaton. Related to the Lewis characterization, Laurel can be viewed as the Idiot, and Hardy as the Kid. Lewis admires the work of Stan Laurel and believes that he was not sufficiently appreciated as a creative talent. Lewis has said in *The Total Filmmaker,* "But you take someone like Stan Laurel who had the greatest dignity and the most influence of any man I've ever known. And he was just chucked under the rug. I finally found out the reason for it; most people fear comedy. Because the truth of it is like a bone coming through the skin."

Both Laurel and Hardy are meant to be lovable. They are childish but are unwilling to accept the fact that they may be mentally inferior to others. The viewer feels that, deep down, perhaps—again reflecting basic human fears—they really know their limitations but just don't want to admit them to themselves.

Ollie is very much the Kid, sentimental, vulnerable, able to be hurt emotionally and physically. It is Ollie who is almost always hurt in these films; Stan seldom takes a knock. Ollie is a real-world incompetent. He and Stan, the two parts of the single personality, sustain each other perfectly. Stan cannot function in the real world, but his otherworldliness (which is magical) protects him, always to Ollie's dismay. It is a gift Ollie would like; but, because he is too much tied to human weakness and his hopes for adulthood, he is beyond it. Stan is sustained almost totally by his desire for Ollie's approval. They really seem to love and need one another. They are, in a sense, an acknowledgment of the duality of the human wish—retreat and acceptance—that is embodied in Lewis's films.

We humans are, as we see in the films featuring Stan and Ollie, really not as much in control of ourselves as we want others to think we are. The world really isn't as manageable and understandable as we, as adults, try to pretend it is. Ollie tries desperately to be a functioning adult, but it isn't in him. He is too transparent and not quite bright enough.

Stan supports him, yet we never consider Stan as being able to function in the world without Ollie. Stan knows more about the magic of the mind; he is more innocent and protected—but his mind is less connected to reality, too.

Perhaps, particularly for children, Laurel and Hardy reflect the child's fear that he will be like them when he grows up; that he will be unable to handle the real world, his wife, institutions, and his job—just as adult audiences and individuals often fear that these elements are too much for them to control and handle. At the same time, the films reassure most adult viewers, because we know that we are more capable of functioning than are Laurel and Hardy and that we could cope with the adult antagonist (Jimmy Finlayson) much better than they do.

The Marx Brothers

The Marx Brothers represent a further evolution of the comic genre. As comedy developed, we moved from the individual comedian to the duo of Laurel and Hardy (and, to a lesser extent, Bert Wheeler and Robert Woolsey) and then to the Marx Brothers, at first a quartet and then a trio.

The Marx Brothers made no silent films. Their first film, *The Coconuts,* was made in 1929. The American stock market crashed, and the brothers flourished in film: destructive, bitter, nonsensically attacking decorum. There is no affirmative base in their films, as there was in the films of the comic individuals of the 1920s. While they further the romances of others, for example, they are never involved in sentiment themselves—except for Zeppo, who left the act after playing a romantic relief role in a few of their first films, the only vestige of sentiment in their films is in Harpo. The scenes in which he plays the harp can make one feel uneasy because they are out of keeping with the total destructive feel of the films.

Harpo, although he can display flashes of sentiment, also can turn quickly to lust and anarchic destruction. The silent Harpo is like a broken image of the silent film's comic individual. Groucho and Chico, on the other hand, are nonstop talkers. Their words destroy the meaning of language and the dignity of institutions, two topics that were treated with respect by Keaton and the other early comedians. Harpo's destruction is all physical—his scissors are constantly at work. Unlike the destruction caused by Keaton or Langdon, Harpo's destruction is an anarchic attack upon such objects of society as clothes, pianos, and food.

In *A Night at the Opera,* for example, the brothers ridicule sacred American institutions in their comic speech about the greatest aviators in the world. Their ridicule of the heroism and romanticism of trans-Atlantic flight lessens the serious achievements of Lindbergh and others who followed him. Chico's commentary is particularly blasphemous in undermining the dangers Lindbergh faced: ''First'a time out,'' says Chico, ''we got half way across the ocean and ran outa gas. We had to go back for more gas.''

Their destruction of business and cultural totems is even more audacious. Groucho and Chico tear up a contract, piece by piece, because they are unable to understand its legalese—which they have reduced to gibberish. When Groucho finally arrives at the opera, he asks if he's missed it; told that he still has time for the last act, he admonishes his driver, ''I told you you were going too fast.'' On the level of physical destruction, Harpo demolishes the performance of the opera, tears down props, and sells peanuts. At one point in the film, the brothers' attack upon social control is shown in a sequence in which they constantly move furniture between two rooms in a hotel to drive a police detective mad.

With the arrival of the Marx Brothers, the agony felt by the film genre's comic individual—the clown performer who tries to come to terms with American society, although he is torn between affirmation and rejection—became bitter social irony and attack. The Marx Brothers, during the depression years, were part of the system; yet they were seeking to ridicule and destroy it—just as the viewer was almost certainly part of a system upon which he was totally dependent and by which he was totally frustrated.

Woody Allen

A central theme in Woody Allen's films is that of the outsider seeking sex and finding love. Like the traditional and comic performers, Allen often deals in genre parody and satire as springboards from which to launch his image. Allen's character constantly finds himself in situations that, at first, he cannot control—his fantasy overcomes him. Like Jerry Lewis before him, Allen eventually gains control and the girl by controlling his fantasy world. He gives us visions of the terrible mother, the weak father, the motherlike wife he has lost. Ultimately, like Dorothy in Oz, he is a creature sustained by a generic fantasy. In *Take the Money and Run,* he sinks into the role of criminal, screws it up, and winds up with Janet Margolin. In *Bananas,* he fouls up his role as a revolutionary and gets Louise Lasser. The revolutionary film (*Bananas*), the sex film (*Everything You Always Wanted to Know about Sex*), the science-fiction film (*Sleeper*)—all carry him through his fantasy experience to success with his fantasy of the ideal woman.

Play It Again, Sam, which he wrote and starred in but did not direct, deals with generic identification with Bogart's screen persona and the final triumph of the protagonist by being totally absorbed into his fantasy of *Casablanca.* He does not get to keep the girl, but he gets to identify totally with Bogart's image, which is just as good—perhaps better. It is only in his later, more serious films from *Annie Hall* on that the Allen protagonist is so absorbed in his ego that he loses the ideal woman.

Allen's character is physically weak, openly neurotic, and a victim of a society he can only face in fantasy. His women are liberated objects, sometimes more liberated in attitude than he and, except for Diane Keaton, usually more mature and grounded in the real world than Allen's character. They are sex objects for Allen, who wants no maternal relationship; yet they are more maternal than the ideal women of other comic directors.

The secondary characters in Allen films are predominantly confident male figures whose confidence is ridiculed. They are WASPish, generic contrasts to Allen. As such, they are ridiculed because we are intended to see Allen as more honest, not able to hide behind the image of the successful (usually sexual) male.

The general plot of an Allen film concerns the Allen character seeking sexual fulfillment or experience and, secondarily, love. He tries to prove his right to these *Playboy* goals by behaving like an American film hero. Partly as a result of recognizing his vulnerability and openness, the ideal woman gives herself to Allen's character.

The settings for Allen's films are as varied as the genres. New York seems to be the central location of his films, and Allen generally grounds the "reality" of his films there, although they range in location from South America to Los Angeles to the future and the past.

Allen's film *Zelig* (1983) presents a summary questioning of the American struggle for acceptance, a struggle which has been at the heart of individual comedy in film since the earliest days of Chaplin. While we have discussed the anguish of naive individuals struggling to be accepted, Allen has presented an alternate American comic vision, the nonindividual, Zelig, who has no struggle because he has given up his individuality for acceptance. Zelig will be anything history needs, just so he will be accepted. He gives up the vital, eager, and often pathetic persona which the earlier comic figures not only could not escape but which formed the core of what audiences then and now recognize as comic.

As an example, Cheech and Chong, in contrast to Allen, have gone back to the roots of American naive comedy. In their films, Cheech and Chong alternate between wanting to be part of their bizarre fantasy of society and wanting to escape from it. Instead of having childish naivete as part of their birthright, Cheech and Chong, as characters in their films, have chosen naivete and childishness, have chosen to be children, aided by drugs and fantasies. They can never be accepted into normal society, which they generally ridicule, except in their own numbed fantasy. The difference between Cheech and Chong and Woody Allen is the difference between rebellion and commentary.

Mel Brooks

Mel Brooks's central concern appears to be with the pragmatic, absurd union of two males, which starts with the more experienced member trying to take advantage of the other member and ending with a strong friendship and paternal relationship. The dominant member of the union is Zero Mostel in *The Producers,* Frank Langella in *The Twelve Chairs,* and Gene Wilder in *Blazing Saddles* and *Young Frankenstein.* The weaklings in the films include Wilder, Ron Moody, and Cleavon Little.

There is no escape in generic fantasy in the Brooks films, since the films take place totally within the fantasy. There is no regard, as in Allen's films, to the pathetic nature of the protagonist in reality. In fact, the Brooks films end as the reverse of the Allen films. With his new friend, the protagonist moves into a comic fantasy of friendship. *The Producers* ends with the pair in jail, planning another scheme because they enjoy it. *The Twelve Chairs* ends with Langella and Moody working together even though they no longer have in common the quest for the chairs. *Blazing Saddles* ends with Little and Wilder supposedly *as* Little and Wilder, getting into a studio car and going off together into the sunset as pals, much as *History of the World, Part I* concludes. *Young Frankenstein,* an atypical Brooks film, departs from the pattern, with each of the partners, monster and doctor, sexually committed to women.

While the basic pattern of male buddies continued when Brooks began to act in his own films, when Brooks is the hero/star, he winds up with the woman (*High Anxiety; Silent Movie; The History of the World*). A contrast with Allen is in the nature of the jokes and gags. Allen's humor is basically adult embarrassment; Brooks's is infantile breaking of taboos.

Brooks's central figures are of two kinds. First, there is the strong dominant member of the duo—confident, but ill-fated. The second member of the duo is generally physically weak and openly neurotic. He, however, becomes the victim who wins; he learns from his experience and finds friendship to sustain him.

The women in Brooks's films are totally grotesque objects, ridiculed sex figures to be rejected. They are either very old or sexually gross and simple. The love of the friend is obviously worth more than such an object. The secondary male characters, as befitting the intentional infantilism of the films, are men-babies given to crying easily. They are set up as negative examples of what the weak protagonist can become without the paternal care of his reluctant friend. Brooks sees all people who hide behind costumes—cowboy suits, Nazi uniforms, clerical garb, homosexual affectations—as silly children to be ridiculed.

The plots of Brooks's films deal with an experienced and an inexperienced man searching for a way to triumph in society. They seek a generic solution or are pushed into one. In *The Producers*, they try to manipulate show business. In *The Twelve Chairs*, they try to cheat the government. In *Blazing Saddles*, they try to take a town. In *Young Frankenstein*, they try to gain society's respect for their accomplishments—scientific, human, and entertainment. It is always two men alone against a corrupt and childish society. Their schemes fall apart—or are literally exploded (*The Producers; The Twelve Chairs*)—and they have each other. It is interesting that Brooks always tries to distance himself from the homosexual implications of his films by including scenes in which overt homosexuals are ridiculed. It is particularly striking that these overt homosexuals in *The Producers*, *Blazing Saddles*, and *The Twelve Chairs* are stage or film directors.

Brooks's 1983 film, *To Be or Not to Be*, is an appropriate one with which to end this examination of individual comic performance. Like so many others before him, including his contemporary Woody Allen, Brooks has felt the need to turn seriously to those social structures he has previously attacked through comedy. Chaplin, Langdon, Lewis, and others made a move to serious film only to discover that the vision of struggle might not be accepted by audiences without the performer's comic persona. In *To Be or Not to Be* (a remake of the Ernst Lubitsch film of 1942 starring Jack Benny), Brooks has attempted to retain the comic persona against the serious background of a social issue, fascism. The attempt has been made before, most notably perhaps in Chaplin's *The Great Dictator*. In a real sense, Brooks, like Allen with *Zelig*, is drawing upon a tradition of comic performance and helping to revitalize it.

Readings on Film Comedy and Individual Comedians

Books

Adamson, Joe. *Groucho, Harpo, Chico, and Sometimes Zeppo: A Celebration of the Marx Brothers*. New York: Simon & Schuster, 1973.

Agee, James. "Comedy's Greatest Era." In his *Agee on Film*. Boston: Beacon Press, 1958.

Aumont, J., J. L. Comolli, A. S. La Barthe, J. Narboni, and Sylvie Pierre. "A Concise Lexicon of Lewisian Terms." Translated by Paul Willeman. In *Frank Tashlin*, edited by Claire Johnston and Paul Willeman. Colchester, Essex, England: Vineyard Press, 1973.

Barr, Charles. *Laurel and Hardy*. Berkeley and Los Angeles: University of California Press, 1968.

Bazin, André. "Charlie Chaplin." In his *What Is Cinema?* Vol. 1. Translated by Hugh Gray. Berkeley and Los Angeles: University of California Press, 1967.

Bazin, André. "The Myth of Monsieur Verdoux." In his *What Is Cinema?* Vol. 2. Translated by Hugh Gray. Berkeley and Los Angeles: University of California Press, 1971.

Bergman, Andrew. *We're In the Money: Depression America and Its Films*. New York: Harper and Row, 1971.

Byron, Stuart, and Elisabeth Weis, editors. *Movie Comedy: The National Society of Film Critics on Movie Comedy*. New York: Grossman, 1977.

Chaplin, Charles. *My Autobiography*. New York: Simon & Schuster, 1964.

Durgnat, Raymond. *The Crazy Mirror: Hollywood Comedy and the American Image*. New York: Dell, 1969.

Eyles, Allen. *The Marx Brothers: Their World of Comedy*. New York: Warner Paperback Library, 1971.

Flinn, Tom. "Out of the Past: Harold Lloyd and W. C. Fields." *The Velvet Light Trap,* no. 3 (Winter 1971/1972), pp. 6–7.

Henderson, Brian. "Romantic Comedy Today: Semi-Tough or Impossible?" *Film Quarterly* 31, no. 4 (Summer 1978), pp. 11–23.

Jordan, Thomas H. *The Anatomy of Cinematic Humor*. New York: Revisionist Press, 1975.

Kerr, Walter. *The Silent Clowns*. New York: Alfred A. Knopf, 1975.

Lax, Eric. *On Being Funny: Woody Allen and Comedy*. New York: Charterhouse, 1975.

Lewis, Jerry. *The Total Filmmaker*. New York: Random House, 1971.

Lloyd, Harold. *An American Comedy*. New York: Dover Books, 1971.

McCaffrey, Donald W. "An Evaluation of Chaplin's Silent Films, 1916–1936." In *Focus on Chaplin,* edited by Donald W. McCaffrey. Englewood Cliffs, New Jersey: Prentice-Hall, 1971.

McCaffrey, Donald W. *The Golden Age of Sound Comedy*. New Brunswick, New Jersey: A. S. Barnes, 1973.

McCaffrey, Donald W. "Introduction." In *Focus on Chaplin,* edited by Donald W. McCaffrey. Englewood Cliffs, New Jersey: Prentice-Hall, 1971.

Manchel, Frank. *The Talking Clowns: From Laurel and Hardy to the Marx Brothers.* New York: Franklin Watts, 1976.

Mast, Gerald. *The Comic Mind: Comedy and the Movies.* 2d ed. Chicago: The University of Chicago Press, 1979.

Mills, Ian. ''Chaplin's Mutual Films: The Life of Comedy.'' *The Velvet Light Trap,* no. 3 (Winter 1971/1972), pp. 2–5.

Moews, Daniel. *Keaton: The Silent Features Close-Up.* Berkeley and Los Angeles: University of California Press, 1977.

Robinson, David. *Buster Keaton.* Bloomington: Indiana University Press, 1969.

Sarris, Andrew. ''Make Way for the Clowns!'' In his *The American Cinema: Directors and Directions 1929–1968.* New York: E. P. Dutton, 1968.

Schickel, Richard. *Harold Lloyd: The Shape of Laughter.* Boston: New York Graphic Society, 1974.

Wead, George. *Buster Keaton and the Dynamics of Visual Wit.* New York: Arno Press, 1976.

Periodicals

Donnelly, William. ''A Theory of the Comedy of the Marx Brothers.'' *The Velvet Light Trap,* no. 3 (Winter 1971/1972), pp. 8–15.

Du Pasquier, Sylvain. ''Buster Keaton's Gags.'' Edited and translated by Norman Silverstein. *Journal of Modern Literature* 3, no. 2 (April 1973), pp. 269–91.

Flinn, Tom. ''Out of the Past: Harold Lloyd and W. C. Fields.'' *The Velvet Light Trap,* no. 3 (Winter 1971-1972), pp. 6–7.

Henderson, Brian. ''Romantic Comedy Today: Semi-Tough or Impossible?'' *Film Quarterly* 31, no. 4 (Summer 1978), pp. 11–23.

Mills, Ian. ''Chaplin's Mutual Films: The Life of Comedy.'' *The Velvet Light Trap,* no. 3 (Winter 1971-1972), pp. 2–5.

Mundy, Robert. ''Woody Allen.'' *AFI Report* 4, no. 3 (July 1973), pp. 6–7.

11
THE GENRE DIRECTOR
The Films of Donald Siegel

Every year brings one, sometimes two Hollywood films directed by Donald Siegel. Starting with two Academy Award–winning shorts in 1945 (*Hitler Lives,* a compilation documentary, and *Star in the Night,* a two-reel Christmas story), Siegel's name as director has appeared on over thirty-five films. His horror film, *Invasion of the Body Snatchers,* a nightmarish, philosophical feature, is often cited by critics as one of the best and most intelligent films ever made in the horror genre; in addition, it is, according to the film company that owns it, one of the three most requested films on television. *Riot in Cell Block Eleven* is a powerful, relentless, womanless prison genre picture, against which other prison films are constantly measured. And his *Baby Face Nelson* is a violent gangster film that reminds one of, and predates by ten years, Arthur Penn's *Bonnie and Clyde.*

With only a few exceptions, Siegel's films are distinct genre works: gangster films, Westerns, war stories, police stories, horror films, melodramas, and comedies. As a genre director, he received little attention from critics until *Cahiers du Cinema* singled him out as an auteur in 1964. Retrospective showings of Siegel's films have been held in Paris and London. French director Jean-Luc Godard, a great admirer of the American director, visited him and named a character in one of his films, *Made in U.S.A.,* "Donald Siegel." Godard also drew heavily on *Invasion of the Body Snatchers* in making his film *Alphaville.*

Siegel's popular appeal can be seen in the fact that he is one of the few remaining directors to be under contract to a major studio (Universal) and that his films are consistent money makers. *Dirty Harry,* in fact, is among the top box-office films of the past twenty years.

Donald Siegel is not an auteur in the accepted sense that, as a film's director, he has had total control over all aspects of each of his films—until recently. Most often, Siegel has worked with stories he did not select. He was often channeled into film violence by virtue of his success as a second-unit director on many Warner Brothers action films of the 1930s. In addition, studio influence or producer control often over a particular film have forced him to go in directions to which he was opposed, and his desire to direct additional films sometimes led him to compromise where he would have preferred to remain resolute. (See *Don Siegel: Director,* by Stuart Kaminsky [New York: Curtis, 1973].)

Still, the essence of Siegel's creativity can be seen in the extent to which he has been capable of controlling the individual genre films on which he has worked, often guiding them in directions that allowed him to express himself. Had he been given the opportunity to do so, he might well have chosen to work in genres that did not include violence. However, the fact that he was so channeled did not preclude his self-expression. The manner of expression and the points of view of such dynamic directors as Howard Hawks or John Ford frequently have been enhanced by their working in established genres.

The extent to which Siegel is consciously aware of thematic content in his handling of a particular genre is of interest but not totally relevant to his work. Each film must stand by itself and cannot be judged upon the basis of the director's intent. It is not necessary for genre artists to have a conscious understanding of the underlying themes of their work. Such themes are a part of themselves—their culture, existence, and the manner in which they successfully express them in their films are a gauge of their artistry. In many of his films, consciously or unconsciously, Siegel has created a generic expression, in popular art, worthy of serious consideration.

Siegel's films show a distinct evolving attitude toward individuals and their relationship to society, people and their search for meaning, and the relationship between men and women. His treatment of each of these themes shows artistic growth. An understanding of these attitudes and their presentation is essential to an appreciation of Siegel as a serious genre director.

The thematic pattern of Siegel's films, despite occasional variations, involves an initial rash act by the protagonist. This is followed by a sense of guilt and a seeking of justice through personal action. A father-figure is usually present to warn the protagonist, telling him that personal action will not bring justice and peace of mind, even if he comes to understand his impulse; that socially accepted ways of seeking justice are essential and that a person who tries to act like God will be defeated. The protagonist does not heed this warning. He plunges ahead in the hope that he can determine his own fate. Usually, the subject of his quest is an antagonist whose character is an extension of his own. The affirmative villain is vibrant—perhaps mad—but his very madness is affirmative, for spontaneous violent madness is pattern-breaking and life-affirming. The hero and villain are both flawed; an act of violence divides the two. The protagonist, to get justice, must destroy the mad villain, the uncontrolled essence of the total personality. The protagonist has little help in his quest for justice, his desire for confrontation with his villainous mirror image. His friends are of value only because of their professional qualities. A Siegel hero makes friends for no other reason than professional competence. Friends also represent the more conservative aspects of one's personality. Either the villain or the hero can be shown as having friends who are actually supportive projections of the character's conscience and personality.

Women are of no help at all to either the protagonist or the villain. Siegel's women are tempting, deceitful creatures, forever playing Eve. They can't be denied, but they must never be trusted. Often, in the course of his pursuit of justice and vindication for his mistake, the hero discovers that he can't isolate himself by refusing to feel or to be affected by others. The hero knows that human existence has no meaning, but he finds that he should not—in fact, that he cannot—insulate himself, protect himself from the pain of life. Violence is not enough. Trust and social affirmation must be tried, even if they are doomed, for to avoid them is to avoid existence.

Finally, after he attains some kind of justice, the hero finds himself both victorious and defeated at the same time. His wild self is dead; the violent affirmation he once felt has been subdued. The protagonist sinks back into oblivion, lost without his simple course of violent action, his cause of vengeance and feeling of guilt. As the film ends, the hero is no longer of interest. Siegel is ready to look for another flawed hero, another mad villain to play out another variation of the psychodrama of existence.

Literary analogies to Siegel's films can be found most strikingly in

Don Siegel during the filming of *Dirty Harry*.

Lee Marvin and Angie Dickinson in *The Killers*.   Andy Robinson in *Dirty Harry*.

174

Joseph Conrad, especially in terms of the doppelganger villain as a psychological mirror image (*The Heart of Darkness*) and of self-vindication for rash action (*Lord Jim*). Strangely, Siegel's concepts of order, society, and the presumptuousness of assuming power are extraordinarily like those of the Swiss writer Friedrich Durrenmatt (*The Marriage of Mr. Mississippi, An Angel in Babylon, The Pledge,* and *The Quarry*). Cinematically, Siegel's mentors (by his own admission and the evidence of his films) were genre directors Michael Curtiz, from whom he learned much of his cinematic technique, and William Wellman, from whom he learned little technique but whose iconoclastic view of society he admired and accepted.

With this background in mind, one can see that Siegel views humanity as being torn between two extremes of behavior in the attempt to come to terms with existence. Despite being drawn toward both extremes, one may be able to survive—with some semblance of dignity and peace of mind—if one can find a balance between the two extremes. Whether this balance is possible is the probing question asked incessantly by Siegel, as he makes use of the icons, themes, and characters of various genres and brings to the foreground those concerns at the core of each genre.

At opposite ends of the spectrum of existence lies madness. On one end is the drive toward conformity, characterized by a protective lack of emotion and involvement and a seeking of insulation and social acceptance. Those who exist at this end of life's spectrum tend to plunge into hyperprofessionalism, to have little fear, and to display a total disregard for life. In essence, to Siegel, they are pods—a descriptive term for the emotionless, vegetable-humans of *Invasion of the Body Snatchers*. Much of humanity experiences an extreme drive toward this manner of existence, which Siegel despises but toward which he too feels drawn. The mad, or extreme, examples of this behavior include all the pods—especially Larry Gates—in *Invasion of the Body Snatchers*, Eli Wallach and Robert Keith in *The Line-Up*, and Lee Marvin in *The Killers*. The chief inspector in *No Time for Flowers* approaches this madness. Contemporary society in most Siegel films tends to favor this end of the existence spectrum, as exemplified by the townspeople in *Count the Hours, Flaming Star, Stranger on the Run,* and *No Time for Flowers*.

On the other end of the spectrum is the wild, spontaneous, emotional, life-affirming joyousness that is, nonetheless, mad. The representatives of this end of the spectrum, to which Siegel is also drawn, are sponta-

neous, violent, free-spirited, without control, vital, filled with exalta-
tion, often humorous, and totally unpredictable. That these unfettered
madmen are more psychologically appealing to Siegel than the emotionless pods is clear in his presentation of them and in their cinematic interest.

These free spirits are out to destroy whatever stifles society, but they
themselves must also be destroyed if any sense of order is to remain
within the protagonist and society itself. Such unfettered madmen in-
clude Jack Elam in *Count the Hours*, Mark Rydell in *Crime in the
Streets*, Mickey Rooney in *Baby Face Nelson*, Mickey Shaughnessy in
Edge of Eternity, the warlord in *China Venture*, Clu Gulager in *The
Killers*, Eddie Albert in *The Gun Runners*, Leo Gordon in *Riot in Cell
Block Eleven*, Steven Ihnat in *Madigan*, and Andy Robinson in *Dirty
Harry*.

The human societies that approach this unfettered state without going
mad and that are able to retain their self-affirmation are the primitive,
natural societies that have been threatened or subjugated by more dominant and prevalent podlike societies. Such affirmative primitive societies in Siegel films include the Indians in *Flaming Star*, the mountain
people in *The Hound Dog Man*, the prisoners in *Riot in Cell Block
Eleven* and *Escape from Alcatraz*, and the slum dwellers in *Crime in the
Streets*.

The film protagonists, with whom Siegel seeks a sense of balance and
a means of accepting and dealing with existence, are pulled in two directions: toward primitivism and unfettered madness on one side and toward social order and conformity on the other. Those who choose the
primitive extreme—the violent, unfettered course of action—can only
meet with defeat in a Siegel film. This is true of Neville Brand in *Riot in
Cell Block Eleven*, John Cassavetes in *Crime in the Streets*, Stuart Whitman in *The Hound Dog Man*, and Elvis Presley in *Flaming Star*.

Many of Siegel's protagonists are wild, unpredictable men who make
an attempt to accept society and seek the solace of conformist existence.
Invariably, such protagonists must first overcome their primitive, unfettered urges and then take a step away from the direction of emotional
involvement—a step which will bring them closer to a balance between
the two dominant human drives but which may not result in personal
happiness. Other protagonists begin a Siegel film as podlike, conformist
creatures. By the film's end, they have taken a first tentative step toward
emotion and vitality through an act of violence in which they destroy the

unfettered madman, the wild side of themselves. This step is a key to possible hope. Such protagonists include Ronald Reagan in *Night unto Night,* Robert Mitchum in *The Big Steal,* MacDonald Carey in *Count the Hours,* Richard Kiley in *Spanish Affair,* Henry Fonda in *Stranger on the Run,* Clint Eastwood in *Coogan's Bluff* and *Dirty Harry,* and Michael Caine in *The Black Windmill.*

A few Siegel protagonists who appear at the start of some later films are at the very center of the spectrum, apparently at peace with existence. But even in these later films, Siegel's conclusion is that, if a man is able to come to terms with his own existence, other forces—primarily sexual betrayal—will destroy him. This conclusion is true of the characters portrayed by Clint Eastwood in both *Two Mules for Sister Sara* and *The Beguiled* and the character played by Ken Wahl in *Jinxed.*

Seen as a whole, Siegel's films do not build toward a thematic solution. Instead, they explore the problem of existence in the terms already discussed. Siegel's films also explore the director's ideas and feelings concerning personality, guilt, madness, and death. His protagonists are plagued by mirror images of themselves: characters who represent a key part of the protagonist's own personality drives and who force the protagonist to recognize their existence. The villains generally display distorted aspects of the hero's personality, the extremes of podlike conformity or of unfettered madness.

Siegel's skill is such, however, that considerations of psychological structure are not evident on the surface. Even the mad characters are not only psychological equivalents of the generalities encountered by Everyman or John Bunyan's Pilgrim. Nor are these characters allegorical creations, like those that appeared in early Ingmar Bergman films. The psychological complexities of character in a Siegel film are totally integrated into the structure of genre entertainment. Siegel's mode of expression lies within the confines of genre and Hollywood, for it is in such contexts that he has learned to express himself. Although this analysis holds true in all of Siegel's films, it is possible to examine its execution in five distinct genres: the detective film, the gangster film, the war film, the Western, and the horror film.

The Detective Film

In *The Verdict* (1945), protagonist Sidney Greenstreet loses his job to Buckley, played by George Coulouris. Coulouris, a podlike extension of society, is the epitome of the same self-satisfied pride that once ruined Greenstreet, caused him to lose his job, and resulted in his sending an innocent man to the gallows. The character of Coulouris, however, is lacking in depth and dimension. The viewer (and Greenstreet) sees him working in Greenstreet's office, preening himself, being officious and vindictive and gloating. His behavior becomes an exaggeration of Greenstreet's early behavior in the film. Greenstreet becomes obsessed, not with finding the real killer, but in proving that Coulouris is vulnerable. Greenstreet's vindication comes in destroying Coulouris, in exposing his false pride. By erasing Coulouris, he expiates his own guilt.

It is as if, after sending the innocent man to the gallows and later discovering his error, Greenstreet has split into two characters: he becomes a cinematic schizophrenic, a recurrent theme in American police-procedure films. One of the characters is Coulouris, whose portrait in a high military collar dominates the office of Grobman, played by Greenstreet. The other character, Grobman, is a guilt-ridden, somber man who must destroy Coulouris because he represents that aspect of himself that was responsible for his immoral action. Ironically, Greenstreet cannot destroy Coulouris without dying himself. His confession of guilt, at the end of the film, is intentionally self-destructive. Coulouris will lose his job, be figuratively destroyed; in a sense, Greenstreet will murder the figurative dark side of himself—kill the guilty podpart of his personality—in the belief that doing so will free him.

Peter Lorre, Greenstreet's friend, represents an affirmative side of Greenstreet's personality, a side that has never developed. Lorre is outgoing, hedonistic, vulnerable; he is not an unfettered madman, but he certainly exists on that side of the spectrum. Significantly, Greenstreet attempts at one point to murder Lorre, the affirmative side of his personality. The explanation given in the film is hardly adequate to explain an attack upon a real friend. The psychological possibility that Greenstreet also feels guilty about the existence of the hedonistic, emotional side of himself is a more likely reason for the attack. He wants to destroy both sides of his being in order to find peace. Lorre, however, survives the attack, and serves ultimately as Greenstreet's conscience. Without an exchange of confidences, Lorre suddenly arrives at Greenstreet's apartment, and the two of them, in perfect understanding, go together to the police superintendent's office, where Greenstreet makes his confession.

In *Private Hell 36,* the personal dichotomy is clearly evident in the relationship of Steve Cochran and Howard Duff. The two men are partners, friends. They work as a unit with no apparent difference, professionally, between them. They do not even have to converse when they are on a case. They know the right thing to do, and they share an air of professional rapport. Since the Siegel hero can, or wishes to, feel no emotion at first, or strives to hide it, he can only relate to himself and others professionally, through some kind of physical code of behavior.

This relationship is true not only of Duff and Cochran, but also of Neville Brand and Leo Gordon in *Riot in Cell Block Eleven,* Steve McNally and Audie Murphy in *Duel at Silver Creek,* Greenstreet and Lorre in *The Verdict,* Edmond O'Brien and Barry Sullivan in *China Venture,* John Cassavetes, Sal Mineo, and Mark Rydell in *Crime in the Streets,* Eli Wallach and Robert Keith—and Warner Anderson and Emile Meyer—in *The Line-Up,* Elvis Presley and Steve Forrest in *Flaming Star,* Steve McQueen and the members of the squad in *Hell Is for Heroes,* Clu Gulager and Lee Marvin in *The Killers,* Michael Parks and his gang in *Stranger on the Run,* Richard Widmark and Harry Guardino in *Madigan,* and Clint Eastwood and Reni Santoni in *Dirty Harry.* The physical code of professional behavior is the only thing that keeps the hero from being totally isolated from society; frequently, the professional rapport and control provide him with the needed edge to destroy the uncontrolled part of his being. The protagonist is left, at film's end, free of his weight of guilt—but somehow having lost an important part of himself.

In *Private Hell 36,* Duff and Cochran appear to differ only in their private lives. Duff is a family man; Cochran, a rootless bachelor who takes up with Ida Lupino, who wants money. The single professional unit, made up of the two men, is destroyed when Cochran, in one rapid sequence of decision, goes mad; unfettered, he steals some money and involves Duff. Duff experiences a moment of hesitation and weakness at the sudden destruction of the partnership. Cochran has become a mad, uncontrollable personality. Even when Ida Lupino says she no longer wants the money, he cannot turn back: the personality split has already taken place. Duff begins to fall apart, to drink, to weaken, to hate himself. A father-figure, Dean Jagger, emerges; he counsels caution, restraint, conformity.

In an effort to get rid of his guilt, Duff insists that he and Cochran return the money they have stolen. Cochran then attempts to kill Duff. The two protagonists represent a schizophrenic duel between the two sides of an apparently single personality. To the point of the theft, it is clear that both Cochran and Duff are rather conventional heroes. It is not until the theft that the break takes place, and the mad side—in almost *Dr. Jekyll and Mr. Hyde* fashion—tries to destroy the conforming side before it is destroyed itself. In *Private Hell 36,* however, Jagger, the father-figure, arrives in time to kill Cochran, after Cochran has shot and wounded Duff. Despite Jagger's intervention, Duff—the severed being—may be incapable of existence. It is possible that people may not be able to exist meaningfully, or at all, without some uncontrolled drives—another possibility explored by Siegel, again without a positive answer.

Madigan opens with an assault by Richard Widmark and Harry Guardino on an apartment where they believe a suspect is hiding. The resulting schizophrenic encounter is preceded by the sudden smashing of the apartment door by Widmark and the sudden confrontation of the protagonist with his dreaded wild self—the mad killer, Steve Ihnat, who is to plague Widmark and Guardino. The door suddenly opening or falling down is used frequently by Siegel to dramatize a violent confrontation, usually between the protagonist and the mad character (or some other person) who reflects a facet of his personality that the protagonist suppresses but with which he is shatteringly faced. In *The Verdict,* Greenstreet bursts through a door and *appears* to discover the dead body of the murderer. Later, we find that Greenstreet had *actually* broken down the door and then killed the man. In *The Killers,* Marvin and Gulager push their way through the door to face Angie Dickinson, who has betrayed them. In *Coogan's Bluff,* Eastwood kicks in the door to face Tisha Sterling, who betrays him. In *Dirty Harry,* the door of Andy Robinson's room is kicked in by Eastwood in the sequence in which he first meets and tortures Robinson.

The sudden act of violence ties the protagonist—or the female betrayer who has led him into a clash—with the violent part of himself he must confront. Siegel's interest in the physical encounter, including a visual presentation of confrontation and violence, also can be seen in his frequent use of large pistols—often fitted with silencers to make them look even larger. The guns' capacity for destructiveness is underscored in terror-filled images. The cool mania of those who wield such guns—Eli Wallach in *The Line-Up,* Steve McQueen in *Hell Is for Heroes,* Edmond O'Brien in *China Venture,* Lee Marvin in *The Killers,* Clint Eastwood in *Dirty Harry,* Michael Caine in *The Black Windmill,* John

Wayne in *The Shootist*—is emphasized by the mechanistic device of the grotesque weapon.

The instrument of violence, a gun, propels the film audience into some consideration of the gravity of the psychodrama we see enacted before us as entertainment. Although the audience is entertained by the film, the viewer is probably grotesque himself if he is not, at the same time, repulsed by the cool killers—those mad pods who are extreme conformists. Like the free-spirited mad killers at the other end of the spectrum, the conforming mad killers must also be destroyed. The viewer wants to see the destruction of the killer who exists at either end of the spectrum. In many cases, the viewer's feeling is a thrill of being mad along *with* the killers—especially with Jack Elam in *Count the Hours*, Leo Gordon in *Riot in Cell Block Eleven*, and Mickey Rooney, Mickey Shaughnessy, Clu Gulager, Steve Ihnat, and Andy Robinson in the other films. Our repulsion is mixed with understanding.

In *Madigan*, the first scene sets the psychological tone of the film. It is clear that Widmark and Guardino know Ihnat well, for they all are on a first-name basis. Ihnat proves to be the film's uncontrolled personality; Guardino exerts a more conventional pull on Widmark. Guardino seems to have made a satisfactory emotional compromise. He is one of Siegel's few contented characters with whom the viewer feels sympathy, yet the scenes of domestic rapport in *Madigan* (which show Guardino in contrast to Widmark) are flat, almost caricatures, a throwback to the Duff and Dorothy Malone domestic scenes in *Private Hell 36*. Henry Fonda represents the conforming end of the spectrum in the film. He goes by the book, tries to feel nothing, and is willing to destroy his own best friend when the friend deviates from the law. Widmark is caught between the extremes of Fonda and Ihnat and, of the two, his rapport with Ihnat is clearly better.

Ihnat gets away when Widmark glances at a naked girl. In a sense, this scene is a capsule variation on Siegel's theme of betrayal by women; but it is also an indication that Widmark's sexual interests are not vastly different from those of Ihnat, his mad double. The remainder of the film is devoted to Widmark's futile attempt to make a compromise with his life: to destroy his mad side, Ihnat, and come to terms with his conforming side, Fonda. The film's model for a successful compromise is, of course, Guardino.

At the conclusion of the film, Widmark elects to face his mad self. The confrontation is stark and strange. Ihnat and Widmark shoot it out, guns in both hands, at point-blank range, after Widmark kicks down the door. Ihnat's last words are to ask Guardino if he has killed Widmark. He then dies, satisfied that Widmark has not been able to effect a compromise—to exist without him or to reject him. The affirmation in the film comes through Fonda, the intractable semipod, who, as the survivor of the psychological-personality struggle, indicates that he will take a step into emotional concession by not destroying the career of his friend James Whitmore.

Coogan's Bluff followed *Madigan* by less than a year. Although the two films are similar, *Coogan's Bluff* shows a more explicit working out of the affirmation that Siegel sought. He and Clint Eastwood, who agreed with Siegel's view of the film, were in control of the later film's script in a way the director was not in *Madigan*. *Coogan's Bluff* is in many ways a reworking of the *Madigan* theme. The locations and some instances of character development are interesting in comparison. Again, the center of *Coogan's Bluff* is the twenty-third precinct in Manhattan. The same location and offices are used in both films: the office of the lieutenant in *Madigan* is the same as Lee J. Cobb's in *Coogan's Bluff*. The lieutenant in *Madigan* wore his hat in the office, as Cobb does, and appeared angry for no clear reason except that, as the film's father-figure, he continually warns the protagonist—wearily, cynically, and with no expectation of success. The villain in *Coogan's Bluff* is Don Stroud, who played Ihnat's contact in *Madigan*. In *Madigan,* he mentioned that he lived with mother and frequently repeated that he had many girls. He plays a slightly more formidable version of this character in *Coogan's Bluff*. The key to the second film is its apparent simplicity. The story is more direct, for there is no attempt to juggle two stories, with various subplots, as Siegel tried to do in *Madigan*. *Coogan's Bluff* is also more visually alive, and its characters more ambiguous. The twenty-third-precinct building is alive with people—criminals, victims, perverts, and police. The same changes are true of the city and its inhabitants. In *Madigan,* Widmark encountered grotesques, two-dimensional figures whom he dominated. In *Coogan's Bluff,* on the other hand, Eastwood encounters a vibrant mixture of personalities, with whom he has great difficulty coping.

Coogan's Bluff is, ultimately, a highly conservative film that clearly looks forward to Siegel's *Dirty Harry*. In *Coogan's Bluff,* Eastwood comes to New York to pick up a prisoner. Father-figure Cobb tells him to wait. Eastwood, who denies having any feeling for others (the viewer has seen him behave without compassion for the Indian he brought in at the start of the film and then sees him treat Susan Clark as a simple sex object) decides not to wait; he gets his prisoner, Stroud, instead. He then loses the prisoner; and, in pursuing him, Eastwood lives through some of the same kinds of events that have made Stroud the urban animal he is—just as reservation living had made an animal of the Indian Eastwood had captured earlier. Eastwood confronts Stroud's bizarre mother, meets Stroud's friends, plunges into the hangouts Stroud frequented, and even goes to bed with Stroud's girl. At one point, Eastwood tells Susan Clark a story about how he had once been responsible for the death of a prisoner and that the guilt of that experience has caused him to retreat into nonemotion.

In the course of pursuing Stroud, Eastwood begins, reluctantly, to identify with him. The final confrontation between the two takes place in Fort Tryon Park and is almost an affectionate chase. Eastwood catches Stroud but does not destroy him. Instead, he accepts both the rules and Cobb's advice. His contact with Stroud has not destroyed him but has caused him—like Fonda, in *Madigan*—to make an emotional move, to reject nonemotion and to acknowledge human contact. The change in the *Coogan's Bluff* Eastwood is slight, tentative; but it exists. He gives Stroud a cigarette, an action he had refused to perform for the Indian, and seems willing to respond to Stroud. The conclusion is clearly an affirmative one, as Eastwood takes the first steps in joining society.

Dirty Harry is another example of Siegel's exploration of man and his uncontrolled self. The film is a ruthless return to the psychodrama in an attempt to find a new direction, to explore another avenue, and to carry the search for affirmation to its extreme conclusion. The killer in *Dirty Harry* is the most totally mad of all Siegel killers. He is nameless, intent upon the wanton destruction of society. His violence is hideous. There is less to salvage in him, as an affirmative force, than there had been with Siegel's other mad villains.

The killer opens the film by murdering an innocent woman (perhaps in retribution for the female devourers of *Two Mules for Sister Sara* and *The Beguiled*). Although there is a serious question about whether any woman in a Siegel film can be completely innocent—because they all prey on men—this killer in *Dirty Harry* performs insane acts of murder that previous Siegel madmen had never even imagined. After murdering the woman, he kills a small boy and then a young girl. He goes after a priest but finally settles on a busload of children. It is all of society that he wishes to destroy—without compromise. Eastwood, in contrast, is a throwback to the emotionally stunted protagonists of such films as *The Hanged Man, Stranger on the Run, Madigan,* and *Coogan's Bluff.* But in *Dirty Harry,* Eastwood's character, like the killer's, is more accentuated. He is a bigot, a willful killer who likes his dirty work and is out to avenge the death of his wife. He appears to have no home and to exist only so that he can destroy with his oversized Magnum pistol. He is a protagonist who, again, retreats into nonemotion and a near podlike state. These two extremes must settle the world between them; and all of society—the mayor, the judge, the public—must stand aside and watch fate being resolved in the clash of two madmen. The viewer's sympathy is clearly with Eastwood, however, whose act of revenge is prescribed; for, in destroying Robinson, Eastwood will also perform an act that benefits society, since Robinson's acts are totally monstrous.

By the time of their final confrontation, Eastwood has given hints that he might be willing to try to live in society again, willing to feel emotion; but the hints that he gives are small, almost undiscernible, and almost exclusively attached to his feeling for his wounded partner and the partner's wife. When Eastwood and Robinson finally meet, they are beyond society—beyond law. Eastwood has been told not to confront the killer but to give in to all his demands. To Eastwood, that response will bring about chaos—and an unsatisfactory conclusion. He must face the killer, his unfettered self. When he does destroy Robinson, however, he himself is *not* destroyed by his schizophrenic act; still, as a result of that event, Eastwood throws his badge away. He has gone beyond the confines of law and society, and he will surely be fired or have to quit. There is no happy ending for him, no return of feeling, no real function. When the camera slowly zooms away, it leaves him alone and lost. The viewer can conceive of no future for him. In one sense, Siegel has explored through this film another path to inevitable conclusions—and has found no solace. The director can only continue to affirm himself by making movies and by recasting the age-old puzzle of existence and meaning.

The Crime Film

With *Baby Face Nelson,* Siegel began to explore a new area of his thematic preoccupation—this time, within the form of the gangster film. Mickey Rooney is not a hero torn between stifling conformity and the total social alienation of madness. Rooney, who is firmly settled in the gangster genre context, clearly is already mad when the viewer first encounters him. In this film, Siegel is exploring what might happen if the totally nonconforming side of a person dominated—if there were no stabilizing drive toward conformity and acceptance. This exploration is, as Friedrich Durrenmatt has said, a carrying through of a metaphysical aesthetic theme to its logical conclusion.

Rooney, as John Dillinger tells him in the film, is totally uncontrolled. The psychological metaphor employed by Siegel is that of the madman as a child-primitive, stunted physically and emotionally, who has never developed a sense of control, emotion, or conformity. The images of the film constantly tell us that Rooney is small, that he is childlike; we see him having tantrums, carrying on a meeting in a park while his feet dangle from a child's swing, wearing costumes, striking out at adults, and clinging to his surrogate mother/mistress, Carolyn Jones. She even gives him her name, Nelson, while his father-figure, Dillinger, calls him Baby Face. In this bizarre context, it is Dillinger who warns Nelson that he must control his emotions and be cool. But Dillinger senses that Nelson is beyond such advice; and Nelson, like other Siegel protagonists, pays no heed to the fatherly suggestion. Nelson, the unfettered madman, is destroyed both by society and—ironically—by his mother/mistress, who consents to his death when he tells her that he would have killed two children who almost ran into him in the woods.

In *The Line-Up,* Dancer (Eli Wallach) is totally without feeling. He kills efficiently, professionally, with no regard for his victims as human beings. He is a pod killer, an emotionless madman who exists at the opposite end of the spectrum from Baby Face Nelson. Instead of the film's terror being inherent in the madness of violence and unpredictability, it lies instead within the restrained, unemotional, conforming, podlike personality. The terror generated by the Siegel villain Wallach portrays in *The Line-Up* surpasses that which we feel about any of Siegel's outgoing mad villains and is similar to that aroused by Lee Marvin in *The Killers.* (In fact, the two films share a number of interesting parallels. See chapter 4 for a detailed examination of *The Killers.*)

Wallach's drive for conformity is depicted perfectly. When we first see him, his mentor, Julian (Robert Keith), is teaching him grammar—the use of the subjunctive. Wallach studies because he wants to *be* someone in the organization—as Julian says, "How many characters on the

street corner can say, 'If I were you'?'' The images of conformity associated with Wallach and Keith are among the most chilling in the film.
The two act as businessmen, with Keith as the coach of an up-and-
coming executive. Wallach carries a briefcase that contains a pistol with
a silencer, the tool of his profession. When he plans to kill a woman and
a girl, Wallach opens his briefcase and begins to go through it, looking
for the gun, just as if he were trotting out a contract or a bill of sale.
Wallach's drive for conformity is epitomized in his massive flaw: he has
a great desire to meet his employer, the nameless man—''The Man''—
who has hired him to pick up smuggled heroin. At first, Dancer simply
wants to meet The Man; but later, he wants to see him to explain why he
and Julian have not turned in all the heroin. While The Man is evidently
the secret head of the crime syndicate, he is also a metaphorical repre-
sentation of God—control, the being who can answer metaphysical
questions. When Wallach finally encounters The Man (who is
crippled—a flawed God) at the amusement pier, The Man will not listen
to him. The pod, the social human—for all his attempts at conformity
and lack of emotion—can find no peace, no acceptance, no meaning.
The Man refuses to listen to Wallach's confession—or to remove his
sense of guilt. His only words to Wallach are, ''You're dead,'' and,
''No one sees me and lives.'' The God-like epitome of conformity and
acceptance rejects Wallach, who responds by killing The Man—
pushing him off the high platform to an ice rink several floors below.

His world demolished, Wallach then turns upon Keith, his mentor,
who has systematically collected the last words of Wallach's victims.
He kills Keith because his advice advocating conformity has been use-
less. (It is interesting that the dying words that please Keith the most are
those of a Japanese houseboy, who at the last expresses servitude and
concern for his master's property.) In the final wild chase sequence,
Wallach bursts out of his conformity and is trapped at the end of an un-
finished freeway, with nowhere to go. He falls to his death, like The
Man, after a gun battle with the police. The totally cool, conformist
madman has fared no better than Siegel's totally uncontrolled madmen.
Either extreme is unacceptable to the society within the film.

The Hanged Man is a remake of Robert Montgomery's *Ride the Pink
Horse,* but Siegel's concern with man's groping for the meaning of existence and search for a satisfying place in the spectrum—somewhere
equidistant from a completely emotional existence and one of uncontrolled, violent passion—pervades his version and does not exist in the

Montgomery film. In *The Hanged Man*, Robert Culp, a petty gangster, is out to avenge the death of his friend Whitey. His plan is to kill the man who he believes is Whitey's murderer, union leader Edmond O'Brien. Culp is not adept enough to carry the execution through; but, by tempting him, O'Brien's wife (Vera Miles) convinces him to blackmail her husband. It is clear that, of the two men in the original partnership, Whitey was the leader, the mentor, the stronger personality. Since Whitey's death, Culp feels that he is only part of a man, that the sudden violence has left him with nothing to do but exact his revenge and die. He attempts to be emotionless but his deep feeling of loss saves him. Unable to kill O'Brien, Culp cannot divorce himself from his feelings and so is an easy victim for Vera Miles. Culp is a protagonist who has never worried about defining the meaning of his existence because he relied totally upon his vicarious existence through Whitey. When Whitey reappears—alive—and informs Culp that he, Culp, has been used as a tool to get money out of O'Brien, Culp feels defeated, is hardly able to respond. He reminds us of Steve McQueen in *Hell Is for Heroes*, for he now exists in a situation in which all possible meanings are closed to him. Like other Siegel protagonists, Culp had refused to listen to the paternal warnings of tax investigator Norman Fell; instead, he has gone ahead with his plans for revenge, not caring if they resulted in his own destruction.

The ending of *The Hanged Man* is an abrupt turnabout, in which all the danger warnings prove false and Culp is suddenly alive and well. Whitey is suddenly destroyed and an apparently dead Culp proves to be alive. This conclusion may strike the viewer as a tacked-on irony, a resurrection that contradicts the film's meaning, an affirmation where none ought to exist. And yet, Siegel used it to end both this film and the more recent *Rough Cut* (starring Burt Reynolds)—just as F. W. Murnau accepted the ironic, happy ending of *The Last Laugh* and Ingmar Bergman turned the darkness of *The Magician* into light and humor in his finale. Siegel put the ending there by choice, as an imposition of hope or a flouting of the evidence, in an apparent belief that people can come to terms with their existence in spite of the fact that the viewer has seen nothing in the film to support this conclusion.

The Western

In *Duel at Silver Creek*, Stephen McNally loses his father-figure and conscience, Dan Music. He immediately finds Audie Murphy and assumes the role of father to him, for Murphy has also lost his father. Both Murphy's father and Music have been killed by the villain's gang, and the recurrent Western/biblical theme of revenge is initiated. The new father-son relationship is extended when Murphy falls in love with McNally's girl (Susan Cabot), whom McNally willingly relinquishes. When a gunfight is about to take place in the street, Murphy wounds McNally to save McNally's life and then takes his place to kill the villain, Johnny Sombrero (an embryonic unfettered madman). The psychological complexity usually found in Siegel's films, and the resultant cycle of emotion, guilt, and acceptance, is not strongly evident in *Duel at Silver Creek*—but the psychological relationship is certainly present. McNally's extreme enmity for Johnny Sombrero is shown, throughout the film, as a reaction to Sombrero's flamboyance and uncontrolled freedom.

Flaming Star, on the other hand, is completely uncompromising: the social and emotional schizophrenia is clearer here than in any other Siegel film. The genre is the Western, and the theme is racial conflict, but the basic meaning of the film is psychological imbalance. The world of the film is divided into whites and Indians. Presley is in the middle; the pulls upon him come from both sides, for his mother is Indian and his father, white. It is clear from the first encounter with both the frightened whites and the militant Indians that Presley is considered an Indian. His totally white half-brother, Steve Forrest, is his mirror image, which comes into play later. Presley and his family try to live at peace with both Indians and whites but are not allowed to do so. They are forced to make a decision, to pick a side.

The Indians are clearly more elemental in existence; they are not mad, but they are emotionally natural people who live in the James Fenimore Cooper tradition of the noble savage. Their free emotionalism, however, is curtailed by self-control and social order. The whites, who are physically isolated, strive for safety in strict conformity, almost like pods. Their conformity, however, is upset by occasional acts of violence—violence born out of fear.

The townsmen are very similar to other groups of people who represent society in Siegel's movies. In general, Siegel views society as a milieu that tends to accept conformity and unemotionalism. Society, as a larger unit, is taken over by pods or consists of those persons who are unwilling to accept any feeling except a desire for noninvolvement. Any social extension of unfettered action must be killed because the existence of society (which is treated with sympathy by Siegel only when the nonconformist is a madman who has failed to control his violence and animalism) depends upon either conformity by the individual or destruction of the nonconformist.

The townspeople of *Flaming Star* are perfect examples of society's basic need for conformity, as are the residents of Santa Mira in *Invasion of the Body Snatchers.* Certainly, the townspeople in *Count the Hours,* who want Craven to be executed without benefit of an attorney, are similar to the townspeople of *Flaming Star* and *Invasion of the Body Snatchers* in their frenzied desire to get rid of the nonconformist, the person who might force upon society the realization that violence and emotional freedom are concepts worthy of existence. It is not simply that the townspeople want justice; through their actions, they call for complete and utter destruction of the offending person. That many viewers may find this attitude a true reflection of society diminishes neither the power with which Siegel presents it nor his uniform tone and concentration upon this aspect of social reaction.

Actually, however, Siegel seldom concerns himself with showing society as a whole. Even in the midst of a large city, the social encounters made by his protagonists or villains—with the basic exception of those films cited above—are superficial and clearly subservient to the encounters between the principals during the film. Three additional exceptions to Siegel's general bypassing of society are *The Hound Dog Man, Madigan,* and *Coogan's Bluff.* In *The Hound Dog Man,* the expressive, primitive mountain people are portrayed in a sympathetic manner, in keeping with Siegel's positive approach in this film, which portrays the social-psychological situation in affirmative terms. In *Madigan* and *Coogan's Bluff,* the individual representatives of society are grotesques: either they are failures in their attempts at conformity and mindlessness, as in *Coogan's Bluff* (Betty Field, Seymour Cassell, the hippies, and Tisha Sterling), or they are pathetic ineffectuals, as in *Madigan* (Harry Bellaver, Raymond St. Jacques, and Sheree North).

Against this social background of mindless, frightened conformity, Elvis Presley in *Flaming Star* chooses in favor of the Indians. When he joins them, the schizophrenic break is made, and his brother becomes his enemy, for Presley has chosen natural behavior, rejecting society. The incident that brings about Presley's choice is the murder of his mother by a crazed white survivor of an Indian massacre. Shortly afterward, Steve Forrest decides to seek vengeance when his (and Presley's) father is murdered, with little reason, by a group of Indians. The brothers—the divided sides of a personality seeking its purpose in life—must face each other when Forrest battles a band of Indians that includes Presley. Presley cannot kill his brother, his other self. He saves Forrest and, instead of being killed by society or by his brother/friend (the usual occurrence in a Siegel film), Presley—the representative, by choice, of total involvement—chooses to die at the hands of the Indians he has betrayed by saving his brother.

It is interesting to note that, at the end of the film, Presley—who has announced that he is so badly wounded that he is as good as dead—rides to the town to say goodbye to his brother. He does not enter the town, the symbol of conformity: Forrest comes out to meet him. Presley advises Forrest to stay in the town, to make the best of it, and to accept the loss of the unfettered part of their dual personality, which Presley represents. The movie, as originally written and filmed, ended with the girl and Forrest choosing to follow Presley as he goes out to die. Siegel refused to use this psychological compromise, however, or to hold out any possible interpretation of hope. He cut the film so that it ends at the moment when Presley turns to leave, implying that a bitter Forrest will remain with the whites—living in the conformist society but never coming to terms with it.

These same observations are largely true of *Stranger on the Run,* for a psychological split exists in this film also. At one end of the psychospectrum is Henry Fonda, the drunken drifter hiding in guilt for the death of his wife; trying to be emotionless, he exists as a meaningless, unhurt, and uninvolved animal. He is plunged into life again when he performs one small act engendered by emotion: the carrying of a message for a friend causes him to be implicated in the murder of a young girl. He finds himself running from this death just as he had from the death of his wife, which was not his fault.

Fonda's psychological counterpart is Michael Parks, a man who is regarded as a living legend—volatile, in control, and emotionally alive. Parks keeps his gang of semi-madmen together by the force of his personality in much the same way as did Neville Brand in *Riot in Cell Block Eleven* and John Cassavetes in *Crime in the Streets.* In *Stranger on the Run,* the desire for conformity, respectability, and a stable position with the railroad nags at Parks. When he goes after Fonda with his gang, it is to destroy an unknown being who has disturbed him. As the film progresses, the two men begin to alternate, to change and merge. Fonda gradually loses his cowardice and gains self-respect. He comes out of his guilt to find himself both capable of existence and willing to open up emotionally and find satisfaction in others. At the same time, Parks becomes less admirable and less unpredictable; he turns away from Dan Duryea, his mentor and surrogate father. The destruction of Fonda has become essential to Parks, even before their moment of schizophrenic encounter takes place, because Fonda's change reminds Parks of his own weaknesses, his own drives to compromise or lose his identity.

The father-figure, Dan Duryea, is a powerful man who represents a clear bridge between Fonda and Parks. He warns Parks that he is losing his identity and his self-respect; on another occasion, he presents himself to Fonda as a model of honor and self-assurance. When Duryea frees Fonda after the latter has been captured, he also frees the pent-up remnants of protective fear that exist within both himself and Fonda. Fonda runs again and then realizes that he can't get away from Parks: he can't escape from the suppressed part of himself. When Fonda finally confronts Parks, it is Parks who is destroyed, who realizes that he cannot kill Fonda and that his own unfettered madness cannot be controlled. Thus, it is Parks who must be destroyed, and Fonda who survives and moves affirmatively to join Anne Baxter and her son. Again, as in the *The Hanged Man,* the implication of *Stranger on the Run* is that a man can pull himself away from the pod-protected end of the psychospectrum and learn to adapt and exist—once he has faced, recognized, absorbed, and destroyed the animal part of his nature. The schizophrenic confrontation at the end of *Stranger on the Run* does not destroy the protagonist but releases him.

Two Mules for Sister Sara contains many of the same dramatic considerations as earlier Siegel Westerns, but the psychological elements are not so strongly present. The reason for the absence of psychodrama may well be that this particular film is a comedy and that Siegel never really involved himself in it—at least not as a serious statement of feeling—despite its excellence. There is no individual villain in the film; instead, the villains are the French, who remain a faceless corporate group. There is no friend for the protagonist to talk with and no father-figure to warn him. Like *The Beguiled,* which follows it, *Two Mules for Sister Sara* is an exploration of the relationship between men and women and the effect that relationship has upon the protagonist, who has somehow come to terms with life and who is betrayed by a woman. Eastwood, the protagonist in both *Two Mules* and *The Beguiled,* is neither a pod nor a madman. He is the Eastwood who has made peace with society at the end of *Coogan's Bluff.* He is not discontent with his position in life, and he seems to feel no internal struggle concerning the meaning of his existence. However, Siegel seems to be saying in these two films that even if a man somehow finds peace of mind—the psychological acceptance of existence for which he strives and toward which the protagonists of Siegel's previous four films seemed to be heading—he is still doomed. In a sense, *Two Mules* and *The Beguiled* are considerations of the possibilities of continued survival for the previously unemotional man who now is willing to enter the real world of pain and pleasure.

In *Two Mules,* Shirley MacLaine comically betrays Eastwood just as certainly as Angie Dickinson betrays John Cassavetes in *The Killers.* At the conclusion of *Two Mules,* Eastwood is rendered ridiculous; he has become the manipulated and confused pawn of the happy prostitute, in an ending that was not in the original script but that Siegel himself added. Apparently, Siegel believes that the man who commits himself and survives will eventually fall victim to his needs, particularly to his sexual-emotional desires, and that, by giving in to these needs, he will also destroy himself.

Conversely, Siegel's *The Shootist,* the final film of John Wayne, reverses the image, and J. B. Books (Wayne) destroys himself; but he does so by choice and with dignity. In the final confrontation of *The Shootist,* Books faces his mad enemies—the wild Richard Boone, the podlike Hugh O'Brien—and takes them with him. At one point, Books states his simple philosophy: "I won't be wronged. I won't be insulted. I won't be laid a hand on. I don't do these things to others, and I require the same from them." These words summarize, not only Wayne's persona, but also Siegel's idealization of human nature.

The War Films

In *China Venture,* Edmond O'Brien portrays a hard-boiled Army officer who has come to the Chinese jungles with a small group of men to take part in a dangerous mission (see also the section on the war film genre in chapter 11). He makes an attempt (as Steve McQueen does later in *Hell Is for Heroes*) to insulate himself from the war and tries not to react emotionally to the death of his men. He is faced with the personification of the two sides of his personality in Barry Sullivan, a naval officer, and in an insane Chinese warlord played by Leon Askin. Siegel's early pattern of man and his mirror image of unfettered madness, coupled with the same man's mirror-image of conformity, becomes a firmer pattern in *China Venture*. Sullivan, the conformist, is steadfast and resolute in wanting to see the mission through, although he doesn't understand its value. The mission, whatever it is, is a matter of duty and must be done; it all boils down to being an instance of conformity, of performing the proper heroic action. O'Brien finds Sullivan's determination foreign to his own nature, but he acknowledges that he, too, must take part in the mission, even though he is not fully in tune with Sullivan's concept of almost podlike acceptance of social demands. In fact, O'Brien says at one point that, unlike Sullivan, he is only a temporary officer.

At the opposite extreme from Sullivan's conformity is the warlord, a gracious, vulgar rogue who executes a lieutenant and then plays a comic drunk scene. O'Brien volunteers to stay with this man, as a hostage, while the other patrol members escape. He volunteers, in short, to sacrifice himself for his society; he feels he must join his mad ego and try to destroy that madness. In the eyes of Siegel and his film protagonists, as interesting and invigorating as are madness and its accompanying violence, it cannot be allowed to take over our world—or even our own mind. It will and must be destroyed. The other psychological extreme, complete conformity, is almost equally distastetful, because it is dull, unthinking, and unemotional—thus inhuman. O'Brien, like the other Siegel protagonists, must try to settle for what is usually an unhappy middle ground. The compromise required by existence is not a happy one for Siegel, as is evidenced by the fact that, when his protagonists have destroyed their alter ego, they do not appear to be much better off. Happy endings are almost nonexistent in Siegel films.

In *China Venture,* the dilemma is solved by compromise: Sullivan decides to stay behind as the hostage. By taking a special medicine, he can hold his liquor better than O'Brien—but not as well as the warlord. The patrol leaves and, in a Freudian confrontation, Sullivan kills the warlord. Sullivan himself dies as he talks to O'Brien on a radio. O'Brien has been freed from both extremes, which have destroyed one another. Supposedly, O'Brien will complete his mission and then continue to live his middle-ground existence, the unhappy compromise offered by society.

This psychological level of meaning is not shouted at the viewer. It is understated; and perhaps it is not even apparent to Siegel, who talks about such meaning incisively, but only obliquely. The consistency with which the psycho-spectrum appears in Siegel's films, however, and the contribution the psychological compromise makes to the understanding and appreciation of the power of a Siegel film, are undeniable; it is possible that this level of meaning lies at the core of appreciation of the personal statement Siegel presents in his films. The boundary line between fine and popular art becomes less distinct and less meaningful if the work of a popular artist, like Siegel, is understood on the same plane of metaphysical consideration as that of Ingmar Bergman.

Hell Is for Heroes is an extension of the motif of conformity and freedom, pod-ism and unfettered madness. Steve McQueen has been so numbed by the war, and is so much in opposition to all society, that he does not live beyond the world of violence. Violent action is his whole being, but his is an unthinking, mechanical violence. There is no madness and no life in his actions, only a dull stare, an agile mechanical movement, and an element of understanding. McQueen's closest counterparts in Siegel's films are Eli Wallach in *The Line-Up* and Lee Marvin in *The Killers*. Like them, McQueen in *Hell Is for Heroes* is a professional killer; but, for him, the act of killing, like the use of violence, is not an affirmative act. He strives for a total mindlessness and retreats into a dedication to killing that is completely antisocial; but, ironically, McQueen is a soldier, fighting in a war in which social destruction is rewarded. He has become almost a robot killer—a pod with a gun—but he is tortured by his inability to single-handedly destroy society.

There is no place for McQueen outside the war, for he is neither freed by his madness nor comforted by mindlessness. He tries, like O'Brien in *China Venture,* to feel nothing for the other members of his squad. But, in *Hell Is for Heroes,* as the squad members die, after becoming involved in the professional act of war with him, McQueen feels himself breaking, feels that he is somehow responsible for their deaths. His act of sacrifice at the end of the film is a form of suicide—perhaps the only possible escape for a man who is tortured by his inability to live at either end of his psycho-spectrum or to compromise by simply existing in some middle ground.

Siegel had shot an affirmative ending for the film; but, as he was editing it, he came upon a shot of McQueen destroying himself and the German bunker, followed by one of the American soldiers advancing. In his further editing, Siegel magnified the image, intensified the screams of the dead and dying, and ended the film with the war in progress—with no answer to McQueen's dilemma and with a very hell of existence present before our eyes. Siegel's comment is not upon the war alone, but upon the lack of an answer to the psychological question of existence and compromise. Again, the film has a generic context, war, and a strong thematic point of view—it is clearly an antiwar film, but its real strength lies in its presentation of McQueen's psychological dilemma.

Almost uniformly, the reviewers who analyzed the film when it first appeared were puzzled about what was troubling McQueen, why he was so bitter, so tormented and, apparently, mad. An understanding of McQueen's state of mind, and a total intellectual appreciation of the film, can come about only by studying the psychological milieu of Siegel's work as a whole.

Another thematic motif that emerges clearly in *Hell Is for Heroes* is Siegel's distrust of women, his almost post-Adam fear of the duplicity of women and of the destructive, self-serving qualities he attributes to them. In part, this feeling of distrust accounts for the weakness or lack of dimension of so many of Siegel's female characters in the films made before *Hell Is for Heroes*. The women in the early films who are most vivid are those who are the prototypes of the tempting, destructive females Siegel was to develop a few years later. Some early examples of the tempting, destructive female character are Joan Lorring (though her character is not fully developed) in *The Verdict*, Faith Domergue in *Duel at Silver Creek*, Ida Lupino in *Private Hell 36*, Dana Wynter (at the conclusion) in *Invasion of the Body Snatchers*, Adele Mara in *Count the Hours*, and Gita Hall in *The Gun Runners*.

These women are far more vividly portrayed than the more conventional women of the early Siegel films. The reason for their depth appears to be that Siegel felt that what he was doing with the destructive female character was more honest and more in keeping with his own feelings about women than were the characters of his conventional heroines, including Viveca Lindfors in both *Night unto Night* and *No Time for Flowers*, Susan Cabot in *Duel at Silver Creek*, Teresa Wright in *Count the Hours*, Dorothy Malone in *Private Hell 36*, Diana Lynn in *An Annapolis Story*, Patricia Ownes in *The Gun Runners*, Victoria Shaw in *Edge of Eternity*, Carol Lynley in *The Hound Dog Man*, and Barbara Eden in *Flaming Star;* later conventional heroines included Brenda Scott in *The Hanged Man*, Anne Baxter in *Stranger on the Run*, and Susan Clark in *Madigan* and *Coogan's Bluff.*

Siegel's most vivid female characters, by far, begin to appear in *Hell Is for Heroes* and often are portrayed as being totally evil and dangerous. Monique, the girl at the bar in *Hell Is for Heroes,* is one such female, as are Angie Dickinson in *The Killers,* Vera Miles in *The Hanged Man,* Tisha Sterling in *Coogan's Bluff,* Shirley MacLaine in *Two Mules for Sister Sara* (although the context of her character is comic), Delphine Seyrig in *The Black Windmill,* and all of the females who appear in *The Beguiled,* with the possible exception of Elizabeth Hartman. In four of his five most recent films, more affirmed and dynamic female characters have appeared, including Janet Suzman in *The Black Windmill,* Lauren Bacall in *The Shootist,* and Leslie Anne Downes in *Rough Cut,* and Bette Midler in *Jinxed* as a revitalization of the comic dominating woman portrayed by Shirley MacLaine in *Two Mules for Sister Sara.*

The relevance of this motif to the broader consideration of the psychosocial struggle is that the goal of the double-dealing woman is to use the man and then destroy him. She does this by convincing him to become interested in her, to relate to her emotionally, and to commit himself affirmatively to her and to existence. This kind of woman, in Seigel's films, is a false path to understanding and resolution.

By extension, sex answers nothing; it, and women, are a dead end—an inevitable one that cannot be resisted, but that gives the protagonist a false solution. Those protagonists who succumb to the tempting woman, and to emotional and sexual involvement with her, are destroyed. In *Duel at Silver Creek,* Stephen McNally is almost destroyed by Faith Domergue, in spite of the warnings of Audie Murphy. Steven Cochran is destroyed because of his involvement with Ida Lupino in *Private Hell 36.* Stuart Whitman is almost killed as a result of his attraction to Claude Akins's wife in *The Hound Dog Man*—an attraction she has encouraged. It is certainly John Cassavetes's being taken in by Angie Dickinson in *The Killers* that results in his destruction (and, in a sense, Lee Marvin's being taken in by her also results in his destruction). Vera Miles's attempt to use Robert Culp almost results in his death in *The Hanged Man.* Certainly, one of the reasons for Richard Widmark's demise in *Madigan* is related to his wife Inger Stevens's lack of understanding of his psychological problem and her attempts to use him as a provider and to force him to be an ambitious husband. In *Coogan's Bluff,* Tisha Sterling uses Clint Eastwood; she tempts him, abets his seduction of her, and then betrays him. Just as certainly, but in a comic vein, Shirley MacLaine betrays Eastwood in *Two Mules for Sis-*

ter Sara; and the epitome of Siegel's conception of female destruction of the male takes place in *The Beguiled.*

In *Hell Is for Heroes,* this motif is presented in a clear, conscious form. In a small French tavern, McQueen encounters the only female who appears in the film. He plays sexual word games with her and watches her make equally suggestive motions. She tells him that she hates the Germans and has never collaborated with them. He doesn't believe her, but he pretends to get taken in by her lies. He proves her duplicity when he gets her to respond naturally to a question he has asked in German. At this point he laughs, his only laugh or smile of the film. His view of women and their destructive role has been confirmed; his total pessimism has been supported. He is so protected from emotion that she cannot tempt him or use him.

The Horror Film

Invasion of the Body Snatchers is central to the work of Siegel and is the film that most clearly and overtly deals with the dichotomy of the pressures to conform and adapt that exist on one side of the psycho-spectrum, and the uncontrolled madness found on the other extreme. In *Invasion of the Body Snatchers* (as in *Private Hell 36*) the conclusion that Siegel wanted his audience to reach was that there is no answer, that all of society is doomed to struggle and to lose out to pod existence. The horror film's metaphor is perfectly conceived. Pods, the emotionless, conforming, living dead, begin to replace humans; they take over human bodies and use them. The genre theme is remarkably similar to that of Howard Hawks's *The Thing,* which preceded this film; Jean-Luc Godard's *Alphaville* and Francois Truffaut's *Fahrenheit 451,* which came after it, are clearly influenced by the Siegel film.

In *Invasion of the Body Snatchers,* Kevin McCarthy gradually realizes that the town of Santa Mira is being "taken over"—that each resident is being replaced by a duplicate. To fall asleep is to be replaced, or to die, with only the human body continuing to exist—painlessly and meaninglessly. The pod spokesman, a psychiatrist (Larry Gates), powerfully presents their case. Living, he says, is painful. Being a pod is painless—easy and, above all, inevitable. Once a person accepts being a pod, he is content. He looks no different from his nonpod neighbors, but his pain is gone.

Siegel plays upon the idea of the difference between people who have become pods and people who are not pods. The viewer can't tell the difference simply by looking at them, but the pods have no extremes of behavior, no mad side, only a totally conforming side. Clearly, this is how Siegel views the mass of humanity. Becoming a pod or going mad is inevitable for all of us. Life is so structured that we all give in wearily to the solace of total acceptance, to a lack of imagination. The characters in *Alphaville* or *Fahrenheit 451* are pods who exist without need for explanation by a semiplausible science-fiction genre. *Invasion*'s Kevin McCarthy struggles to remain awake, however, to preserve his individuality, his pain, and his imperfect independence.

The pods never use violence. They need only wait, for society will always win. Violence in *Invasion* and in other Siegel films is reserved for the nonconformists, those who are mad or violently alive.

McCarthy knows he must leave the valley that enclosed Santa Mira and escape from the pod world that is certain to absorb him. (The name Santa Mira means ''Saint See''—a combination of religious-metaphysical symbol and earthly warning.) He escapes only to find that the pods are beyond his valley—that there is no escape. He also finds that there is no warning one can give to others because the takeover is inevitable. Siegel explained to the author of this book that he wanted the last shot of the film to be the one in which McCarthy turns to the camera and shouts, ''You're next.'' Although Siegel had to add an epilogue to the film, in which it appears that it may be possible to combat pods after all, Siegel's original ending is clearly a totally pessimistic one. The film is an artistic metaphor of the human condition as it is seen by Siegel.

Almost twenty years and eighteen feature films later, as he told the author, Siegel continues to think of *Invasion of the Body Snatchers* as the film that best expresses his world view. His choice is not surprising, considering the nature of the horror film genre's thematic concern with mortality. Siegel continues to talk of the world in terms of pod behavior and humanity's losing battle against being absorbed by emotionless, soothing conformity. The mindlessness of this emotionless conformity also is central to the horror genre. When McCarthy tries to destroy the pods in the conventional ways that horror films use to bring about the destruction of monsters—burning, a stake through the heart—and fails, the viewer has gone beyond the affirmative destruction of horror (which is so cathartic in conventional horror films) and has emerged with a new horror.

Readings on Donald Siegel

Books

Hutchinson, Dave. *Don Siegel.* L.S.F.T. Society, London, March 1968.

Kaminsky, Stuart M. *Don Siegel: Director.* New York: Curtis Books, 1974.

Lovell, Alan. *Don Siegel.* London: The Education Department of the British Film Institute, 1968.

Periodicals

Bogdanovich, Peter. ''Working within the System: Interview with Donald Siegel.'' *Movie,* Number 15, Spring 1968, pp. 1–17.

Eichelbaum, Stanley. ''Rooftop Drama in North Beach.'' [On the making of *Dirty Harry*] *San Francisco Examiner and Chronicle,* May 9, 1971.

''Interview with Don Siegel.'' *London Times,* March 8, 1968.

Maltin, Leonard. ''Conversation with Donald Siegel.'' *Action,* Directors Guild of America, July-August 1971.

Siegel, Donald. ''The Anti-Heroes.'' *Films and Filming* 15, no. 4, January 1969.

Table 11.1
Donald Siegel Films

Title	Year	Principal Actors
An Annapolis Story (Britain: *The Blue and the Gold*)	1955	John Derek
Baby Face Nelson	1957	Mickey Rooney, Carolyn Jones
The Beguiled	1971	Clint Eastwood, Geraldine Page
The Big Steal	1949	Robert Mitchum, Jane Greer
The Black Windmill	1974	Michael Caine, Janet Suzman
Charley Varrick	1973	Walter Matthau, Felicia Farr
China Venture	1954	Edmond O'Brien, Barry Sullivan
Coogan's Bluff	1968	Clint Eastwood, Susan Clarke
Count the Hours (Britain: *Every Minute Counts*)	1953	MacDonald Carey, Teresa Wright
Crime in the Streets	1956	John Cassavetes, Mark Rydel

Table 11.1 *(Continued)*
Donald Siegel Films

Title	Year	Principal Actors
Dirty Harry	1971	Clint Eastwood, Andy Robinson
Duel at Silver Creek	1952	Stephen McNally
Edge of Eternity	1959	Cornel Wilde
Escape from Alcatraz	1978	Clint Eastwood, Patrick McGoohan
Flaming Star	1960	Elvis Presley, Steve Forrest
The Gun Runners	1958	Audie Murphy, Eddie Albert
The Hanged Man	1964	Robert Culp, Vera Miles
Hell Is for Heroes	1962	Steve McQueen, Fess Parker
Hitler Lives	1945	(Documentary)
The Hound Dog Man	1959	Stuart Whitman, Fabian
Invasion of the Body Snatchers	1956	Kevin McCarthy, Dana Wynter
Jinxed	1982	Bette Midler, Rip Torn
The Killers	1964	Lee Marvin, Ronald Reagan
The Line-Up	1958	Tom Tully, Eli Wallach
Madigan	1968	Richard Widmark, Henry Fonda
Night unto Night	1948	Ronald Reagan, Viveca Lindfors
No Time for Flowers	1952	Viveca Lindfors
Private Hell 36	1955	Steve Cochran, Ida Lupino
Riot in Cell Block Eleven	1954	Neville Brand, Leo Gordon
Rough Cut	1976	Burt Reynolds, Leslie Ann Downs
The Shootist	1975	John Wayne, Lauren Bacall
Spanish Affair	1957	Richard Kiley
Star in the Night	1945	Donald Woods
Stranger on the Run	1967	Henry Fonda, Michael Parks
Two Mules for Sister Sara	1969	Clint Eastwood, Shirley Maclaine
The Verdict	1946	Sidney Greenstreet, Peter Lorre

12
THE GENRE DIRECTOR
Character Types in the Films of John Ford

Enduring popular literature is based on universal character types: personae who reflect both a basic meaning for their own time and one that is universal. The inability of some critics to recognize the late John Ford's handling of type in this manner, and their confusing it with stereotyping, has—in part—kept much of Ford's best work, his Westerns, from being appreciated. Robert Ardrey (writing in *The Reporter*) indicated that Ford was once regarded as a serious director but that, partly as a result of his resorting to types (but principally for turning to the Western), he had lost his merit as an object of serious attention. "And the same John Ford who once gave adults *The Informer*," writes Ardrey, "must now give children *The Searchers*." It seems almost perverse to me that one could fail to see the merit of *The Searchers,* but such perversity exists and manifests itself in critical terminology such as "stereotype," "cliché," "trite," and "truism." In the case of Ford's films, in general, and his use of type, in particular, such critical responses are signs of the critic's intellectual prejudice and an inability to recognize archetypal patterns and quintessential characters.

The works of Geoffrey Chaucer, William Shakespeare, Mark Twain, Charles Dickens, Henrik Ibsen, Anton Chekhov, and Vladimir Nabokov are based upon character types just as surely as are the films of Sergei Eisenstein and V. Pudovkin; but all of these creators have the distinct advantage of being removed in time, culture, or genre—or all three—which gives the types with which they work a protective distance. Familiarity with the myth of Abraham Lincoln tends to alienate American audiences from Ford's *Young Mr. Lincoln,* precisely because Ford has shown so well in his film what we think about the myth of Lincoln.

The artist, if he is to achieve a universality that keeps his work meaningful beyond a few years, either consciously or unconsciously must recognize the existence of universal characters, situations, reactions, and artifacts. It then becomes the task of the artist to give meaning to these universal elements within the context of his or her own time and the genre being used. Whatever life and vitality Chaucer's or Chekhov's characters display is heavily dependent upon our recognition of the type through a familiarity based upon our own reading, listening, or personal contact. Literature and life are as full of distilled and undistilled Ringo Kids, Jeeter Lesters, Old Man Clantons, Owen Thursdays, Ethan Edwards, Frank Skeffingtons, Marty Purcells, and D. R. Cartwrights as they are of Poloniuses, Falstaffs, Lady Macbeths, Hedda Gablers, Pnins, and Tom Sawyers.

Such well-known examples transcend the supposed limitations of character type. But even if a type portrayal adds no new dimensions, its reinforcement of genre in popular works is worth attention. Those who are concerned about aesthetic extensions would insist, I am sure, that the true artist must give new dimension to each type. This statement is often taken to mean that radical deviation from expectation is essential to artistry—an assumption that often leads to confusion between the concepts of performance and acting. Ford's characters give added dimension to character type without great deviation from generic expectation. Ford demands acting, not performance. One might even argue that, in a narrative, especially film—which is limited to dramatized action—a character type that deviates too greatly from the viewer's expectations and understanding stands the risk of losing the audience's interest by being unrecognizable. Directors who wish to emphasize the degree to which they are deviating from type will often go to stylized performers, people who do not merge their own personality with that of the character but instead use the character to build a performance. Such actors as Marlon Brando, George C. Scott, Rod Steiger, and Laurence Olivier, for example, are performers; and it is difficult for a member of an audience to see his or her own character as merging with that of the role these men are portraying. Generally, the response, ''Wasn't that

Olivier marvelous?'' is a condemnation of the film, for it means that the viewer has concentrated less on the story than on the performer and his deviation from type and character expectation.

In a Ford film, however, there is a tacit assumption that the individual actor is reflecting an essential part of himself in the film role, that he is the type of character that he portrays. In actual fact, as far as Ford's principal characters are concerned, the character can have radical differences from the actor; but Ford is always careful to play upon the viewer's basic expectations of an actor and type from previous works and general assumption. The difference between Henry Fonda's Lincoln and his character as Colonel Thursday is great, but connecting threads exist between these apparently different characters. This is also true, for example, of the characters John Wayne has played in such films as *Stagecoach, The Long Voyage Home, She Wore a Yellow Ribbon,* and *The Searchers.*

As a related aside, I would contend, however, that any work that seeks to depict a character type or types merits attention. Even an exact copy—as exact as exact can be—is not necessarily, by definition, the same as stereotyping; it may well be an example of homage, or allusion, or even creation (as Andy Warhol has demonstrated and Jorge L. Borges has considered). The weakest Italian ''spaghetti'' Western, to the degree that it recognizes its genre (by making use of types and playing upon our expectations concerning them), can have reinforcing value or critical meaning. Whether the viewer likes the work or not carries us into the realm of taste instead of description. One man's stereotype may be another man's archetype—which leads us back to John Ford.

One major basis of Ford's status as a director in general and a director of Westerns in particular is his mastery of character type. Ford works on our expectations and expands our understanding of basic American folk characters, such as the silent hero, the hard-drinking but essentially romantic professional, the whore with the heart of gold, the lovable and loyal giant, the lovable and somewhat pathetic old retainer, the righteous father, the savage idiot, the meek who shall inherit the earth, and the paternal villain. It is not so much that Ford has created new characters and types, but that he has portrayed, as Alexander Pope once wrote, ''what oft was thought but ne'er so well-expressed.''

Ford's types derive from two dominant, related referents of great importance to the director. All of the types exist in frontier literature, from James Fenimore Cooper to dime novels to Bronco Billy Anderson, Tom

Mix, and William S. Hart. In addition, Ford's characters have distinct echoes of the Bible, as do his films. A familiarity with the Bible's book of Exodus is as important to the viewer's understanding of Ford's films and characters as is a knowledge of the Western genre. For Ford, popular culture and the Bible are a rich heritage from which to draw.

Other points to bear in mind when considering character and type in Ford films is that the same types run through all the films—changing, evolving, often being played by the same actor but with a different name. Four character actors who portrayed the same basic type (under a variety of names) were J. Farrell MacDonald, Jack Pennick, John Carradine, and Alan Mowbray. It is essential to remember that Ford's character types are always revealed, not only by their dialogue—which often, in the hands of another director, would just be a hollow reminder of past movie dialogue—but by the location in which the character is found, how he states his lines, who we see reacting to him, and how the scenes in which he appears are filmed. All of these elements contribute to a Ford type: his dialogue often is minimal and sometimes is not as essential as his image.

For example, reading the *Stagecoach* screenplay is interesting because it is a valuable and literate Ford/Dudley Nichols script that clearly shows the writers' knowledge of the Western genre. The script is peopled totally by types or, as John Cawelti and others have pointed out, archetypes. Without Thomas Mitchell's face and movement, however, and without the pained visual reaction of Donald Meek to Mitchell, the two types these men play would lack aesthetic meaning. Doctors—the film variety, anyway—have called for lots of hot water until the cry has become a cliché. Ford reuses the phrase himself in his later film *Drums along the Mohawk*. It is the viewer's knowledge of who and what Mitchell is in *Stagecoach*, where the action is taking place, and whose baby he is to deliver that leads us, with Ford, into seeing Mitchell's character grow in confidence, respect, and (as a result of a change in camera angle) size. A discussion of the evaluation of character types, and how they are used by Ford, thus breaks down into a question of dialogue, actor, camera, and cutting—all of which are central to an understanding of Ford's work.

In one sense, Ford's films display universal aspects of allegory not greatly removed from *Pilgrim's Progress, Peer Gynt,* or *Everyman.* It is a tribute to Ford's skill as a director that we seldom see the films in this light until after we have viewed and considered them. As Henry

Fonda has said of Ford's films in an interview with the author, "You don't see the wheels work." Compare this understated allegory with, for example, the obvious allegorical implications of Ingmar Bergman, whose work cannot be viewed without understanding that he is working on a consciously intellectual level. Like the director who uses conscious allegory, Ford uses the film genre of the Western to bring his types into contact, conflict, and crisis—to test them and the viewer. It is essential to an understanding of how Ford deals with types to deal briefly with the situation in which the types come together—the generic background of the film.

Ford films, particularly the Westerns, can be seen as religious, mythic quests: they are journeys from east to west, going from civilization to wilderness; but essentially they picture the mythic quest of the West that was indicated by Henry Nash Smith in *The Virgin Land* and Lewis Mumford in his essay "The Romanticism of the Pioneer." The Ford hero is in search of something—some basic mythic grail, a garden paradise, or revenge. The biblical connotations of exodus and vengeance influence the character types we encounter in the film, and that which they say and do, while the icons of the wilderness and the movie's music remind us of American historical traditions. The songs of sentiments and joy and religion sustain the characters during their journey— a journey through history.

The characters in a Ford Western are involved in the myth of carving greatness from a hostile wilderness. This is the great American dream of the frontier and also the great American nightmare, for it is peopled with savages, starvation, murderers, and bigots. Always present behind them is the outdoors, the West—often Monument Valley—a barren, compelling vision of nature. Ford's people look small against their background of the mountains. This image is particularly striking in all the films shot in Monument Valley, from *Stagecoach* on. Men and the artifacts of civilization are vulnerable, weak, in the face of nature or human savagery. However, the characters are sustained by the rituals of courtship and dance and by a pragmatic religion. In *Wagonmaster,* a character even compares the mountains to a cathedral, and in *Three Godfathers,* we see a Western wilderness parable of the Three Wise Men and the Infant Jesus.

Seldom does the audience see the Ford characters succeed in their quest. We generally leave them before they achieve their success, although we know they have been strengthened by their trials by nature

John Wayne in *The Searchers*.

Jane Darwell and Henry Fonda in *The Grapes of Wrath*.

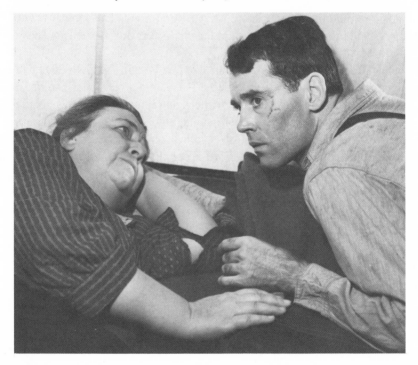

and God. Ultimately, the essence of Ford's films is the testing of his universal types (tempered by American popular tradition) against the legends of history.

At the heart of Ford's films, especially his Westerns, is the dominant American character type, the hero. Ford primarily used four actors to reflect basic character types who exemplify heroic response: Harry Carey, John Wayne, Henry Fonda, and Jimmy Stewart. Other Ford Westerns have featured different actors who represent variations of his original heroes; but Carey, Wayne, Fonda, and Stewart still can be seen as the four aspects of American character type that Ford prefers to present. In all four cases, Ford plays upon the particular skills and personality of the actor.

In Carey's films for Ford, the actor plays a man who is slow to anger, protective toward the weak, fearless, and bemused by human folly. Frequently, he is either entertained by life or perplexed by it; he often pauses to watch some foible of humanity, then scratches his head and displays an amused smile. Carey's face, his calmness and equilibrium, are reassuring and traditionally paternal. Will Rogers, in Ford's *Steamboat Round the Bend,* and *Judge Priest,* is an extension of the Carey character.

In the first two Ford films in which John Wayne starred, the actor was cast as a silent, determined, youthful, shy hero (*Stagecoach; The Long Voyage Home*). Later, in *They Were Expendable,* Wayne's youthful shyness begins to give way to Wayne as the hot, explosive—but paternal—figure. Thus, it is possible to look upon a film like *Wagonmaster*—which was made between the two Kirby Yorke films (*Fort Apache* and *Rio Grande*) and in which Wayne's mature type first emerged—as a schizophrenia of character type. In *Wagonmaster,* the younger Wayne-type character is played by Ben Johnson and the older Wayne-type character by Ward Bond. Clearly, for Ford, Wayne represents the best of American idealism; yet, Wayne's character is tempered and sorely tried by disillusion as he ages, as shown in *The Horse Soldiers* and *The Searchers.* Still, Ford's Wayne is determined to persevere, for he is convinced that something is worth saving.

On the other hand, Ford's Henry Fonda, from the days of *Young Mr. Lincoln, Drums along the Mohawk,* and *The Grapes of Wrath,* is an idealist; he is silent, confident, and seldom falters in his determination. When Ford chooses to question the dangers inherent in American confidence in rigid ideals (in *Fort Apache*), Fonda's idealism and determination—which reached a zenith in *My Darling Clementine* and faltered in *The Fugitive*—turn into inflexibility and fatal stubbornness.

At another corner of Ford's heroic picture is James Stewart. Although he played a Fonda-like role in *The Man Who Shot Liberty Valance,* he also portrayed a man of seedy, totally hedonistic weariness and near-comic paranoia in *Two Rode Together* and then parodied Fonda's portrayal of Wyatt Earp by turning the character into a hedonistic, ineffectual, comic grotesque in *Cheyenne Autumn.*

In a Ford film, Fonda seldom is moved to even minor displays of anger or emotion; Wayne is moved to anger and emotion in the face of attack on or violation of such basic American ideals and principles as love of mother or friends, patriotism, and loyalty; and Stewart is moved to anger, even in *Liberty Valance,* when people are not pragmatic. For Wayne, action and killing are matters of traditional American principle; for Stewart, action and killing are matters of pragmatism—you don't kill unless the killing will be of value to you. Thus, Ford does not present a single, inflexibly defined heroic type; he varies his heroic character type because he realizes that different actors have strengths and associations that can be called upon to reflect the attitude of the filmmaker.

Just as the heroic type varies, so too does the romantic object of the hero's affections. In Ford films, there are actually only two kinds of romantic women: the whore with a heart of gold and the virginal madonna. The whores, the tough yet gentle women, are often urban in origin, tainted by the corruption of the city (their names even reflect the city background: Denver, Dallas, Chihuahua). But once in the wilderness, and given the opportunity to gain both personal idealism and the love of a man with ideals and affirmative goals, the woman takes on a clear identification with the reformed Mary Magdalene (Claire Trevor in *Stagecoach,* Linda Darnell in *My Darling Clementine,* Joanne Dru in *Wagonmaster,* even Ava Gardner in *Mogambo*).

For Ford, although a public loss of innocence, of virginity, may diminish a woman in the eyes of society (even when, as in the case of Linda Cristal in *Two Rode Together,* that loss is caused by rape), it is the character's own self-esteem that really matters. In a Ford film, the tough yet gentle woman remains visually pure.

Also at the heart of Ford's films during the journey through the wilderness is a drinking, disillusioned professional: a doctor (Thomas

Mitchell in *Stagecoach;* Chill Wills in *Rio Grande;* William Powell in *Mister Roberts*); an actor (Alan Mowbray in *My Darling Clementine* and *Wagonmaster*); or a newspaper editor (Edmond O'Brien in *The Man Who Shot Liberty Valance*). This character has participated fully in the conventions of society—he can quote from Shakespeare or the Bible—but has rejected society, and America, out of cynicism (although he still clings vaguely to the hope that, although the journey through life has been too much for *him,* others will have the strength to see it through). He is a paternal type, who reflects a weak but enlightened old guard.

Another major Ford type—one with biblical implications—is the sacrificing friend, who can be found at the side of the protagonist and who recognizes in the hero a superior value worth saving and sacrificing oneself for. The idea of sacrifice (with its connotations of death for country and ideals) is embodied in such Ford sidekick characters as Victor Mature in *My Darling Clementine* and John Wayne in *The Man Who Shot Liberty Valance*; total dedication and subordination to the protagonist can be seen in the child-father figure of Victor McLaglen in *Fort Apache* and *Rio Grande,* Ed Brophy in *The Last Hurrah,* and J. Farrell MacDonald in Ford's last silent Western, *Three Bad Men.*

Surrounding these central characters are a bevy of Ford character actors who represent distinct visual icons and type responses: the Irish old-timer and confidant, J. Farrell MacDonald (*Submarine Patrol; My Darling Clementine*); the strong, silent giant, Jack Pennick (*Prisoner of Shark Island; Submarine Patrol; Stagecoach; The Long Voyage Home; They Were Expendable;* the calvary trilogy of films; *The Sun Shines Bright;* and other films); the lovable, slightly pathetic, not-too-bright old retainer, Francis Ford (*My Darling Clementine; Steamboat Round the Bend;* and *Wagonmaster*) or Charley Grapewin (*Judge Priest*). Ford also presents a series of sage idiots, clowns who would have felt at home with the madness of King Lear; the most notable examples of this type are John Qualen (*The Grapes of Wrath*), Hank Worden (*The Searchers*), and Jane Darwell (*Wagonmaster*).

Extensions of Ford's biblical character types are the meek who shall inherit the earth. The most striking examples are Donald Meek, who portrays, ironically enough, a whiskey drummer with five children (*Stagecoach*) and John Qualen (*The Searchers*).

Ford's villains also have biblical echoes in their characters. The paternal villains, including Charles Kemper (*Wagonmaster*), Ford Rainey (*Two Rode Together*), Walter Brennan (*My Darling Clementine*), and Tom Tyler (*Stagecoach*) and their families of grotesques are mock reflections of the more stable, affirmative families who appear in Ford's films. Invariably, the paternal villain who is willing to violate the will of God loses his family and dies, screaming or mad, much like Lear.

Nonwhites have always been a political and ideological problem for Ford. The Indian character type in Ford's films gradually moves from a portrayal as an unsympathetic savage to that of a highly respected superior being. It must again be recognized, however, that Ford does not see the reality of his Indian characters beyond their types. That Ford types most nonwhites into two camps (in much the way D. W. Griffith does) can be seen in his use of actor Woody Strode. Strode, a black, has played an Indian in *Two Rode Together,* a Chinese (actually, an extension of the savage Indian) in *Seven Women,* and a black servant in *The Man Who Shot Liberty Valance.* In *Sergeant Rutledge,* a much more sympathetic film than most critics have given it credit for being, Strode played a variation of the black servant: he was a steadfastly loyal cavalry sergeant. In all these films, the minority character played by Strode has been depicted either as a powerful, proud savage or as a docile servant. The affirmation of the character derives almost totally from the degree of loyalty he can demonstrate toward the film's hero. A loyal nonwhite—one who is loyal to the hero, or the United States, or his tribe—is affirmed. Seldom is a prominent nonwhite type shown to be disloyal (although it might be argued that Stone Calf, who is portrayed by Strode in *Two Rode Together,* dies because he fails to obey his chief) as long as he displays a sympathetic feeling for nonsavage society. In general, in the films before *The Searchers* (1956), the nonwhite aboriginal was used by Ford as a savage tool of divine testing of the white man; in a group, these nonwhites are a faceless mass of terror, be they (actually Caucasian) Arabs (as in *The Last Patrol*) or Indians.

These have been some rather tentative, and somewhat random, observations of character type in the work of John Ford. They are not qualitative judgments, for they only indicate the direction and progression that can be observed in Ford's work. Looking at Ford's total body of work, in terms of his manipulation of variety of generic elements—of which type is but one—helps the viewer better to understand the stature of John Ford as a genre artist.

Readings on John Ford

Books

Baxter, John. *The Cinema of John Ford.* New York: A. S. Barnes, 1971.

Bogdanovich, Peter. *John Ford.* Berkeley and Los Angeles: University of California Press, 1968.

Burrows, Michael. *John Ford and Andrew V. McLaglen.* Cromwell, England: Primestyle, 1970.

McBride, Joseph, and Michael Wilmington. *John Ford.* New York: DaCapo, 1975.

Place, J. A. *The Western Films of John Ford.* Secaucus, New Jersey: Citadel, 1974.

Sarris, Andrew. *The John Ford Movie Mystery.* Bloomington: Indiana University Press. 1977.

Sinclair, Andrew. *John Ford.* New York: Dial Press, 1978.

Stavig, Mark. *John Ford and the Traditional Moral Order.* Madison: University of Wisconsin Press, 1968.

Wootten, William Patrick. *An Index to the Films of John Ford.* London: British Film Institute, 1948.

13
THE GENRE DIRECTOR
The Grotesque West of Sergio Leone

The West of John Ford or Howard Hawks is, for Sergio Leone, an arena in which to explore his own sad, comic, grotesque, and surreal vision of life. Leone is no more interested in what could or did happen in the West than he is in any conception of surface reality in his films. Leone's Westerns—*Fistful of Dollars* (1966); *For a Few Dollars More* (1967); *The Good, the Bad, and the Ugly* (1968); *Once upon a Time in the West* (1969); and *Duck, You Sucker!* (1972)—are comic nightmares about existence.

Basic Themes in Leone's World

The feeling of unreality is central to Leone's work (for a discussion of Leone's gangster film, *Once upon a Time in America,* see chapter 3). His is a world of magic and horror. Religion is not only meaningless; it is false, a sham that hides honest emotions. Civilization is inevitable, pervasive, an extension of the human need to dominate and survive by living off others. The Leone world is essentially womanless. It is not just that women are ill-treated or handled indifferently; they hardly exist at all (Claudia Cardinale is a striking exception in *Once upon a Time in the West.*)

Leone's world is set up for an interplay of male style in the face of world horror. In this, he is very like Howard Hawks. In Leone's world, as in Hawks's, death erases a man. A man who dies is a loser. The measure of a man is his ability to survive, to laugh at death. This is not a bitter point in Leone films; there are few lingering deaths and very little blood. Even the death of Ramon (Gian Maria Volonte) in *Fistful of Dollars* takes place rather quickly and with far less blood than the comparable death in *Yojimbo*. A man's death is less important than how he faces it.

The only thing worth preserving in Leone's world is the family—and his world is such a terrible place that few families survive. In *Fistful of Dollars*, Clint Eastwood's primary emotional reaction is to the attempt to destroy the family of the woman Ramon has taken. In later films (*The Good, the Bad, and the Ugly*; and *Once upon a Time in the West*), the only family life we see that is affirmed as "a good thing" is destroyed early by the evil character. As wild as Rod Steiger's family is in *Duck, You Sucker!*, it is the closest thing there is in the film to any genuine feeling—and it is destroyed.

Leone's Characters

In each of Leone's Westerns, there appears a character who can, somewhat ironically, be described as the "good guy" (Eastwood in the first three films; Charles Bronson in *Once upon a Time in the West*; James Coburn in *Duck, You Sucker!*). There is also a "bad guy" (Volonte in the *Dollars* films; Lee Van Cleef in *The Good, the Bad, and the Ugly*; Henry Fonda in *Once upon a Time in the West*). The assignment of this role to any character in *Duck, You Sucker!* is less easy, because Leone's work shows an evolution toward a more complex idea of the world of good and evil. But even in *Duck, You Sucker!*, the evil role can be given to Gunther, the egg-sucking young German-Mexican colonel who murders peasants and eventually kills Coburn.

The final primary character in the films is "the ugly." This role appears in neither of the *Dollars* films, which are less complex than the later films, although the embryo idea does exist in the character played by Van Cleef in *For a Few Dollars More*. The "ugly" character appears as Eli Wallach in *The Good, the Bad, and the Ugly*, Jason Robards in *Once upon a Time in the West*, and Rod Steiger in *Duck, You Sucker!*

The "good guy" for Leone is consciously aware of the kind of world in which he finds himself. He is amused (and Eastwood shows this most clearly) and aloof from the grotesque world, the human manifestations of which he destroys like flies even though he knows it is to no effect— the world spawns evil far beyond his capacity to destroy it. Although the "good guy" seeks material satisfaction, money, he seems to have nothing particular he wants to do with it. He is more interested in living according to a certain style, showing others that he knows how to live, how to face danger without fear, and, if necessary, how to die. In this sense, he becomes an almost mystic survivor, a new Christ offering a way to face life. Eastwood's appearance out of the smoke and his survival of Ramon's shooting is staged as a mystic experience to unsettle the killer. In *Duck, You Sucker!*, Coburn's first appearance out of the smoke of his explosions is seen by Steiger as a semimystical omen, a hopeful sign that he equates with religious experience.

The importance of style and the amused detachment from death can be seen in Eastwood's telling the coffin maker to get three coffins ready in *Fistful of Dollars,* only to have to apologize later when he shoots four men. In *Duck, You Sucker!,* Steiger rants angrily as he and Coburn wait to face the Mexican regiment alone. Coburn appears to be sleeping. We see below his hat that he is intentionally giving this impression, that he is amused by Steiger's annoyance. The indifferent quest of the "good guy" for material wealth is also strikingly seen against his lack of interest in sex, a disinterest that ties in with his ascetic style, his distance from ordinary men. In none of the Leone films—except for the flashback sequence in *Duck, You Sucker!*—does a Leone "good guy" show anything but minimal interest in women. The only thing that seems to move the "good guy" to emotion is a threat to a family. Even Bronson's hatred of Fonda stems from the murder of Bronson's family *by* Fonda.

The "bad guy" in Leone's films is, in many ways, similar to the "good guy." Neither is defined in his goodness or badness by traditional morality. Certainly, Eastwood's illegal activities in *The Good, the Bad, and the Ugly* and *For a Few Dollars More* make his goodness definable in terms of some kind of morality above moral law. His is an Old Testament morality of veneration of family, vengeance, and personal style. The "bad guy" in Leone films appears to have all the skills and style of the "good guy," but he is totally immoral, willing to serve anyone for money and to do anything for it—but he must retain his dignity while doing so. He is willing to destroy anyone, good or evil, who stands in his way. He lives only by his word, not lightly given; but, once his word is given, he will destroy anyone—men, women, and children, i.e., even the family—to fulfill it. The gratification of needs of the "bad guy" is cold; even his sexual responses are clinical—acts of corruption rather than fulfillment of desire. Fonda's sadistic rape-seduction of

Above and below: Eli Wallach and Clint Eastwood in *The Good, The Bad, and The Ugly.*

Claudia Cardinale in *Once upon a Time in the West* is a prime example. The ''bad guy'' is, ultimately, able to achieve satisfaction only in living out his accepted role.

Often the ''bad guy'' sees in the ''good guy'' another character who lives by a code of style. Again, this is much like Hawks. The roles of John Wayne and Christopher George in *El Dorado* indicate this kind of respect. The ''good guys'' and ''bad guys'' in a Leone film respect each other, see the possibilities in each other of alternate existence, and recognize early that their styles demand that they eventually shoot it out in a morality combat.

The ''ugly'' character is hyperhuman; he can show great affection and great hatred and violence. He has no cunning, is open and direct, and shows an earthy simplicity and sense of humor. In one sense, he is a threat to both of the other primary characters, for he needs no style with which to define himself. When he lusts for gold or women, he sees in them the fulfillment of drives and the chance for enjoyment. He is unpredictable, a liar who eats with verve and gusto and complicates the simplicity of life as seen by the ''good'' and the ''bad.'' We react with amusement and affection to Wallach, Robards, and Steiger, although they are shown to be murderers. The murders they commit are all matters of survival or angry emotions, without calculation; and this is seen by Leone as sympathetic. In all three films in which this character appears, the emotional distance of the ''good guy'' is penetrated by the honest earthiness of the ''ugly.'' In *The Good, the Bad, and the Ugly,* Eastwood humiliates but spares Wallach and leaves him part of the money. In *Once upon a Time in the West,* Bronson clearly grows to respect Robards and honors his final wish of a solitary, dignified death. In *Duck, You Sucker!,* Coburn's façade is broken by his growing affection for Steiger, which eventually destroys Coburn's confidence in his own simple approach to good and evil.

Leone's Visual World

Visually, Leone has some marked obsessions that contribute to his thematic interests. Many directors could work with and develop the same themes and characters, but Leone's forte lies in the development of these themes and characters in a brilliant and personal visual world.

No director, with the possible exception of Sam Fuller, makes as extensive use of the close-up as does Leone; and Leone's close-ups are often extreme, only a portion of a face, usually the eyes of one of the three main characters. It is the eyes of these men that reveal what they are feeling if they are feeling anything; such characters almost never define their actions in words. Henry Fonda appeared for his first day of shooting in *Once upon a Time in the West* wearing brown contact lenses to harden his image. Leone, who had gone to great lengths to get Fonda for the film, insisted that the lenses be taken out. "He had bought my blue eyes for that first close-up after I kill the family," Fonda told me.

The extreme close-up is a major device of Leone's for getting to his primary concern: character. Plot is of minimal interest to Leone. What is important is examination of the characters, watching how they react, what makes them tick. It appears almost as if everything is, indeed, happening randomly, as if we are watching with curiosity the responses of different types of people, trying to find a meaning in the slightest flick of an eyelid. The visual impact of water dripping on Woody Strode's hat or of Jack Elam's annoyed reaction to a fly is of greater importance to Leone than the gunfight for which the two appear in *Once upon a Time in the West*. Both Elam and Leone told me that the fly appeared by chance while the scene was being shot and that Leone liked it so much he insisted upon shooting all of Elam's reactions to it, mainly in close-ups.

In addition to using extreme close-ups to define character responses, Leone uses them for irony, most notably in the close-ups of the stage-coach passengers in *Duck, You Sucker!* These aristocrats are seen with food crumbs on their lips to emphasize their proximity to the kind of animal behavior they ridicule.

The use of the pan in Leone's films is also remarkable. The pan in *Duck, You Sucker!* from the firing squad past the church and to behind the poster of the governor, where Steiger watches in bewilderment through the poster's eyes, is a prime example. The shot ties the execution to the indifferent church and to the nonseeing poster and then to the responsive Steiger in one movement. The dizzying pan that follows Wallach around the graves in *The Good, the Bad, and the Ugly* is another example of such a movement for thematic purpose—in this case, to show the frenzy of Wallach in the midst of massive death.

At some point in each Leone film, the screen reveals the grotesqueness of battle, the dreamlike horror of multiple death. Visually, his handling of large crowds is as good as anything in De Mille or Lean. The battlefield scene at the river in *The Good, the Bad, and the Ugly* is vast, complex, and compelling. Interestingly, many of Leone's massive scenes of death are at border rivers whose waters offer no distance or separation for protection. The massacre of the Mexican soldiers in both *Fistful of Dollars* and *Duck, You Sucker!* are other examples.

Generally in his films, the destruction of hundreds seen on the screen is more nightmarishly appalling than in more conscious antiwar statements in too many films. For Leone, this destruction within his myth is an extension of the meaningless destruction of life by man. *The Good, the Bad, and the Ugly* is played against the destruction of the Civil War—a scourge that Eastwood, Van Cleef, and Wallach either ignore or make use of. The North and the South are indistinguishable. In one sequence, in fact, Wallach and Eastwood mistake a dust-covered column of Northern cavalry for the grey-uniformed Southerners.

The apparent joy and even comedy of mass destruction and battle in Leone films are often followed immediately by something intimate in horror, some personal touch that underlies the real meaning of the horror that, moments before, had been amusing. In *The Good, the Bad, and the Ugly,* Eastwood encounters the dying young soldier after the river sequence. In *Duck, You Sucker!* the battle at the bridge is immediately followed by the sight of the dead revolutionaries and Steiger's family in the dark cave. The comedy and zest of the battle are immediately undercut visually in both aftermath scenes. There is little dialogue. The vision of youthful dead dominates.

Visually, Leone shows towns isolated in a vast wilderness with great space between them. When people in conflict appear together in a room, they, too, are often separated by relatively great distances. The rooms and interiors themselves are generally grotesquely large. The inside of the stagecoach in *Duck, You Sucker!* looks like a small, plush dining salon. The huge saloon in which enemies Fonda and Bronson meet in *Once upon a Time in the West* is opposed to the closeness in the earlier saloon scene in which potential friends Bronson and Robards meet.

At the same time, Leone's fascination with the spontaneity of living, his zeal for existence in the midst of his morality films, can be seen in his handling of details. For example, food in his films is always colorful and appetizing, and people eat it ravenously. Food is tangible, real, and good. Wallach's gusto in eating the several bowls of food given to him by Van Cleef in prison is animal and honest. It makes the beating he suffers moments later all the more vivid and disturbing.

Another recurrent Leone image is the circle of the final shootout. The shootout is often held in a literal circle, a miniature arena into which a man finally steps and defines himself without an audience. In *For a Few*

Dollars More and *The Good, the Bad, and the Ugly,* the shootout involves all three of Leone's principal characters. In all these cases, when the "bad" one enters the arena—as he must if his life-style is to have meaning—he dies. His death is both welcome and admirable, since he is evil. However, it is disconcerting to see Van Cleef tumble into the open grave or to see Volonte thrown onto the wagonload of meaningless dead grotesques. Once dead, a man loses meaning.

Every Leone film has visual moments as vivid and powerful as the final shootouts. In *Fistful of Dollars,* there are the shootings of the "evil" family of father, mother, and son as they emerge from the burning house; the slaughter of the soldiers; the exchange of Ramon's mistress for the hostage while the mistress's young son and husband watch; and Eastwood's crawling escape from town after the beating he suffers. In *For a Few Dollars More,* there are the bank robbery, Eastwood's first meeting with Van Cleef, Van Cleef's duel on horseback with the gunmen, and Volonte's speech in the church pulpit. In *The Good, the Bad, and the Ugly,* there are: the opening sequence ending with Wallach in a freeze-frame, chicken leg in hand, flying through the window; Van Cleef's calm murder of the family and the man who hired him for the job; Wallach's confrontation with his priest brother; Wallach and Eastwood's trek through the desert; the battle at the river; Eastwood's loading of his gun behind a door just in time to meet the killers, who break in; the graveyard search for gold; and Wallach's stealing of the gun. In *Once upon a Time in the West,* the vivid and powerful visual moments include Elam and Strode waiting in the station; Fonda killing the family; the card game on the train; Robards's death; and the final, long ride of Bronson into the distance, as the railroad station is being built in the foreground. In *Duck, You Sucker!,* there are the stagecoach ride, Coburn's first appearance, the attack upon the bank, the executions in the rain, and the final battle, with Steiger's confused reaction.

Leone's Politics

The obsession of Leone protagonists and villains, major and minor, with the attaining of wealth can be seen as growing out of a dominant strain in American-made Westerns. The extent to which all the characters—with the exception of Bronson in *Once upon a Time in the West* and Coburn in *Duck, You Sucker!*—are driven by a desire for gold goes far beyond American sensibilities and into Italian intellectual poli-

tics and attitudes toward American capitalism. The implied Marxist attitude in Leone's early films appears to become explicit in *Duck, You
Sucker!* (which was originally titled *Once upon a Time, the Revolution*).
Much of this concern with killing for money can be seen as mere bor-
rowing from Western conventions, as in the ruthless railroad tycoon
plunging west in *Once upon a Time in the West.* Yet one can see hints,
shadings of Leone's sensibility at work even here. Leone shows this
capitalist as a man with a diseased body. Fonda tells him, ''I've watched
the rot progress,'' and, ''A normal man would put a bullet through his
brain.'' The tycoon feels pain despite his wealth and power; he cannot
say, as Fonda does, that ''sitting behind this desk feels good—like holding a gun.''

In *The Good, the Bad, and the Ugly,* there are some thematic brothers
to this ruthless tycoon. Early in the film, Van Cleef comes to see the
boss who has paid him to get information from the man who is to be
killed after talking. The boss is in bed suffering from TB. In a scene of
typical Leone black humor, Van Cleef tells the boys that, before dying,
his recent victim gave him money to kill the boss. Van Cleef muses that,
once he is paid, he must always follow through; and he proceeds to
shoot the boss through a pillow—an uncharacteristic way to kill someone in a Western.

Thus Leone's treatment of money can sometimes carry extensive
meanings that go beyond the ordinary use of Western conventions. The
fact that the money in *The Good, the Bad, and the Ugly* is buried in a
graveyard can have immense Marxist and Freudian overtones—the association of death and money. Sometimes the treatment of money sur-
faces in the dialogue. One of the most striking lines in all the Leone
films occurs when the railroad tycoon in *Once upon a Time in the West* is
told that, even when he is dead, ''You'll always leave a slime behind
you—two shiny rails.'' There is a passage of dialogue with more political overtones in *The Good, the Bad, and the Ugly,* when Eli Wallach
finds his brother, a monk in a monastery. Wallach says that the only
ways to escape from the poverty they were raised in is to go into the
Church or to become a bandit, and he tells his brother that he chose the
Church because he was too cowardly to become a bandit. The scene is
not really essential to the film structurally, but it is important to Leone.

In the above ways, Leone bends the framework of the Western to express his own personality. Studying Leone's play upon this relationship

between money and killing, one discovers it is dangerous to label his outlook as simply "European" or "Marxist"—even in *Duck, You Sucker!*—but one must at least recognize it as his own and certainly as atypical of the Hollywood Western.

Leone's Religion

The scene between Wallach and his brother in the monastery is one of the few times Leone refers to the Church. In that scene, Leone evokes the Western tradition of two brothers on opposite sides of "the law"; yet the scene actually expresses Leone's own dark vision. His West, which can offer becoming a monk or a bandit as the only alternatives, is certainly more of a desert than it is a garden of opportunity. Leone's monastery is not perceived as a civilizing institution or even an arm of imperialism, but as a bleak means of survival.

Also, in *The Good, the Bad, and the Ugly* are a few bits of irreverency by Wallach, as when he crosses himself distractedly when referring to a man he has just killed. We remember that one of the law's charges against him, stated early in the film, is stealing sacred objects, and he eyes some of the things in the monastery. These details just add some color to the Wallach character, "the ugly," and increase his contrast to his reverent brother. There are also Volonte's sermon in the ruins of a church in *For a Few Dollars More* and the biblical language spoken at the funeral of the family in *Once upon a Time in the West,* but Leone does not seem to have a strong attitude toward religion. Clearly, religion is to Leone a false hope that hardly merits venom.

Leone's Development

Leone's films are explorations of the mythic world he has created. Unlike many directors, he is not simply repeating the same conviction in a variety of ways. Each successive film takes the same characters and explores them in greater depth. Leone's involvement with this exploration is intense. Both Fonda and Eastwood emphasize that Leone likes to act out the roles of his principal characters to show how he wants them done. He falls into character, lives the role. "He is a short, heavy fellow," Eastwood told me; "but when he acts out his roles, you can see what he wants, and you know that he really feels himself tall and lean, a gunfighter."

Leone's first Western, *Fistful of Dollars,* portrayed the nameless man, Eastwood, as sure of himself, a force for good, invulnerable.

There are no alternatives to his behavior. He is a cleansing force, the only character with whom we care to identify.

In *For a Few Dollars More,* the ambiguous character of Van Cleef inserts a new kind of honor, a new complication that undermines Eastwood's image as an invulnerable force for good. Van Cleef proves to be more clever than Eastwood in their nonfatal shootout in the street. Evil is still total evil manifest in an individual, Volonte; but Leone shows that something worthwhile exists between the moral extremes.

In *The Good, the Bad, and the Ugly,* the trinity emerges, and Eastwood, the moral man, is forced to accept the amoral man, Wallach, as part of a worthwhile existence. There are not, in short, simple good and evil to contend with, but undeniable animal feelings, which are neither good nor evil but part of us nonetheless.

In *Once upon a Time in the West,* the positions are further blurred. Bronson's moral goodness stems from a desire for specific revenge. He is not simply a cleansing force; he is, like Van Cleef in *For a Few Dollars More,* a tormented man. Robards is not simply amoral; he has an earthy wisdom and a sense of honor and self. And for all of Fonda's evil, his honor and courage are admirable.

In *Duck, You Sucker!,* the questioning of the morally good man, Coburn, is carried further. Coburn's confidence is shaken by Steiger's desire to exist within his family and Steiger's conviction that revolution is meaningless. Steiger's contention is that the poor need no moral champions, that they only suffer at these moralists' hands. Indeed, Coburn tricks Steiger into fighting for the revolution and causes the destruction of the amoral man's (Steiger's) family. This is further complicated by Coburn's realization that his killing of his IRA friend had not been as clear-cut a righteous act as he had thought. Further, there is not simple extremity of evil in the person of a ''bad guy.'' There is no person to destroy to end a cycle, to complete the morality play. The Mexican colonel dies; but he has had no real personality, no presence. When Coburn dies, his moral certainty dies with him. In the end, we are left with Steiger in close-up, alone, unsure of whether he can exist alone without family and moral conscience.

One can see Leone's films as mythical explorations of the human attempt to find meaning in life and his main characters as conflicting poles within each of us, with a moral confidence pulling against immoral urges and an amoral, animal self being torn between. With each film, the answer grows more complex and fascinating.

Readings on Sergio Leone

Books

Frayling, Christopher. *Spaghetti Westerns.* Boston: Routledge & Kegan Paul, 1981.

Periodicals

Fonda, Henry. Interview. *Dialogue on Film.* American Film Institute, November 1973.

Gili, Jean. "Sergio Leone." *Cinema 69,* November 1969.

Jameson, Richard. "Something to Do with Death: A Fistful of Sergio Leone," *Film Comment* 9, no. 2 (March-April 1973), pp. 8–16. Note on pp. 32–33, *Film Comment* 10, no. 2 (March-April 1974).

Kaminsky, Stuart. "The Italian Western beyond Leone." *The Velvet Light Trap* 12, Spring 1974, pp. 31–33.

Sarris, Andrew. "Spaghetti and Sagebrush." *Village Voice,* September 19, p. 53; Sept. 26, pp. 51–52.

Simsolo, Noel. "Sergio Leone Talks" (interview). *Take One* 3, no. 9 (May 14, 1973), pp. 26–32.

14
CONCLUSION AND SUMMARY
The Importance of Film Genre

A genre that can be traced through films for a distinct period of time has a basic formal and thematic importance for those viewers who return to it. A genre variation can originate with one or two films, an adaptation from a work of popular literature, or the headlines from yesterday's newspaper. If the first film has a basic meaning for its audience, and if it is allowed to reach that audience, the film will likely be financially successful—and the success of the first film will lead others to follow it. Those that follow will often do so because they are viewed as a product in a business, and it has been demonstrated (at the movie theater) that this particular product—the Western, the gangster film, the police film—is marketable. To produce this marketable product, the entrepreneur-producer finds a story or has one written and works with a team of professionals led by a director; together they produce a genre film. The genre work must contain the basic elements of the original if it is to appeal to the same audience; yet, at the same time, it must not be a carbon copy. It must show some kind of variation or development.

The writer, director, art director, director of photography, and other contributors to the motion picture play on the elements of the established genre, adding to it their own talents and ideas, often refining details and clarifying the archetype. Clearly, the creative abilities and concerns of the director and the collaborators can make the genre film distinctive and personal at the same time that it serves to retell an old

story. Often, directors like Ford, Siegel, and Leone are at their most
creative when working within familiar genres. The genre thus becomes
part of our contemporary folklore, part of our popular culture—the way
we order and see our lives.

Each genre has its roots in myth, which strengthens the argument for
serious examination of the American genre film. It might be worth-
while, for example, to investigate the concept of the hero in the myth of
Perseus in relation to the heroes in *Sharkey's Machine, Dirty Harry,* and
The French Connection or to deal with the generic elements common to
Dante's *Inferno* and *The Poseidon Adventure.*

Certain genres are clearly universal, depending upon archetypal patterns common to all civilizations. Northrop Frye points out in *Anatomy
of Criticism* that creative narratives, such as a film, can be examined in
terms of categories of images, as cycles of movement. Such archetypal
elements include: the process of death and rebirth of a god (an element
in many horror films as well as in religious myth); the daily journey of
the sun across the sky (the journey often made in Westerns or biblical
films); and the cycle of waking and dreaming—the belief that a great
libido awakens when the sun is asleep, and that the light of day is frequently the darkness of desire (an idea common to several genres but
certainly the essence of the films noir). Frye also mentions such categorical images as ''the tragic process of life cut off violently by accident, sacrifice, ferocity, or some overriding need, the continuity which
flows on after the tragic act being something other than life itself.'' In
addition, Frye lists such archetypal elements as: the cycle of the sea-
sons; the organic cycle of growth, maturity, decline, death, and rebirth
in another individual form; and water symbolism. These patterns are as
evident in Budd Boetticher's *Comanche Station* and Walter Hill's *48
Hours* and *Southern Comfort* as they are in John Milton's *Paradise Lost.*
It is not necessary to deprecate the Western and extol the epic poem.
Genre criticism should recognize the value of both and be based upon
what the works *do,* rather than try to establish certain criteria of quality.

Genre studies in film should lead to an understanding of the work in
question and explore the reasons for the persistence and change of
myths, types, forms, and formulas. If a work endures or a form persists
and is responded to by a particular culture, it is of value to explore the
meaning of that work or works. Such study helps us to understand what
we respond to and how we find meaning in existence.

Tastes change, as was mentioned earlier; and thus Alexander Pope or

Robert Burns might decline in one generation and burn brightly in the next. All too often, however, critics and teachers try to impose their own views of contemporary taste upon readers and students, to tell them that they should be responding to the "art" of Shakespeare or William Faulkner. People respond to that which has meaning for them, although they may not be able consciously to understand that to which they are responding. To bludgeon one's students or readers into shame for not liking Luchino Visconti's *Death in Venice* (a film I happen to like) and to refuse to respond seriously to films like *Poltergeist* or *Firefox* (which I like also) is to ignore the generic validity of the latter two films—to be unable to treat them as serious generic creations.

Inherent in most discussions of "What is art?" is the general belief in the existence of "high" and "low" art. Popular generic works generally are treated by critics and teachers as examples of low art, which they then equate with inferiority. High art is considered to be more elite, to have rules of procedure that exclude the insensitive. "High" art, all too often, is an elitist concept established to differentiate the "knowing intellect" from the rabble. It is assumed that high art is of the mind and low art, of the emotions. The emotions are inferior, in this argument, because they connote a lack of intellectual control. Being emotional and inferior, they do not merit intellectual attention. Low art is simply "entertainment" to such critics—which is equivalent to a psychiatrist's saying a patient's dream is simply a dream and not worth consideration. It is the totally conscious intellectual artist dealing with a number of purely personal images who is considered, by such critics and teachers, to merit attention and analysis. After all, they argue, this artist is a creator.

The argument of this book has been that the popular generic work also can be analyzed and that the popular work has significant meaning. Time after time, history has shown that popular works have survived to become examples of "classical high art" at least as often as have works of intentional high art. Countless numbers of men and women who now are acknowledged as great painters, sculptors, poets, and novelists were considered to be base popularists in their own time—only to be discovered after their deaths, when a later society realized that they had created works of enduring generic value, that they had molded archetypal patterns and expanded them.

Critics who say that they like a film such as *Once upon a Time in the West* or *Tootsie* but that they must consider such films to be inferior works are—all too often—saying that they are embarrassed at having responded to a work that they had already classified (usually before seeing it) as low art. Their assumption is that any film they consider to be low art does not merit analysis and is therefore inferior. They ignore the fact that, if they have felt a response to the generic work—as have millions of other viewers—then the form and the work are of great value, and an effort should be made to understand both.

It is not harder to understand the films of Ingmar Bergman or Luchino Visconti than those of Burt Kennedy or Roger Corman. In fact, sometimes it is much more difficult to come to terms with a successful Western than with a consciously intellectual film. Bergman, Visconti, and Federico Fellini, for example, are interesting and admirable creators; all three work in a tradition of high art, which has clearly defined rules of conscious symbolism and recognition. It is possible to suggest, however, that the ironic use of Christian symbolism in Bergman's *Winter Light* or Fellini's *8½* is blatantly overt and crude compared to the use of generic symbolic elements in Ronald Neame's *The Poseidon Adventure*. In the Neame film, any symbolism that exists is as an inherent part of the action or the decor. The use of the Christmas tree first as a destructive element (when the boat turns upside down) and then as a symbol of hope (when the small party, led by Gene Hackman, uses the tree as a ladder to escape) is just one example of Neame's use of symbolism. The film also plays upon certain elements of the myth of the *Inferno*—but in reverse—as it shows the ascent from hell by faith, combined with the social reinforcement of personal sacrifice.

In *The Poseidon Adventure,* the stronger members of the party sacrifice themselves for those who are weaker. Hackman's final leap to certain death, so that he can open the valve, is an act of Christian sacrifice; the image of Hackman, hanging, is one of voluntary crucifixion—yet, like every image, it is part of a generic pattern necessary to the content of the film. Never once does Neame employ the frequent device of high-art films—that of thrusting a symbol or bit of dialogue in front of us so that we can respond with a knowing inner glow at being part of an elite group of viewers.

Another example of distortion of generic analysis is the frequency with which war films are examined, or rated as having a claim to high art, on the basis of whether or not they are strong, personal antiwar statements. As generic works, the antiwar element is of minor consideration. To look at *All Quiet on the Western Front,* or even *The Grand Illusion,* as an intellectual plea for peace on earth is to attribute to such films a pretension that has reverberations of elitist response yet has nothing to do with continued public interest in the war-film genre.

The war movie in the United States dates back beyond D. W. Griffith, but conventions can be conveniently pinpointed in his *Hearts of a Nation* and *The Birth of a Nation;* parodies of the war film existed as early as Charlie Chaplin's *Shoulder Arms.* A major thematic consideration in the American war film (those genre films that deal with groups living in isolation, not the war spectaculars that strive to be epics, like *The Longest Day*) is the sense of group unity—the need for varying individuals to learn to cooperate if they are to survive. The war film almost always deals with a small group, a patrol of assorted personalities with a variety of backgrounds. In the course of the film, they are reduced almost to animal status. Because the war film examines the most primitive human instinct—the drive for survival—it is an opportunity for a modern person—the film's writer or director at a particular time in history—to examine basic social attitudes and to present personal feelings about the survivability and value of humanity in a generic context that is familiar to the audience. The central issue of such war films is whether the members of the group will be able to work together and survive in spite of the threat of disruption and chaos that comes, not from the enemy, but from the group's own flawed members.

The war-film genre evolved during the same period of history as the gangster film. Its settings are always stark—open landscapes, bombed-out houses, and an almost expressionistic reduction of detail which is blamed, in the film, upon the destruction of war, but which actually reflects the primitive state of the relationships of the men in the group.

The genre has evolved in terms of the particular war most recently in progress and the reaction of the people of that time to their own feelings about survival. Most war films are made, not during a war, but after it; for this reason, they generally serve as reflections of how the person who fought at that time views the way he behaved and considers his dignity—or lack of it—in survival. The sacrificial affirmation of John Ford's *The Lost Patrol* (which itself replaced the pacifist response of *All Quiet on the Western Front*) or George Stevens's *Gunga Din* is expanded in *The Immortal Sergeant* and *Nine Men.* Following the Korean War, hope for cohesion is questioned but wearily accepted in such films as Nicholas Ray's *Bitter Victory* and Raoul Walsh's *The Naked and the Dead.* But the disillusionment of the time is evident in the ambiguous, unresolved endings of Robert Aldrich's *Attack!,* Donald Siegel's *Hell Is for Heroes,* Sam Fuller's *The Steel Helmet,* Lewis Milestone's *Pork Chop Hill,* and Dennis Sanders's *War Hunt.* Post-Vietnam films such as *Apocalypse Now* and *The Boys from Company C* and even *First Blood* with its final image of the mad Sylvester Stallone, echo the disillusionment of earlier films of other wars.

By the same token, instead of dismissing the police film as a shallow form of entertainment, one might make an examination of the elements of the genre and discover striking similarities in such diverse films as *Dirty Harry, Naked City, The Case against Brooklyn, Rogue Cop, The Big Heat, Cry of the City, The Detective, Detective Story, Madigan, No Way to Treat a Lady, T-Men, Union Station, Laura, Day of the Jackal, Vice Squad, Sharkey's Machine,* and *48 Hours.* The recurrent generic elements, like those of the war film, help to define this genre's meaning for the viewer:

- The police officer becomes emotionally involved with the criminal; his pursuit of the criminal becomes an example of personal and societal revenge (as it is in *Les Miserables,* to cite a literary work that also typifies this genre).
- The police officer begins to identify with the criminal; this reinforces his hatred of the criminal, for the criminal represents elements the policeman hates in society and fears in himself.
- The police officer's family is often threatened or destroyed in order to ensure the protagonist's emotional involvement with the criminal.
- The police officer finds himself driven outside the restrictions of the law under which he has always lived because that law is too narrow to deal with the criminal and too rigid to handle the policeman's emotional need for confrontation. The confrontation between hero and villain is bigger than societal restriction.
- The protagonist is threatened with loss of his job or loses his job because of his emotional involvement with the criminal and his desire for revenge. Invariably, the policeman has a mentor who advises that he stick to the rules, but the protagonist does not heed the advice of this father-figure.
- Frequent parallels are drawn between the life of the police officer and that of the criminal. Often their visual time in the film—the amount of

time each of them appears on the screen—is shared, sometimes through a process of balanced cutting back and forth between the two. At film's end, both men appear on the screen, facing one another, in a final confrontation in which the survivor is in control—but slightly diminished in character.

- The police officer who is threatened by the dark side of himself, which he sees in the criminal, is clearly a middle-class citizen. He wears suits and devotes himself totally to business, spending almost all of his time on the job—much to the chagrin of his wife, if he has one.

- The identity of the criminal is known very early in the film; there is no mystery to solve, as in a private-detective film. The question is not *who* committed the crime, but *why* he did so and how society can control him.

With such descriptive elements to consider, the police film takes on new meaning, new possibilities of exploration, as a reflection of—or comment upon—how a society—and its artists and creators—can present this type of story in mythic form.

The approaches taken in this book are but a few of the possibilities for genre study. Some of the approaches could be interchangeable between genres. It might be of value, for example, to compare American horror films with German horror films; to examine in *I, the Jury* as an archetypal private-detective film, or to explore the sea epic as a subgenre.

Much of what I have said is clearly open to contradiction, variation, or new direction. The value of this book, however, lies not so much in whether each approach given here has been beyond reproach, but in that some basis for response and further analysis has, in fact, been attempted.

INDEX